FOOD INEQUALITIES

FOOD INEQUALITIES

Tennille Nicole Allen

Health and Medical Issues Today

GREENWOOD

An Imprint of ABC-CLIO, LLC
Santa Barbara, California • Denver, Colorado

Library of Congress Cataloging-in-Publication Data

Names: Allen, Tennille Nicole, author.
Title: Food inequalities / Tennille Nicole Allen.
Description: Santa Barbara : ABC-CLIO, 2021. | Series: Health and medical issues today | Includes bibliographical references and index.
Identifiers: LCCN 2020043402 (print) | LCCN 2020043403 (ebook) | ISBN 9781440864308 (hardcover) | ISBN 9781440864315 (ebook)
Subjects: LCSH: Food supply—Government policy—United States. | Food supply—United States. | Equality—United States.
Classification: LCC HD9006 .A785 2021 (print) | LCC HD9006 (ebook) | DDC 338.1/973—dc23
LC record available at https://lccn.loc.gov/2020043402
LC ebook record available at https://lccn.loc.gov/2020043403

ISBN: 978-1-4408-6430-8 (print)
       978-1-4408-6431-5 (ebook)

25 24 23 22 21   1 2 3 4 5

This book is also available as an eBook.

Greenwood
An Imprint of ABC-CLIO, LLC

ABC-CLIO, LLC
147 Castilian Drive
Santa Barbara, California 93117
www.abc-clio.com

This book is printed on acid-free paper ∞

Manufactured in the United States of America

This book is dedicated to all of those working on and in the ground to ensure that we move from food apartheid and food injustice to food sovereignty and food justice.

Contents

Part III: Scenarios

SERIES FOREWORD

Every day, the public is bombarded with information on developments in medicine and health care. Whether it is on the latest techniques in treatment or research, or on concerns over public health threats, this information directly affects the lives of people more than almost any other issue. Although there are many sources for understanding these topics—from Web sites and blogs to newspapers and magazines—students and ordinary citizens often need one resource that makes sense of the complex health and medical issues affecting their daily lives.

The *Health and Medical Issues Today* series provides just such a one-stop resource for obtaining a solid overview of the most controversial areas of health care in the 21st century. Each volume addresses one topic and provides a balanced summary of what is known. These volumes provide an excellent first step for students and lay people interested in understanding how health care works in our society today.

Each volume is broken into several parts to provide readers and researchers with easy access to the information they need:

Part I provides overview chapters on background information—including chapters on such areas as the historical, scientific, medical, social, and legal issues involved—that a citizen needs to intelligently understand the topic.

Part II provides capsule examinations of the most heated contemporary issues and debates, and analyzes in a balanced manner the viewpoints held by various advocates in the debates.

Part III provides case studies that show examples of the concepts discussed in the previous parts.

A selection of reference material, such as a directory of organizations and a bibliography, serve as the best next step in learning about the topic at hand.

The *Health and Medical Issues Today* series strives to provide readers with all the information needed to begin making sense of some of the most important debates going on in the world today. The series includes volumes on such topics as stem-cell research, obesity, gene therapy, alternative medicine, organ transplantation, mental health, and more.

Preface

As the 2019 novel coronavirus (COVID-19) disease began its spread in the United States, it soon became clear that in addition to a health crisis, it would create and deepen food crises and inequality. In addition to health concerns, COVID-19 has created numerous food-related concerns, including those surrounding access, supply, and employment. COVID-19 has meant that many children have been unable to access free and reduced lunches at their schools. Many farmers' fields have lain fallow. Some farmworkers have lost employment, while others are forced to work longer hours under increasingly unsafe conditions. Farm and processing workers are compelled to go to work, whether sick or well, for fear of losing needed hours and missing out on COVID-prompted, promised perfect-attendance bonuses. Some fast-food workers have been told they may not wear masks, and others have been verbally harassed or physically assaulted by customers who refuse to follow government rules and company policy and put theirs on. Contingent workers have had to go grocery shopping or make restaurant deliveries for those able to shelter in place. Untold numbers of people have lost income that would have gone to food. They join those who have had to stand in line for hours to get food from the declining number of open food pantries and soup kitchens. And this has all been in just the early stages of the pandemic.

A March 2020 report from the Food Chain Workers Alliance (FCWA) entitled *What Food Workers on the Front Lines Need Right Now* discusses the vulnerabilities of food workers during the COVID-19 crisis. The report supports the long-held assertions of food workers, their allies, and activists on the importance of their work. Still, in the United States, these workers lack many vital health, economic, and other protections that many nonessential workers continue to enjoy even as they work from home. Through the crisis, food workers are forced to work in very close proximity to others and are not assured the ability to practice social distancing. They often are given inadequate to no supplies such as running water, soap, hand sanitizer, and protective equipment. There has also been a lack of guidance and implementation of safety protocols to limit their exposure to COVID-19. Food workers' working conditions did not shift to offer them the pay, protections, or benefits, such as health care and paid leave, that would have been commensurate with the importance of their labor.

At the same time, many food workers in the restaurant and other parts of the hospitality industry have lost their jobs in the wake of businesses closing their doors to halt the spread of COVID-19 or as declining revenues forced them to do so. Those restaurant and other hospitality workers who remain employed have seen their wages and tips significantly reduced as patrons dwindle and service models switch from dining-in to take-out. The FCWA further highlights the particularly marginalized position of food workers in the informal labor market who do not enjoy even the meager labor protections offered in the formal labor market.

These are some of the most recent examples of the food inequalities explored in this book. Organized into three parts, this work provides an exploration of the many interrelated food inequalities present—and growing—in the United States. The first part of this book addresses both the historical and current contexts of unequal access to food and its consequences. Chapter 1 is an introduction to food inequalities that begins with an overview of how food is important across physical, mental, and social dimensions. It also details how and why inequalities develop in general and how they relate specifically to food. Chapter 2 is an exploration of the history of food inequalities in the United States that begins with colonization and enslavement and continues through the present. The roles of structural racism and stereotypes around food are emphasized in this chapter. Chapter 3 builds on this history in its examination of current unequal access to food, as this is structured by race, class, gender, age, and geographic location. Chapter 4 focuses on ways culture shapes and is shaped by food. It looks pointedly at the idea of taste as a symbol and how that relates to inequalities. Chapter 5 presents a deep examination of the impacts of food inequalities. In it, the ways that macro- and micro-level inequalities in and around food affect individuals, institutions, and other systems are detailed to provide a sense of how pervasive and significant food inequalities are. Chapter 6 illuminates the processes through which food practices and policies both create and remedy food inequalities. It does this as it delves into the decisions, choices, rules, regulations, and changes made by federal, state, and local governments, corporations, and nonprofit organizations. Chapter 7 illustrates more small-scale and grass-roots efforts to improve access to food and end food inequalities as it turns attention to food activism across the nation.

The second part of the book is an examination of six contentious dimensions of food inequalities. Chapter 8 explores the existence of racial and gender discrimination in the food system in hiring, pay, and promotion. Chapter 9 looks at compensation in the food system, with a particular emphasis on the large gaps between those on the front lines of food work and those in the executive suites. Chapter 10 focuses on the creation and maintenance of food deserts in rural and urban communities. Chapter 11 assesses the Supplemental Nutrition Assistance Program, popularly known as food stamps, how it is perceived, and what it provides. Chapter 12 is a study of the ways that agricultural and other food companies deploy social and behavioral science as well as biology and chemistry in shaping consumers' ideas and preferences and policies around food. The last chapter in this section investigates recent changes designed to improve the health and quality of foods offered to children served by the National School Lunch Program. The resistance to these changes is also investigated here.

The third and final part of this book is a series of case studies. The first is on sweetened-beverage taxes designed to reduce sugar consumption and its attendant risks. The second is on reactions to policies designed to create healthier school lunches. The third is on the causes and responses to economic and political crises in Latin America that lead to individuals and families immigrating to the United States and engaging in farmwork. The fourth is on the effort a resident of a low-income African American neighborhood in a food desert must make in order to go grocery shopping. The fifth and last case study is on a parent who is confronted by another customer who sees them using their Electronic Benefits Transfer card to pay for some of their groceries. An interpretation based on parts I and II is given after each case study.

Acknowledgments

Thank you to Kay Bolden, who introduced me not only to the idea that food access is an issue in too many of our neighborhoods but also to the reality that with time, determination, and community, we—and our children—can and do work to solve it. I also want to thank Erika Allen, who is always an inspiration. Your spirit shines, and your dedication is humbling. A special appreciation for patience, encouragement, and feedback is reserved for the editor of this book, Maxine Taylor. I also must say thank you to my father for introducing me to the importance, value, and beauty of growing food. I wish I had listened more; I wish you were still here to teach me and my sons what you knew about tending to tomatoes, greens, cucumbers, and life. Finally, I also want to thank my family, in general, and my husband, James White, and sons, Allen James and Langston Alexander, in particular, for your love, care, company, and faith in me.

PART I

Overview

CHAPTER 1

An Introduction to Food Inequalities

Sevri o'lem mol'yesheka ris ner.

That's how you say *hello* in the language of my kin. *Sevri* means *to dip bread*. *O'lem* means *with all* or *together*. *Mol'yesheka* means *into a common pot*, and *ris ner* means *let us*.

Let's dip our bread into a common pot.

—*An Unkindness of Ghosts*, Rivers Solomon

"Let us dip our bread into a common pot." This greeting signifies the role of food in everyday rituals that unite and define a people. Though these words are written in the fictional language of Ifrek, they have resonance in any language. Across people, across place, and across time, eating together not only provides physical sustenance but also sustains communities. Indeed, sharing meals works to build commonality, mutuality, and support.

What happens when eating together is not possible because of a lack of food? The costs of that—physically, mentally, and socially—are catastrophic, widespread, and long lasting for individuals, families, communities, and society. One impact is hunger. Another is food insecurity. As Feeding America, the largest antihunger organization in the United States, points out on the Understand Food Insecurity page on its website, "It is important to know that hunger and food insecurity are closely related, but distinct, concepts. Hunger refers to a personal, physical sensation of discomfort, while food insecurity refers to a lack of available financial resources for food at the level of the household." Food insecurity, a major component of the food inequalities that are the focus of this book, is defined by the U.S. Department of Agriculture (USDA) "as a lack of consistent access to enough food for an active, healthy life." Food access is another focus. Approximately 25 million people in the United States live in what are called *food deserts*. Food deserts are areas where supermarkets, grocery stores, and other places to buy affordable and healthy foods (such as fruits, vegetables, whole grains, and other unprocessed or minimally processed foods) are not present within a reasonable distance from one's home (commonly accepted as 1 mile within urban environments and 10 miles within rural ones). Food security and access are vital, given the importance of food physically, mentally, and socially.

THE PHYSICAL, MENTAL, AND SOCIAL IMPORTANCE OF FOOD

Physical Importance of Food

It almost goes without saying that there are clear, definitive, and widely agreed-upon links between food and bodies. This understanding has been the basis of marketing campaigns, such as one from the dairy industry in the 1980s that proclaimed that "milk . . . does a body good." It is the basis for nutrition guidelines received from the federal government, physicians, teachers, various family members, staff at the gym, and a host of magazines and passersby, regardless of whether dietary advice has been asked for. When diets are not rich in variety, there is a high risk of missing important nutrients such as calcium, iron, fatty acids, vitamin D, and zinc, which are vital for multiple measures of physical and mental well-being. Indeed, as of 2017 the American Academy of Pediatrics recommends that children be screened for food insecurity in the same ways they are screened for other measures of growth and development.

When pregnant women do not have adequate access to food or nutrition, they are more likely to give birth to babies with birth defects. Children who live in homes where there is food insecurity are more likely to be anemic; be at greater risk for asthma; have nutritional deficiencies, cognitive and behavioral problems, and oral health concerns; be hospitalized; show symptoms of mental health issues; demonstrate higher levels of anxiety and aggression; and have lower levels of overall health, according to research by economists Craig Gundersen and James Ziliak. For adults in homes where there is food insecurity, health issues are similarly found to include higher nutritional deficiencies, rates of depression, and chronic illnesses, such as high blood pressure, high cholesterol, and diabetes. In addition, there are lower rates of sleep and sleep quality, mental and physical acuity, and wellness. Those who live in food deserts are 30 percent more likely to be obese, according to USDA findings. These issues exist over the life course. This is evidenced in people over the age of 65 who are food insecure: they have poorer mental and physical health outcomes and need more help with the tasks associated with everyday life when compared with those over 65 who are food secure.

These patterns are cyclical. As people and families become less able to afford healthy and nutritious foods, their ability to prevent and treat chronic illnesses decreases; the costs of illnesses increase, diverting money, time, and other resources away from food, which exacerbates illnesses, costing more money, time, and other resources. This also comes at great mental cost, and this stress can lead to more emotional eating, which often diverges from health-conscious, mindful eating. Indeed, there is a strong link between mental states and food.

Mental Importance of Food

As the popular Snickers advertisements note, we are not ourselves when we are hungry. When meals are missed, there are physiological shifts that also manifest themselves emotionally and in ways that are apparent to others. This is the concept behind the portmanteau *hangry*. When hunger goes unsatisfied for too long, it fuses with anger, creating a hangry state. This is seen when people—whether they are 2, 22, 42, 62, or 82—exhibit cranki ness after going too long without a meal or snack. Missing meals causes decreases in levels of glucose, blood sugar, and these trigger the release of the stress hormones cortisol and epinephrine. In addition to tiredness and lack of focus becoming apparent, attitudes worsen and irritability rises as blood sugar drops. Neuropeptide Y, a hormone associated with increased aggression, is also released. This helps explain the relationship between hunger and displays of hostility. Based on the many shifts in how information is processed, understood, and relayed because of hunger, New York physician and medical school professor Deena Adimoolam encourages the public to leave mentally and emotionally challenging matters alone until after they have eaten. The clear-cut links between mood and food are also seen when too much of certain items is eaten, as when blood sugar spikes and then crashes after the consumption of too many carbohydrates, leading to subsequent losses of energy and temper. Food is also related to cognitive and other mental health disorders. Natalia Rawls of the National Alliance on Mental Health notes that what and when people eat is associated with their likelihood of having, managing, or preventing Alzheimer's disease, attention deficit hyperactivity disorder, depression, and schizophrenia.

There are other connections between food and mental states. Some of these are attached to the symbolic, cultural, and representational meanings that are attached to food. Indeed, sometimes the meanings that are associated with food are more powerful and immediate than what food provides physically or nutritionally. Food offers not only nutrition or pleasure but also ways to connect to others. It binds people together with those who are like them and highlights points of disconnection as well. Food is nourishment, food is symbolic, and food is meaningful.

Popular culture illustrates the connections between food and meaning well. Magazines implore their readers to eat this rather than that, to eat like a man, and to eat salads to find the perfect, summer bodies. In doing so, they promote mental association with food. Perceptions of food are decidedly shaped by the mental shortcuts made when considering what goes onto plates and into mouths. In magazines and other elements of popular culture, the power of classed, gendered, racialized, and other stereotypes about food that influence decisions about what to buy and consume is apparent. Just as food has a role in promoting stereotypes and creating inequalities, it also has a role in challenging these. Popular culture can reverse the erasure of identity and experience. In the 2018 Pixar animated short *Bao*, a lonely Chinese Canadian woman has a husband who is always at work and a son who is growing up and moving away from her. One of the constants in her life has been making *bao*—a filled dumpling that is a staple of many Chinese cuisines—for her family's breakfasts. As she begins her journey as an empty nester, her *bao* comes to life one morning, giving her another chance to feel needed again as she raises her dumpling. This critically acclaimed film struck a chord with audience members across the nation. This chord was especially resonant with North American Asians in general, as *Bao* marks the first time an Asian family has been depicted in a major animated release. Those with Chinese ancestry in particular could recognize and appreciate the specific cultural allusions to food, family, and change in the film. In the Americas, people of Asian descent are decidedly underrepresented in film and television. The care and tenderness with which both Asian—in this case, Chinese—people and food are shown in *Bao* are thus remedies for their usual invisibility and erasure as their deep value, love, and meaningfulness are the focus, according to sociologist and cultural critic Nancy Wang Yuen.

Food also challenges oppression in the ways that it sustains those fighting against discrimination and disadvantage. Paschal's Restaurant in Atlanta and Edna's Restaurant in Chicago were both vital in feeding activists, organizers, and leaders in the modern civil rights movement. These places were notable, as they provided staging grounds for protest, legislative, and other strategies to be safely mapped out away from the prying eyes and open ears of interlopers and infiltrators. More recently, television and streaming series by hosts including Rick Bayless, the late Anthony Bourdain, Padma Lakshmi, Samin Nosrat, and Andrew Zimmern seek to not only share culinary knowledge but to also offer paths to remedy injustices in the food system and remove cultural barriers between and across groups. In the wake of a devastating 2010 earthquake in Haiti, famed Spanish chef José Andres established his charity organization, World Central Kitchen (WCK), and since then has provided millions of meals to those in crisis in the aftermath of wildfires in California and hurricanes in Puerto Rico, among others. The work of Andrés and others to feed people in Puerto Rico when the U.S. government failed to do so in the wake of the devastating hurricane that hit the U.S. territory in 2017 is another example of the power of food to address inequalities. This is also the logic behind diversity dinner dialogues, a movement across the United States on college campuses, in racially integrated communities such as Oak Park, Illinois, and other locales. These are designed to bring people together across social differences—whether racial, religious, sexual orientation, and/or political—to explore distinctions and reveal commonalities over shared meals, discussions, and meanings.

Social Importance of Food

In chronicling the hurts and happiness that mark a year in the life of the Joseph family—a fictional African American family at the heart of George Tillman Jr.'s 1997 film *Soul Food*—food plays a central role. Food plays a supporting role in the film as viewers watch members of the Joseph family gather to mark major milestones such as marriages, births, and death; discuss moments in their daily lives that revolve around sibling rivalries, work, and school; and work to maintain their weekly ritual of having the extended family come together around the dining room table to cement bonds and resolve tensions. As shown in this and other films, such as *Like Water for Chocolate* (1992), *Woman on Top* (2000), *What's Cooking* (2000), *Tortilla Soup* (2001), *Pieces of April* (2003), *Waitress* (2007), *The Hundred-Foot Journey* (2013), and *Chef* (2014), food is a central way that strangers, neighbors, friends, families, and rivals come together—and come apart—across generations, places, sexuality, religion, race, and ethnicity, as well as with regard to intimate interpersonal relations. Animated films such as Disney's *Beauty and the Beast* (1991) and *Princess and the Frog* (2009) and Pixar's 2007 *Ratatouille* also explore these themes. These films allow us to see the relationships between food, family, friends, work, and identity. They show that food is about so much more than what is on one's plate. It encompasses meaning and relationships and can both lead to and abate conflicts. A 2002 review of anthropological research conducted by Sidney Mintz and Christine Du Bois presents works that show the role of eating and food in creating economic systems, meaning, and collective and individual memory. They also offer analyses of cooperation, conflict, and war, and explanations for human behavior and biological processes. Because of one's social locations—their collection of social statuses that matter for the ways that they are perceived and treated, including race, class, gender, sexuality, immigration status, and nationality, among others—one may experience increased inequalities and inequities when it comes to being able to attain the benefits accessible through food. This awareness allows a focus on the ways that social inequalities—unequal access to goods, resources, and opportunities, based on group member-ships, such as race, class, gender, sexuality, age, and religion are created, experienced, interrelated, and challenged. Group membership also shapes how and what people eat, as choices and understandings of food are related to their social networks.

Just as the people one knows are important for how one learns about scholarships and obtains jobs, the members of one's social networks are important for how one thinks about food, what one eats, and which dietary, nutritional, and taste trends one follows or dismisses. This is evidenced when people go to a new restaurant because a person they see on the train daily raves about it to anyone nearby. Flash back to when you were in first or second grade and a parent or teacher brought in a new fruit or dish to the class for everyone to try. Were you the first to raise your hand to ask for a bite? Probably not. Did you refuse a taste because the other kids at your table wrinkled their noses in disgust at the thought of eating this unfamiliar item? Probably so. Researchers have confirmed these kinds of impacts on people's philosophies and habits around food.

Research from the Pew Research Center in 2017 shows the social nature of food. One of the findings from the survey is that adults who agree that their "main focus is on eating healthy and nutritious" also have close friends and family members who they would also say the same about. This same poll also shows there is a relationship between adults who say that they have food sensitivities or allergies. While most respondents to the poll do not have food sensitivities or allergies, those who report that they do are more likely to have close friends and family members who also have food sensitivities or allergies. This suggests that social networks can also have an influence on how bodies react to food consumption. While genetics may explain shared food sensitivities and allergies among relatives, it does not do so for friends. The social dimension of food offers one explanation.

According to research such as that done by Adam Fletcher, Chris Bonell, and Annik Sorhaindo, friends have a great deal of influence on food consumption patterns, especially for those who are younger. It can be stigmatizing to note one's food sensitivities and allergies. These are often mocked, ignored, or denied, as shown by the many times there have been eye rolls and jokes about people asking for gluten-free dishes at restaurants, the failure to tell someone with a known issue that there are peanuts in a sauce, or the arguments that can arise when someone asserts an inability to eat a certain ingredient. More benignly, for those who are unfamiliar with food sensitivities and allergies, their seriousness may be unknown and inadvertently not addressed accordingly. In such a context, people may gravitate toward others who also have food intolerances and form social networks that are made up of similar others, which can help reduce the stigma they experience and increase the likelihood that their food needs will be satisfied. Seeking similarities in food consumption among social network members is certainly often true for vegetarians and vegans in the United States, where these food practices are received at best with tolerance in some places in the nation and at worst with outright hostility in others.

Pew Research Center data from 2016 reveal that while 12 percent of adults in the United States identify vegetarians and vegans in their networks of close friends and family, 52 percent of those people who identify themselves as vegetarian or vegan report that some or most of their close friends and family are also vegetarians or vegans. In contrast, only 8 percent of those people who are not themselves vegetarians or vegans could say the same.

Since food is so vital in the ways people socialize, most people agree that providing meals that all can enjoy is important. When colleagues, friends, family, and other guests are around, most respondents to a recent Pew Research Center survey say they should take steps to accommodate the dietary needs and preferences of guests they hosted. Sixty-two percent feel that hosts should ask guests about any food restrictions or allergies. These numbers are even higher among those who themselves have food restrictions or allergies. While in some spaces this may seem burdensome or contentious, most of the replies to that Pew survey data reflect otherwise. More than two-thirds of respondents report that it is not a bother when asked to accommodate special food requests. However, not everyone has access to food, let alone healthy food, or to those who would happily satisfy special food requests. The next two sections detail this further.

THE CREATION OF INEQUALITIES

Max Weber, one of the first sociologists, was interested in the creation of new forms of social inequalities amid the rise of the Industrial Revolution and the shifts in capitalism that accompanied this at the end of the nineteenth and beginning of the twentieth centuries. His work identifies the nexus of inequality in the overlapping categories of control over the production, distribution, and retention of resources; access to and occupation of positions of power; and the status that is denoted in the social prestige and respect that one has relative to others. As social locations are weighted differently—and unequally—inequality will occur based on the combination of these three categories. When society is organized in ways that create unequal valuations and rewards based on resources, power, and status, structural advantages are constructed for some at the same time that structural disadvantages are constructed for others. It is along these lines that inequality occurs and gets cemented. Inequality is also ultimately taken for granted as the way that things should be. This ideology creates systems where small, elite groups come to dominate large groups. In this, inequality also forms hierarchies of privilege and its necessary opposite, oppression. Scholar Patricia Hill Collins theorizes about what she calls the matrix of domination to show how these inequalities work together in ways that can benefit or privilege some and in ways that limit or oppress others. Based on one's social locations, the ways that a person is simultaneously oppressed in some ways and privileged in others can be mapped. This framework also enables the realization that inequality occurs across levels. Inequality has impacts on individuals, in interactions with others, culturally, and across societal institutions. This creates the structural disadvantages—those interlocking inequalities that are systemically built into a society's everyday functioning and throughout its social institutions—that too many in society experience.

Sociologists Linda Burton and Whitney Welsh point out that this inequality is both an antecedent and result of social exclusion. They state that social exclusion has four aspects:

- the lack of full integration of the excluded into society
- unequal access to necessary resources and opportunities for life chances

- oppression by those privileged members of society who retain control of necessary resources and opportunities
- the establishment of clear interactional and interpersonal boundaries between the excluded and the included

Food is clearly mapped on to these four aspects of social exclusion. This concept of social exclusion will be further explored in subsequent chapters. In the section that follows, the ways that inequalities around food exist and the ways that these inequalities matter are explored in more detail.

THE RELATIONSHIP BETWEEN FOOD AND INEQUALITY

This structural disadvantage both leads to and flows from poverty and is clearly seen when it comes to food inequalities in the United States. Those who are socially excluded are kept from fully taking part in the abundant food and related resources available in the United States because of their place in the social hierarchy. As a function of their intersecting race, class, gender, sexuality, nationality, and immigration status, among other socially important statuses, they are made to occupy rungs that are lower on the ladders to what is seen as success in the United States. Racism, classism, sexism, homophobia, xenophobia, and nativism mean that people of color, poor and working-class people, women, LGBTQ people, and immigrants—especially those from Latin American, African, and Arab countries and those who are undocumented—and those who have any of the myriad combinations of these social statuses are most likely to lack resources that would allow them access to affordable, healthy foods. They are also most likely to work in the lowest echelons of the food industry.

Neighborhoods, especially in urban environments, that suffer from unequal and inequitable access to food also tend to suffer from a lack of access to other goods commonly agreed upon as necessary or at least desirable for a good life, such as job availability, employment that offers at least a living wage, high-quality public schools, parks, and libraries, as well as safe and affordable housing, mental health services, and dental and health care. These social structural barriers are implicated in a number of ways related to food inequalities.

Seeing these barriers and inequalities that lead to a lack of food as a problem, in 2006 the USDA adopted a guide to official definitions by the National Research Council to describe access to food by those in the United States. In consultation with a panel of economists, nutritionists, sociologists, statisticians, and other related experts, the USDA's official definition of food security is twofold and includes the ready availability of nutritionally adequate and safe foods and the assured ability to acquire acceptable foods in socially acceptable ways. Socially acceptable ways of getting food are those ways that do not involve resorting to emergency food supplies, scavenging, stealing, or other coping strategies. At the opposite end of the spectrum of access and availability of food is food insecurity. This, according to the USDA, is the limited or uncertain availability of nutritionally adequate and safe foods or limited or uncertain ability to acquire acceptable foods in socially acceptable ways. Based in these understandings, the USDA has established a four-category range of food security. The first is high food security, defined as having no reported indications of food-access problems or limitations. The second is marginal food security, defined as having one or two reported indications of food-access problems or limitations. This often is manifested as having some anxiety over whether one has enough food in the house. While those who have marginal food security are anxious about where their next meal may come from or over whether they have will sufficient amounts of food in the house between paychecks, they also report little or no indication of changes in diets or food intake. The next two categories noted by the USDA are measures of food insecurity. The third category is termed low food security, in which there are reports of reduced quality, variety, or desirability of diet. Those with low food security report little or no indication of reduced food intake. This means that while people with low security are not missing meals nor eating fewer calories, the food they have may rate low on nutrition and/or taste. Low food security could also mean that people have to eat the same meals each day. It could also mean that people do not have the opportunity to eat what they truly want or like to eat. The final category identified by the USDA is very low food security, which is defined as reports of multiple indications of disrupted eating patterns and reduced food intake. Those with very low food security do not know where they will access food or when they will next eat, nor are they able to eat enough. They not only do not have the food they like but also do not have the food they need.

The preceding definitions largely exist on an individual level. Yet hunger or food insecurity can and does exist on a household level as well. For example, while children may have access to free breakfasts and lunches through their Head Start or public school, adults in the house may have a much harder time finding food. Another example is found when food is scarce and older household members eat fewer meals so that younger members may eat in order to have enough physical and mental energy to go to work. As such, the USDA also issues definitions of household food insecurity. In households with high food security, members report that they have no problems or anxiety about consistently accessing adequate food. In households with marginal food security, members report that while at times they have problems or anxiety about accessing adequate food, the quality, variety, and quantity of their food intake are not substantially reduced. In households with low food security, members report that the quality, variety, and desirability of their diets are reduced, but the quantity of food intake and normal eating patterns are not substantially disrupted. Rather than eating what most consider a balanced meal—the kinds that physicians, dietitians, and nutritionists endorse—food-insecure people and households must modify their meals. They may go from eating nightly dinners that include grilled chicken on a bed of couscous with a side of broccoli or a green salad and beans and rice to nightly dinners that consist of only grilled cheese sandwiches or just the beans and rice.

A Feeding America study shows other strains that interlocking connections between food and poverty cause. Respondents report that they have had to make tough choices between food and other necessities. Seventy-four percent have had to choose between food and medicine; 67 percent between food and transportation; 59 percent between food and utilities; and 57 percent between food and housing. The impacts of these are long reaching and consequential. Those choosing food over medicine may become sicker and need increasingly expensive care and, ironically, higher food costs. Those who spend money on food rather than transportation may lose their car and become more dependent on unreliable rides and public transportation, putting their employment, and thus income, at risk. Those who buy food rather than pay utilities may find themselves unable to cook dinner and more likely to eat at restaurants, which comes with greater health risks. They may be unable to pay for air conditioning which may result in trips to the emergency room for heat-related health crises. Buying food rather than paying a full month's rent can plunge a family into unstable housing conditions and homelessness. Choosing the nonfood option also comes with those serious and multiplying costs associated with food insecurity and lack of proper nutrition previously discussed.

In households with very low food security, members report that at times during the year, the eating patterns of one or more household members are disrupted and food intake reduced because the household lacks money and other resources for food. This translates into people who do not know where and when their next meal will come from, people who must ration the amount of food they and others in their homes consume and people who are not able to eat the minimum number of calories to sustain themselves for daily activities because their financial resources and other ways of obtaining food are severely limited. These other resources may include food obtained from food banks, at food drives, or through the use of the Supplemental Nutrition Assistance Program (SNAP) and the Women, Infants, and Children (WIC) program. The latter two are federal programs designed to act as a social safety net for people with low incomes.

Food insecurity is not evenly distributed through the population. Children are at particular risk of food insecurity. Households with children under the age of 18 are more likely to be food insecure than those without children. The presence of children in the household has a clear impact on the ways in which scarce food is distributed and accessed. Recent data show that 16.5 percent of households with children younger than 18 are food insecure. This means that children in 3.1 million households in the Unites States experience some level of food insecurity at some point during the course of a year. Of those, 8.5 percent of households report that it is only the adults who are food insecure, suggesting that available food is reserved to ensure that children are adequately fed and/or that children may have access to (additional) food from schools, community centers, and other external sources. In the remaining 8 percent of households in this population, it is both adults and children who experience food insecurity. In 1 percent of households, food insecurity is so great that children experience both marked decreases in the amount of food they eat and disrupted eating patterns.

A study led by Maryah Stella Fram from the University of South Carolina shows that adults have different experiences of food insecurity than children do. Adults worry about having sufficient amounts of money for food, having enough food that is also high in quality, and accessing it in socially acceptable ways of getting food. They strongly prefer to access food through what they see as legitimate ways, such as preparing low-cost but filling foods such as rice and pasta and avoiding the stigma of federal food assistance programs. Children, on the other hand, worry when they see lower quantities and less variety of food in their homes. They also worry about their parents' stress around food inadequacy. Additionally, they report feeling angry and powerless when they do not have food available to them. Children are also well aware of a lack of food in the household. This is despite adults' efforts to hide that reality from them by using strategies such as not telling children about their lack of food or money, encouraging children to eat first, giving children larger servings of food than they give themselves, or skipping meals altogether to ensure children's nutritional needs are met.

Instead of not knowing the dire financial straits they live within, children in food-insecure households develop strategies of their own to limit what they eat and reserve food for times when it is less abundant. This is evidenced when children tell their parents they are not hungry or when they eat only partial amounts of meals and save the rest for later or for another family member. They also seek food from neighbors, friends, and family members and come up with ways to earn money for food, such as cutting grass for neighbors or through part-time jobs. Adults are often unaware that children feel and act in these ways, according to the researchers, who find that there are discrepancies between what children said about their own food insecurity and what adults report children would say.

Those 60 years of age and older are also disproportionately impacted by a lack of access to food. In a 2018 Feeding America report, 8 percent, or about 5 million people, in this age range are food insecure. Approximately 4 million more are marginally food secure. Food insecurity for people in this age range has more than doubled since 2001. Some impacts of this food insecurity manifest as lower consumption of calories and important nutrients and higher rates of physical and mental illness compared with those who are food-secure seniors, as noted earlier.

Across place, age, and race, access to food—and lack thereof—is a key cause and consequence of poverty and other intertwined social inequalities. The historical roots of these are explored in the next chapter.

CHAPTER 2

History of Food Inequalities in the United States

Philadelphia: Two African American men await a third person for a meeting over coffee at a Starbucks. As they wait for their guest to arrive, a white manager calls the local police department on them, claiming they are loitering.

Suburban Los Angeles: A Latinx man places an order for a white chocolate mocha and an iced caramel macchiato and gives his name—Pedro—to the barista. When he gives one of the drinks to a colleague, she notices the name typed on the cup is "beaner," a racist slur targeting people of Mexican descent.

New York City: Two Latinx customers and a Latinx waiter are speaking Spanish at a restaurant. A white, male customer rages at them, ultimately threatening to call Immigration and Customs Enforcement to have them deported, unveiling his racist assumption that they are undocumented migrants.

Oakland: An African American man is barbecuing in a popular local park, as is customary there. A white woman calls the local police department on him, claiming he does not have the proper permit.

San Francisco: An eight-year-old African American girl is selling water in an effort to raise money for a trip to Disneyland. A white woman calls the local police department on her, claiming she does not have the proper permit.

Met with public castigation, official apologies, traditional and social-media attention, and in the case of Starbucks, the shuttering of all corporate-owned locations for an afternoon of diversity training, each of these examples that took place during the spring and summer of 2018 show responses to people of color deemed out of place around food. They also illuminate some of the deep-seated prejudices, stereotypes, and racism that fuel inequalities associated with food in ways that are both clear and direct as well as subtle and more obscure. These examples exist on a through line of inequalities related to food in the United States since its founding that will be further explored through this chapter. This chapter also details how ideas in the United States around food are in fact socially constructed and how they relate to inequalities. These include what foods are considered to be in good taste, what foods are considered to taste good, and what foods are considered to be good for you. It engages the work of French sociologist Pierre Bourdieu to better understand how cultural tastes associated with food lead to and reflect social hierarchies and inequalities.

Colonization and Enslavement

As the Declaration of Independence, the founding document of the United States of America, asserts, "We hold these truths to be self-evident, that all men are created equal, that they are endowed, by their Creator, with certain unalienable Rights, that among these are Life, Liberty, and the pursuit of Happiness." Though many today would argue that the *all* in the text is in fact inclusive, that word modifies the noun *men*, thus excluding all women. Furthermore, as Native, or Indigenous, Americans and people of African descent living in the colonies were seen and legally designated as savages and enslaved respectively by the founders of what would ultimately become the United States, it was only white men who were considered fully eligible for the promises made in the document that established the U.S. experiment. This experiment is one that catalyzed race, colonialism, enslavement, and capitalism into the systematic inequalities that continue today. It is impossible to tell the story of food in the United States without also telling the story of race, class, gender, and their intersecting oppressions.

The land that is now the United States is stolen land. The labor that built the United States—symbolically and literally—is stolen labor. Indeed, the agricultural practices and trade relationships that made the United States, since its inception, into the capitalist powerhouse it has long been show it was built on the backs of the enslaved and on the land of the Indigenous. This was a truly global enterprise. A look at Great Britain is instructive here. British colonies throughout the Americas were used to provide food in the colonies and throughout Britain. Indeed, British citizens could find themselves in Cambridge sipping cups of tea that was harvested under forced labor conditions in China and sweetened with sugar that was planted and refined in Brazil under enslaved labor.

In the United States, while many schoolchildren celebrate Columbus Day every October by reciting the rhyme, "In fourteen hundred ninety-two, Columbus sailed the ocean blue," others mark Indigenous People's Day and learn that with Columbus's voyage also came the beginnings of a perilous and deadly process of colonialism. When Christopher Columbus first arrived in Hispaniola—the shared island home to both modern-day Haiti and the Dominican Republic—the Indigenous population in North America is conservatively estimated to have been around 50 million. Today in the United States, Indigenous, or Native, Americans constitute the nation's smallest racial group, with around 1 percent of the population, or 2.9 million people, as of the latest U.S. Census.

This is the history that leads Planting Justice, a nonprofit organization in California's Bay Area to describe colonialism as a violent project. This is true both physically and culturally, as people are concurrently taken away from their land and their foodways, or their historical and cultural beliefs, practices, and traditions around food. There was certainly violence as Indigenous people resisted being forced from their land. The wars beginning with colonialism and ending at the dawn of the twentieth century, waged by white settlers, the U.S. armed forces, and other state-sponsored agents against Native Americans and policies are examples of said violence.

One such policy occurred in an 1823 Supreme Court ruling that ironically held that Native Americans could live in the United States but could not hold the lands they lived on, as the United States had a right of discovery that superseded Indigenous peoples' right of occupancy. The most notable policy was the 1830 Indian Removal Act, which is commonly referred to as the Trail of Tears. This was a series of removals lasting 20 years that forcibly relocated tens of thousands of Indigenous peoples from their lands in the southeastern United States to so-called Indian Territory west of the Mississippi River. In addition to the massive land and cultural losses this entailed, thousands died and others fell ill due to disease, exposure to the elements, and a lack of food. The 1871 Indian Appropriation Act and 1887 General Allotment Act, which resulted in the loss of more than 100 million acres of land, were other dispossession policies enacted by the U.S. federal government. These ended the practice of Native Americans holding land collectively. After the twentieth century, U.S. federal policies around Native Americans largely moved from physical to cultural violence as forced assimilation replaced land dispossession and war.

Physical and cultural violence were also the rule for those Africans kidnapped from the interior of West African countries such as Benin, Cote d'Ivoire, Ghana, Nigeria, and Senegal during the transatlantic slave trade. Once in the United States, these West Africans were made into enslaved people through tortuous conditioning processes that involved harsh physical punishment, family separation, forced reproduction, sexual abuse and violation, and rape. They also experienced the dehumanization of not being able to speak their language, retain their names, come and go of their own volition, or have autonomy over their own bodies. They were sold, traded, and used to secure loans and satisfy debts, as enslaved people were considered chattel—property—and not people at all. This was codified into law, including in the U.S. Constitution, where the enslaved had no rights and were not even fully human under the law, which defined each of them as merely three-fifths of a person. This dehumanization was what was necessary to support an entire society where one group of people was made to do the most arduous agricultural labor, cultivating animals and crops as well as planting, harvesting, and processing commercial and food crops. They produced crops such as indigo, sugarcane, tobacco, sweet and white potatoes, rice, peas, and citrus with no compensation and no legal or other autonomy recognized by whites.

LAND, AGRICULTURAL LABOR, AND RACE FROM THE LATE NINETEENTH THROUGH THE MID-TWENTIETH CENTURIES

This land appropriation from Native Americans and forced labor of enslaved Africans and their descendants is what created the United States' wealth and influence as the new nation sought to become a global power. The profits from the work of the enslaved certainly created wealth for the enslavers and in those places where enslavement was legal. Wealth was also created through the entirety of the United States, as burgeoning industries such as finance, insurance, and mass textile production were intricately tied to an economy fueled and, in many cases, generated by the enslaved. The Industrial Revolution was premised upon the technological innovations made on plantations by the enslaved and enslavers, according to historian Edward Baptist.

As Julie Guthman, a social scientist at the University of California, Santa Cruz, explains, the late nineteenth and early twentieth centuries continued patterns, practices, and laws that were privileging to whites while oppressing people of color. The experiences of multiple groups of people of color has certainly fortified the color line around who was allowed to own property in the United States and who was not in ways that were started in colonization and enslavement and that reverberate today. Shortly after the Union won the Civil War and enslavement ended in 1865, a plan was initiated to provide the 4 million formerly enslaved people with land as some small measure of compensation for their stolen bodies and stolen labor, which is estimated to be worth $6.4 trillion in contemporary money. Issued by the Union Army general William T. Sherman as Field Order 15, this plan, better known as 40 acres and a mule, called for miles of land abandoned or confiscated during the Civil War of white enslavers' land across a region that included the agriculturally rich South Carolina, Georgia, and Florida. This plan to establish the formerly enslaved with the ability to be self-sufficient was one of the most radical and important elements of the postwar Reconstruction era. After President Abraham Lincoln's assassination, his successor, Andrew Johnson, overturned that order and had the land returned to its former white owners. This was detrimental to the newly emancipated African Americans. It also heralded the beginnings of new forms of systematic racist oppression. Sharecropping and Jim Crow laws and customs were put into place to re-create the social, political, and economic conditions that emancipation and Reconstruction were supposed to end. Today, the value of the land promised by Sherman is approximately $1.3 trillion. If the order had not been rescinded, each contemporary descendant of enslaved people in the United States would have approximately $400,000 in wealth derived from it. In other parts of the United States at this time, the federal government gave away millions of acres, mostly west of the Mississippi River, for free under a series of Homestead Acts that began in 1862. Taking advantage of this policy were 1.6 million homesteaders, some single women and almost all white, increasing the number of property owners in the United States dramatically. Just as during earlier periods of colonization, however, this land was expropriated from Indigenous people.

Land was also taken from the former Mexican citizens whose land became the United States and home to its settlers after the United States won the Mexican-American War in 1848. As the U.S. borders expanded into what had been Mexico, the rich farmland and productive ranches throughout Arizona, California, Colorado, Nevada, New Mexico, Texas, Utah, and Wyoming were incorporated into the nation while the people living there were not. They were instead deprived of their land, rights, culture, and their ability to work and accumulate wealth, in accordance with white supremacist reasoning. Deprivation was also cemented through practices of educational and housing segregation and acts of violence that continued well after the end of the war. This process is the reference point for the oft-used activist phrase heard from their descendants as they assert their right to life and prosperity in the United States: "We didn't cross the border; the border crossed us." Similarly, Puerto Ricans and Native Hawaiians were colonized at the end of the nineteenth century for access to the rich soil, bountiful crops, and lucrative supplies of sugarcane, coffee, rum, and pineapples. Indeed, a large number of residents of the U.S. colony Puerto Rico were recruited to relocate to the U.S. colony Hawaii after a series of devastating hurricanes created a global sugar shortage in 1899. Puerto Rican cane workers were compelled to labor in Hawaii sugarcane fields in order to meet the worldwide demand.

Rich agricultural land was also expropriated from Asian immigrants and their descendants. Workers from Asia—specifically, men from China, Japan, and the Philippines—were brought to the United States to work in agriculture after enslavement's end and sharecropping's start, in addition to being recruited to work in mining and on railroad construction. These workers all faced low pay, social stigma, stereotypes, and discrimination. Those who were able to secure enough money to accrue land were treated as a threat by other landowners, white citizens, and politicians who wrote and passed a series of Alien Land Acts that restricted the ability to own land in the United States by immigrants deemed ineligible for citizenship. The Naturalization Act of 1870 allowed all whites and people of African ancestry the ability to become citizens of the United States while excluding other groups and revoking citizenship from people of Chinese descent. As people deemed ineligible for citizenship, Chinese and Japanese people in the United States were banned from long-term land leases and land ownership. In California alone, large swaths of land were seized from Chinese and Japanese migrants and their families under the Alien Land Acts as a result. At the beginning of World War II, most Japanese Americans worked in agriculture. Despite those Alien Land Acts preventing them from owning and leasing land, 40 percent of the vegetables grown in California were grown by Japanese immigrants and their American-citizen children, according to reporting from National Public Radio's Lisa Morehouse in 2017. After the United States' entry into the war and President Roosevelt's Executive Order 9066 in 1942, tens of thousands of Japanese immigrants and Japanese Americans were forced to relocate into internment camps, leaving the communities, homes, and businesses behind. Once settled into one of the nation's 10 internment camps, women, men, and children were compelled to work harvesting, tending, and planting food and commercial crops, as well as keeping livestock such as chickens and pigs, even as they were dispossessed of their own land. Furthermore, they received less than one-fourth of what other farmworkers were paid and had stiff fines imposed upon them if they did not work, showing the lack of choice they had.

The internment camps were strategically placed on land that was part of national irrigation projects or had some potential for agricultural production that the government wanted to exploit during and after the war. Some of the camps had such abundant and fertile farmland that workers were made to harvest food for themselves and others interned at different camps. Food and other crops from their labor were also sold on the open market, though the profits never flowed to those who produced the farm goods. After the war's end, the land that had been worked and improved by Japanese and Japanese American internees was distributed as homesteads to white soldiers returning from battle. After their release from the camps, though some internees returned to agriculture, many never did, citing the horrors they had undergone and the time, land, and equipment that was taken away from them. By 1960 only approximately 25 percent had gone back to farming. Their losses were estimated at some $4 billion in today's money. Compensation for what the internees endured and lost would not come until more than 40 years later, in 1988, when survivors were issued an official apology and $20,000 in reparations from the federal government.

The current food system's use and exploitation of immigrant labor of those from Mexico and Central America is a long-standing process. The history of Mexican farmworkers in the United States is itself rooted in patterns of inequality, exploitation, and exclusion. Once racist immigration policies restricted and barred immigrants from Asia, U.S. employers turned to their southern neighbor, Mexico, for agricultural workers. Further instances of this practice of recruiting labor from Mexico are found as the United States entered World War II. As U.S. men went off to fight on fronts in Africa, Asia, and Europe, the farms they had been working on needed laborers. Growers lobbied state and federal legislatures into starting the nation's first official guest worker program, so the United States launched a massive importation plan that moved Mexican farmers north in 1942. This Mexican Farm Labor Program Agreement, or Bracero (which roughly translates to "manual laborer") program, provided more than 4 million Mexican farmworkers until 1961. Their work kept the U.S. agricultural industry afloat, yet they were subjected to deportations, public and political scorn, low pay and poor working conditions, and, ironically, both a lack of food and poor-quality food. Additionally, they experienced segregation and other discriminatory treatment.

Through these forms of food-related exploitation and oppression, people of color in the United States have not been passive. In each one, they have mounted resistance campaigns. For example, the interned Japanese retained their culture by preparing more intimate family meals rather than eating in mess halls, and they refused to work for low pay and under unsafe conditions, even as this meant they would be court-martialed, placed under martial law, and ordered into stockades within their already restrictive living conditions. Many Mexican braceros protested, went on strike, and organized labor unions to improve their food, pay, and work conditions.

Anthropologist Ashanté M. Reese posits that African Americans have long employed a politics and culture of self-reliance when it comes to assuring their needs amid contexts beginning with enslavement in the sixteenth century and especially during times of transition such as during the shift from enslavement to freedom, the Great Migration, and the end of legal discrimination with the modern civil rights movement of the 1960s. Securing food for themselves and other community members has been one key way this has taken shape in practice. To supplement the meager diets afforded them by their enslavers, the enslaved used knowledge, traditions, and seeds they brought with them from West Africa to plant gardens near their quarters. After emancipation, African American intellectuals and leaders such as W. E. B. Du Bois, a noted activist and founder of American sociology, and Booker T. Washington, a formerly enslaved man who would go on to become president of Tuskegee University, espoused the importance of African Americans growing, distributing, processing, and otherwise controlling their own food as paths to true freedom and community control in the decades after enslavement's end. During the civil rights movement, key figures, such as Mississippi's Fannie Lou Hamer founded national cooperatives for African American farmers who were shut out from white-controlled agricultural networks, financing, and opportunities.

Like other Black resistance movements, including the civil rights movement, funded through efforts of Black women and restaurant owners who made and sold meals, and organizations such as the Nation of Islam, which made nutrition and health education a key component of its work, the Black Panther Party saw food as a critical component of its work too. In the face of economic inequality and government indifference in African American communities, one of the first missions of the Black Panther Party was to establish several of what they called survival programs. These filled community needs around education, safety, and health. Food was a key part of the survival programs as well as the Panthers' 10-Point Program, which included both land and food in its many calls for justice. The first Panther-sponsored free breakfast program was started in the late 1960s in

Oakland, California, and was quickly replicated by other Panther chapters across the country. Chapters collected cash and food donations from businesses, religious and nonprofit organizations, and individuals as they fed thousands of children in schools, community centers, and churches each week. The success and demonstrable need for the breakfasts spurred the start of national Panther efforts to provide lunches to children and bags of groceries to any in need. Though the Panthers as an organization had been dismantled due to the FBI's repressive Counterintelligence Program (COINTELPRO) by the early 1980s, the Panthers' legacy of providing food had been cemented: their efforts became institutionalized through nonprofit, philanthropic, and, ironically, government-funded efforts. Food programs founded and inspired by the Panthers continue to feed children and adults in free breakfast, food pantry, summer lunch, and other food programs across the country's cities and towns. Children of all races being fed by the federally funded School Breakfast and Summer Food Service Programs today are beneficiaries of programs institutionalized in the wake of Panthers' efforts to feed poor Black children.

STEREOTYPES AND CULTURAL IMAGES AROUND FOOD

Inequalities related to food are not limited to the economic or social realms. They are cultural as well. After enslavement's end and as the era of colonialism ended, immigration of new groups of people fostered stereotypes and other related inequalities within the United States. These took shape through food-derived myths and slurs at times. One example is seen as immigration from Asia in general and China in particular became framed as a social problem in the late nineteenth and early twentieth centuries. Stereotypes of Chinese people eating rodents and animals kept as pets in the United States, such as cats and dogs, began to proliferate and were weaponized as propaganda that allowed racist policies and laws, such as the 1875 Page Act, which essentially barred Asian women from coming to the United States; the 1882 Chinese Exclusion Act, which halted immigration from China; and the various Alien Land Acts in several states that denied Asians in the United States the ability to own land and other properties, to easily pass. (In)famously, a *New York Times* article that asked if Chinese people ate rats was published.

Food companies also have drawn on these images. One example is Pillsbury's use of racist caricatures to sell its Funny Face drink mix to compete with the popular Kool-Aid brand in the 1960s. The buck-toothed/slant-eyed and war-painted/feather-wearing so-called funny faces represented the drink flavors Chinese Cherry and Injun Orange, respectively. In the late 1960s, Frito-Lay launched its character the Frito Bandito, a broken-English-speaking, gold-toothed, handlebar-mustachioed Mexican highway bandit, to sell its corn chips. Though the campaign only lasted four years due to Frito-Lay pulling it from use after protests, its cultural resonance continued far after the character disappeared from advertisements.

Such racist characterizations and the myths and associations with food still exist, as the usage of the aforementioned term *beaner* shows. A number of products have actively engaged these in their marketing and branding well into the twenty-first century. When it was initially introduced in 1944, the Chiquita Banana mascot was a banana dressed in a red dress and high heels, carrying fruit on its head, depicting the racist image of a hypersexual Latina. This image was itself based on Brazilian actress Carmen Miranda and created to justify the sexual and economic exploitation of Latinas in Latin America and the United States. In the 1980s the anthropomorphized banana gave way to a Latin American woman carrying fruit on her head while dressed in a form-fitting dress and heels and still carrying a basket of fruit on her head.

Cultural stereotypes about African American servility have shaped both food work and food marketing and branding. African Americans' forced agricultural labor under enslavement and through the civil rights movement of the 1950s and 1960s made its way to consumers' packaged goods as well, as images of Blacks as servants have been used to sell food through the present. The continued use of images of Aunt Jemima, Rastus, and Uncle Ben draw on a cultural nostalgia for enslavement, according to such scholars as Maurice Manring. Quaker Oats's Aunt Jemima, which originated in 1893, played on the myth of the Mammy. Even after the image was updated from an overweight, handkerchief-wearing, formerly enslaved African American woman to a more contemporary version, the name remained, with its full rooting in enslavement and the Jim Crow era, when whites referred to Black women with the derisive term "Aunt" or "Auntie" rather than their given names. Though African Americans have called for the image and name to be changed since its inception, the Aunt Jemima trademark holder resisted these calls until June 2020 when it was announced that the name and image would be dropped as an overture to racial equality during a summer that began with international protests against racism in policing, housing, employment, and other social systems. Other popular brands have similarly long histories of racial stereotyping. One example is Cream of Wheat and its use of the character of Rastus. The brand invoked this name and caricatured image, which gained popularity in post–Civil War minstrel shows that solidified the myth of cheerful African American servants, in 1893 as well. Rice company Uncle Ben's introduced its smiling, docile elderly Black man's character in 1943. Just as African American women were referred to as "Aunt," whites called African American men "Uncle" to avoid addressing them directly by name. As with Aunt Jemima, in June 2020 Mars Incorporated, owner of Uncle Ben's, announced changes to the brand that would end its racist depiction, after decades of protests. Other brands using racist caricatures of other groups followed suit. One was the Dreyer's Grand Ice Cream–owned ice cream confection Eskimo Pie; Dreyer's announced it was dropping that name and its accompanying imagery after 99 years, since Eskimo is a derogatory term used to refer to the Inuit and Yupik people. Earlier in 2020, Land O' Lakes announced that it would remove the image of a young Native American woman from its butter packaging after using it for more than 90 years and following many years of activism to end its display. Counterprotests were immediately launched in response to each of these decisions to halt these uses of racist iconography in food marketing and branding, showing how attached some people are to these depictions and the ideologies they reinforce.

The combination of factors explored in this chapter, all of which stem from racial discrimination, is an example of what scholars refer to when they discuss structural racism. Structural racism occurs in such a fashion that it is deeply embedded into a society's culture, economy, and politics and can have impacts independent of an individual's personal belief, knowledge, desire, or intent. Structural racism occurs when historical and contemporary social systems, made up of cultural understandings and representations, social norms, social policies, institutional practices, and laws, work together to create, maintain, and deepen racial inequalities for members of racially marginalized groups. In the United States, these groups include those people under the umbrella of the term *people of color*—members of groups the U.S. Census defines as American Indian and Alaska Native, Asian American and Pacific Islander, Black or African American, and Hispanic or Latino. In addition to the colonization, land appropriation, enslavement, xenophobic immigration laws, and Jim Crow racism of the seventeenth through mid-twentieth centuries, contemporary policies and practices of labor exploitation, unequal educational funding and quality, lower wages, redlining, residential segregation, environmental racism, mass incarceration, and discriminatory hiring and promotion practices are some of the ways that structural racism feeds into food inequalities. These are all present in shaping the basis of the next chapter: inequalities in food access and availability.

CHAPTER 3

Inequalities in Food Access

The USDA's Economic Research Service (ERS) discusses food access as key for decisions that consumers make about what to buy and what to eat. These are influenced by the distance they must travel and available modes of transportation to retail outlets, as well as the prices, affordability, and the availability of food. Social statuses and geographic locations mean some have abundance and others have scarcity in their options. Whites, people with incomes above the federal poverty line, households without children, and suburban residents are more likely to be food secure. The corollary is that Latinx and African American people, people with incomes at or below the federal poverty line, households with children and especially those households with children headed by single parents, people living alone, and urban and rural residents are less likely to be food secure.

FOOD INSECURITY

Data from a 2006 USDA study by Mark Nord, Margaret Andrews, and Steven Carlson show the severity of the situation for those with very low food security: almost all reported that they worried that their food would run out before they got money to buy more (98 percent); that the food they bought did not last and they did not have money to get more (97 percent); that an adult in the household had reduced the size of their meals or skipped meals due to a lack of money for food (97 percent); that they could not afford to eat balanced meals (95 percent); that they had eaten less than they felt they should due to a lack of money for food (95 percent); that they had been hungry but did not eat due to a lack of money for food

(68 percent); that they had lost weight due to a lack of money for food (44 percent); and that an adult in the household had done without food for an entire day due to a lack of money for food (33 percent).

Indeed, many people without the ability to obtain the foods they prefer are hesitant to fully disclose their struggle. Instead of discussing their hunger, they may talk about fixing the same meal of rice and beans every night. Others apply for government assistance, only to never use it. Some refuse to ask for help, clinging to their independence even as they go to bed hungry or lose weight from their many missed meals. Research from Feeding America further illustrates some of the techniques those who are food insecure use to manage their scant access to food. These include 83 percent of people who economize what money they do have by buying cheap, unhealthy foods, 53 percent of people who get help from friends, 40 percent who water down their food or drinks, 35 percent of people who sell or pawn whatever valuable personal items they have for more money to spend on food, and 23 percent who plant and grow food in gardens. The pressure to engage in these strategies is quite acute among those responsible for minor children.

As sociologist Kate Cairns finds, children in food-insecure households are very active participants in helping themselves and their families secure necessary food. In her dealings with children and teens working at an urban garden, she noted that kids not only donated some of their checks to the household to buy food but also took home produce from the gardens to supplement meals. They also made sure that younger siblings ate, mirroring strategies used by parents and other adults. A study conducted by sociologists Sinnika Elliott and Sarah Bowen finds children as young as eight are also not only aware of a lack of food and money in their homes but are also actively working to help their families by doing things such as collecting cans and bottles to be recycled for money, refusing snacks, filling up on water, sleeping to ward off their hunger pangs, and telling parents they are allergic to food to ensure that the scarce amounts of food coming into their homes can be stretched across members of the household. It is important to note that these strategies are important for immediate survival. It is also important to note that living in food-insecure households has long-term implications. There are declines in grades, for example. Additionally, children without enough to eat often act out in school and are thus seen as behavioral problems and subjected to harsh disciplinary repercussions in school and increasingly in the criminal justice system. Additionally, there are the less apparent costs, such as lack of energy, lack of focus on schoolwork, and the inability to fully participate in sports and other extracurricular activities. As these are often preparatory for other educational opportunities, food insecurity in early childhood may limit children's ability to gain further education, making it more likely that they and subsequently their children will continue to experience the compounding inequalities associated with inadequate access to food. People in homes where food is overabundant and neighborhoods replete with educational and other resources do not have to consider these implications.

In places where wages are too high for individuals and households to qualify for public assistance programs and too low to afford available housing, food insecurity rates are increasing. Reporting from Tara Duggan asserts that though approximately 10 percent of Bay Area residents do not earn enough to afford the basic costs of living, 62 percent of this population earns too much to qualify for Supplementary Nutritional Assistance Program (SNAP) benefits. Furthermore, though the unemployment rate in the area is lower than it has been in decades, these realities are insufficient when it comes to being able to afford both food and rent. As the costs of housing in particular rise, residents of communities in such places as the Bay Area have to sacrifice food in order to pay for shelter. This is explained by the fact that housing costs are fixed and less likely to be sacrificed compared with food. When choices have to be made and money has to be shifted to meet household needs, housing costs are the last to be touched, and food can be among the first, whether this means buying less from the store, purchasing generics or lower-quality items, or missing meals. Indeed, it is easier to find enough food for basic sustenance than it is to find help paying the mortgage or rent.

There are people working every day who are increasingly unable to afford life in areas that are growing more and more expensive for almost everyone who had been calling it home. One indication of this is found as the gap between an adequate food budget and one that someone earning minimum wage can actually afford is some $652. This shortfall is often made up through people skipping meals, relying on what is available at area food banks and other food charities, and eating cheaper and often less nutritious foods. These are all associated with risks, such as nutritional deficiencies and increased consumption of fats, sugars, and processed ingredients.

Similar findings are present in other parts of the Bay Area and are of serious concern in other rapidly gentrifying communities across the United States. Some charities and churches fill this gap when it comes to food, through the presence of food pantries inside public schools, the San Jose–based Wesley United Methodist Church's provision of free grocery deliveries to those in need, and the opening of several new food pantries in areas where the median housing value of homes is $1.85 million for a single-family home. Indeed, these realities defy the picture that many have of those who are hungry as foraging for food in trash cans, asking for spare change to buy a meal, and sleeping in an old car or a tent city at night.

Recent USDA data show that the majority of people in the United States are food secure. Eighty-eight percent of households have access to enough food. The converse of this statistic is that some 12 percent of households are food insecure. Of these, 7 percent have low food security, and 5 percent had very low food security. Those households with low food security often also rely on food obtained from area food banks and federal food assistance programs to ensure that they have enough food to fulfill basic food needs. Those in households with very low food security do not even have that. Though they may get food from local food banks or through federal food assistance programs, their ability to access food is limited to the point that they may only be able to eat once a day. People with very low food security also may not be able to eat enough at any one meal through the day to eliminate hunger or nutritional deficiencies. Food security is another social reality that is influenced by the social structures that create inequalities based on the intertwined nature of geography, social class, and race.

THE SOCIAL CLASS AND RACIAL DYNAMICS OF FOOD ACCESS

Social Class and Food Access

Research indicates that, on individual and group levels, social statuses shape whether and how food inequalities are experienced. Social class is one lens through which this is crystallized. Though it is true that people with higher amounts of disposable income may spend more to purchase a particular brand and those with less money may be more likely to buy generics or a store brand, the costs of food staples are not income dependent. There is not much variance in the cost of a dozen eggs or a gallon of milk. Price fluctuations for the basics are more closely tied to region rather than to social class. Data from the Bureau of Labor Statistics show that people in the United States spend a lot of money on food annually. Indeed, in 2018, households spent almost $8,000 on food, an increase of 2.5 percent compared with 2017. Food is the second-highest cost for urban dwellers—after housing—and the third-highest for those living in suburban and rural communities, behind housing and transportation, respectively.

There are wider disparities on food spending when income levels are considered. The bottom quintile of U.S. earners, with a mean income of

$11,394, spends more than one-third of their pretax income on food. U.S. earners in the next quintile have a mean income of $29,821 and spend about 19 percent of their income on food. Many of the households in the bottom two quintiles have earnings that are so low they qualify for federal food assistance, even if most do not actually receive such assistance. Those in the middle quintile have a mean income of $52,431 and spend 13.4 percent of their income on food. U.S. earners in the next quintile have a mean income of $86,363 and spend just over 10 percent of their income on food. Earners in the highest quintile have a mean income of $188,103 and spend slightly under 7 percent of their income on food.

It very well may be the case that food insecurity is more severe that an initial exploration of data indicates, given the stigma faced by those lacking enough work, money, and food. A research team led by Debbie S. Dougherty from the University of Missouri finds that in the wake of the Great Recession that started in 2008, people were more comfortable discussing their lack of employment than they were their lack of food. This 2018 study also reveals the pertinence of social class as it shapes the ways that individuals think about and discuss food. It shows that people with lower incomes perceive food as a means of survival while people in the middle class use language that obscures their access to food. This makes it difficult to determine whether they are food insecure. For both classes, perceptions of food make them unlikely to disclose any food insecurity to others who may be able to assist them, limiting their ability to obtain the food they need. This is a key finding, as poorer people may be able to obtain food through less personal institutions, policies, and programs that target them while middle-income people are rarely considered in remedies for food insecurity. The research team finds that for the affluent, food is not seen as a physical necessity but as a social one that facilitates their ability to network with others. This research unveils the existence of food insecurity for not just the poor but the middle class as well. It also unveils the class-based ways that food and food access are understood, discussed, and lived. Poor and working-class study participants are more likely to document physical activities such as hunting and fishing or the scarcity of food in their homes. Middle-class study participants, on the other hand, are more oblique in their discussions of food, describing diets without much variety or healthy options but not admitting that they do not actually have enough to eat.

Race and Food Access

A study led by Heather O'Connell of Rice University indicates that there is a triracial system of inequality at work in the United States that is visible through supermarket access. This assessment is revealed through the example of Houston, Texas, neighborhoods with sizable African American populations having the least supermarket access. This finding is consistent, even when factors including income, college education, employment status, and population density are controlled, or held steady. Based on the way this triracial system of social inequality occurs, whites have the highest access and availability of food resources, followed by Asian Americans, then Latinx people, and finally African Americans, with the least access and availability. Neighborhoods with a predominantly white or Asian American population have a supermarket within a half mile. This is in comparison to neighborhoods with a predominantly white majority and those with a large African American population that have supermarkets that are much farther away.

A report from Jodi L. Liu, Han Bing, and Deborah A. Cohen of the Centers for Disease Control (CDC) reveals that the average distance from U.S. households to the nearest supermarket is just over two miles. Traversing this distance while carrying enough food to supply a household on foot, via public transportation, or while riding a bike is quite different and more difficult than in a car. Without easy passage to supermarkets, individuals and families may be limited to shopping in local outlets. Though more convenient, these typically have more limited selections, lower quality, and higher prices. They are also less likely to have ready access to foods that the CDC calls upon consumers to eat in order to support healthy eating patterns. As noted in previous chapters, healthy eating patterns are important, as are the emotional, mental, and physical benefits that come with being food secure.

GEOGRAPHY OF FOOD ACCESS AND AVAILABILITY

The details of food access and availability are further illuminated when looking extensively at the ways residence affects food options. Those living in rural and large metropolitan communities are more likely to be food insecure than those living in smaller metropolitan areas and suburbs. As USDA data illustrate, 15 percent of households in nonmetropolitan or more rural areas and 14 percent of households in major metropolitan areas experience food insecurity. Food insecurity rates also vary across region. The South has the highest rates of household food insecurity (14 percent), followed by the Midwest (12 percent), the West (12 percent), and then the Northeast (11 percent). Geographic location means that for some, food options are very much limited. It can also mean that foods that are available are often processed and high in preservatives, sugar, sodium, and fat, rather than fresh and high in vitamins, nutrients, and minerals. When compared with neighborhoods where populations are more likely to be white and/or suburban, available food choices are decidedly limited yet more expensive. In addition, while grocery stores are scarce, fast food is not. The saturation of fast-food restaurants with their preponderance of processed foods that are high in fat and sugar and low in nutritional value to the exclusion of healthy food options in some neighborhoods has recently been termed *food swamp*. Whether a small mom-and-pop joint or a multinational chain, fast food is often the most available, accessible, and affordable choice for people living in communities marked by food inequalities. A 2017 study by Kristen Cooksey-Stowers, Marlene B. Schwartz, and Kelly D. Brownell reveals that unhealthy food retailers outnumber healthy food retailers four to one.

A particular kind of food inequality occurs when there is geographic limitation on available foods. These are commonly referred to as food deserts. Food swamps often are found in places marked as food deserts, and both have negative effects on health. Ten percent of the U.S. population live in places that are marked by both low incomes and an absence of supermarkets less than one mile away from their homes, according to the USDA estimates of distance-to-supermarkets report using 2010 U.S. Census data. While there is overlap between food deserts and income, these are not perfectly correlated, as USDA data show that only about half of those who live in food deserts are themselves poor.

Food Access and Availability in Suburban Communities

Though suburban communities are often painted as idyllic, people there may also have limited access to food. Plagued by more limited access to public transportation than urban residents are, those who do not have reliable access to their own transportation but live in sprawling U.S. suburbs that are designed for those reliant on cars are limited in their ability to go to full-service grocery stores, even if such stores are abundant where they live. Often described as "hidden hunger," food insecurity in the suburbs may not look as it does in Baltimore, Chicago, or Detroit but is nonetheless present. Just as in the city, those who need to go grocery shopping in the suburbs may be faced with time-intensive multiple buses and trains and multiple trips in order to get food into their homes. Race and class play important roles in the dynamics of access here as well. In suburban Cook County, Illinois (which is adjacent to its big-city neighbor, Chicago), for example, more than 350,000 people, or some 15 percent of the population, have limited access to food. Throughout suburban Cook County, there are racial differences in residents' access to food as well as the kinds of stores they are able to access, according to a study led by Chicago State University geographer Daniel Block. According to their 2012 report, suburbs with large African American populations have the most distance between supermarkets and residents. Those supermarkets that are present are more likely to be chain discount stores than specialty and full-service chain grocery stores, compared with stores in other communities. Suburbs with large Latinx populations are farther from full-service chain grocery stores but closer to other kinds of stores, such as independent grocers, smaller corner stores, and liquor stores, compared with those with large numbers of white residents. Farmers markets and specialty chains are found in close proximity to white and higher-income communities. Suburban renters, who typically have lower incomes and wealth than homeowners, live closer to drugstores, corner stores, independent and fast-food outlets, and liquor stores, which can affect the kinds of food they eat.

Food Access and Availability in Rural Communities

Reports from organizations such as the Food Trust, a nonprofit founded to provide food and nutrition information and increase access to affordable, nutritious food, show us—though much media and academic focus has been on food insecurity and food deserts in urban communities—that rural locales and Native American reservations are also quite hard hit by unequal and insufficient access to food. Though much of America's food is produced in locations such as these, those who live near the sites of food production often lack financial, transportation, and other resources they need in order to eat easily or eat well.

Approximately 27 percent of people in the United States live in rural areas. USDA data show that 7 percent of rural dwellers live more than 10 miles from their nearest grocery store, meaning they live in a food desert. More than 2 million people live in low-income rural areas that are also more than 10 miles from a supermarket, according to the USDA. They tend to be poorer than their city peers, as 60 percent of those in rural food deserts are themselves low-income. Intersections of race and region matter here as well. Analyses from Sarah Treuhaft and Allison Karpyn of the Food Trust show that the highest poverty gap between urban and rural environs exists in the South. Furthermore, African Americans and Native Americans in the South are most likely to be poor. USDA analyses show the particularly dire situations for Native Americans living in rural, low-income communities. More than 15 percent of this group live more than 20 miles from the nearest full-service grocery store compared with less than

3 percent of those in moderate- and high-income areas. For those living on federally designated tribal lands, including those residing in American Indian Tribal Areas, Alaska Native Village Areas, and Native Hawaiian Homelands, close to 72 percent live in rural areas. Eighteen percent live between 10 and 20 miles away, and 14 percent of this group live more than 20 miles from the nearest full-service grocery store. Of those who are poor, 18 percent live more than 20 miles away from a grocery store. For those living on federally designated tribal lands in urban locations, nearly 50 percent are more than 1 mile from the nearest supermarket and about 44 percent of those who are poor also live more than 1 mile from the nearest supermarket. Here we also see how race is implicated in geographic access to food, a subject explored further in the next section.

RACE, GEOGRAPHY, AND FOOD ACCESS

Though often associated with income levels, race is also very heavily implicated in who has ready access to food and who does not. Social structural factors of segregation, deindustrialization, suburbanization, and urban disinvestment help explain this. In some urban communities, African Americans have to travel more than a mile farther than do white people of the same social class standing to get to the nearest supermarket. African Americans, Latinx people, and Native Americans are more likely to have problems accessing and affording food than whites are. One example of this is apparent, as food deserts are commonly found in African American neighborhoods regardless of the socioeconomic status of the residents living there. In an analysis conducted by the Food Trust, African Americans are 2.5 times and Latinx people are almost 1.5 times more likely than whites to live in places where full-service grocery stores are absent. Even in comparably poor communities, whites have more access to local grocery stores than African Americans do. Perhaps coming as a surprise to some, Kelly M. Bower, Roland J. Thorpe, Charles Rohde, and Darrell J. Gaskin, scholars at Johns Hopkins University, found that high-income African Americans had less access to full-service grocery stores in their communities than poor whites do, due to the dynamics of historic and continuing racial discrimination and segregation in the housing market.

Similarly, in 2007, a team of researchers led by public health scholar and economist Lisa Powell found that, overall, compared with whites, African Americans are half as likely to live in communities where they have easy access to large chain supermarkets. Compared with whites, Latinx people are one-third as likely to live in communities where they have easy access to large chain supermarkets. In African American and

Latinx communities, when supermarkets were present, they were far more likely to be small, independently owned stores than they were in white communities. In addition to a lack of variety, one disadvantage of these small, independently owned stores is that they do not get the price concessions based on order volume that their larger, corporate-owned competitors do. As such, they pass these higher costs along to their customers, further exacerbating the financial and other related inequities experienced by people of color.

A report released in 2018 by Marynia Kolak, Daniel Block, and Myles Wolf documents the difficulty in addressing food deserts in Chicago—the city where the term was popularized in 2006 by Mari Gallagher, a research consultant. The city's officials, policy makers, and business owners describe creating more access to food in those areas of Chicago identified as food deserts as a major priority. As a result, there were commitments to open new stores. The researchers' findings, however, are that new supermarkets were opened in places that already had access to food. This means that supermarket access remains as low in food deserts as before the city's initiatives began. So, while the number of supermarkets in Chicago did increase in the study period between 2007 and 2014, food deserts and the resultant food inequalities remain. One particularly striking statistic reported by the team of scholars led by Northwestern University's Marynia Kolak is that though African Americans account for one-third of Chicago's population, they make up 80 percent of those who lack consistent access to healthy food options. Kolak and her colleagues state that the majority of those new supermarkets are opened in or near food oases, increasing the already prevalent rich assortment of choices in those communities. When supermarkets are opened in low-food-access communities, their presence is too sparse to remedy the lack of food options available to residents. The Northwestern University scholars recommend that the definition of food deserts be changed from the current one, which is based on low-income census tracts where residents must travel at least one mile to reach the nearest supermarket. Instead, they offer a definition that is focused on those places with persistent patterns of limited access to food. This avoids the issue of creating what they call *food desert islands* that do not actually remedy a lack of food access.

Other Factors Related to Food Access and Availability

Access to food does not end at the presence of grocery stores and supermarkets around the corner or two blocks away from one's home. Kolak and her colleagues also note that access means that food is both affordable and fairly priced in comparison to food in other neighborhoods. Transportation also matters for access. If a car is necessary to obtain healthy food options, this disadvantages those with unreliable cars as well as those who rely on rides from others, walking, biking, and public transportation. The conditions of streets, highways, and sidewalks also matter in the ability to easily purchase food. According to Jerry Shannon, a University of Georgia geographer, perceptions of neighborhood safety are also a factor in access to food. This is the case in cities and other locales. Food access is also a matter of time—if food shopping and preparation constitute a lengthy process, then food is less accessible, especially for those with lengthy commutes, nonstandard work schedules, and/or familial obligations. Heavier time debts are also accrued for those who must walk, bike, wait for a ride, bus, or train to get to a full-service store. Food access and affordability are also compromised for people who have never been married and who are divorced or separated, people who rent rather than own their homes and people who are less educated when compared with their counterparts. Policy proposals from the Northwestern research team referenced earlier suggest remedies for a number of components of insufficient food access, such as improved public transportation and increased community-supported agriculture resources to ensure the presence of fresh and affordable produce, and new community economic resources, such as jobs and income.

In places with low levels of food access, there is not just less variety in choices but also higher prices for what is available. In communities with low incomes and low access, food costs are 3–8 percent higher than in low-income, high-access communities; 3–6 percent higher than in high-income, low-access communities; and 3–11 percent higher than in high-income, high-access communities. Poorer households spend a greater share of their income on food, compared with more affluent households. In 2017 poor households spent just over 34 percent of their income on food, while middle-class households spent approximately 14.3 percent of their income on food. Residents of less affluent communities also often have an abundance of restaurants that serve affordable, calorie-dense fast food. This is offset by the high costs of these foods' lack of nutrition, however.

There tends to be an inverse relationship between calorie density and cost, so fruits and vegetables that have fewer calories—and more water—are more expensive per calorie than sugary and salty snacks, for example. One study from University of Washington researchers Adam Drewnowski and S. E. Specter found that while fresh carrots carried with them 250 calories per dollar, cookies packed nearly five times as many calories into each dollar they cost. Calorie for calorie, it is cheaper to drink orange soda than to drink orange juice than to eat an orange, even if the healthfulness of each choice declines with increases in processing. For those who are trying to maximize the energy or calories they get for their money, cookies and orange soda are the logical choices. This helps explain why even with knowledge of the health value of foods low in calories, fats, and sugar, people choose more processed items. It also helps to explain why rates of overweight and obesity are rising in the United States even as a lower share of disposable income is being spent on food. Healthy fats, such as leaner cuts of meat and fish, nuts, and olive oil are also more expensive than less healthy sources of fats. Communities with limited food access tend to have less attractive and poorer-quality produce options—when these items are available at all—making these foods less of an option for consumers. Produce and other fresh foods are also more likely to spoil, leading cost-sensitive shoppers to avoid these items when food shopping. When food costs are high and budgets tight, there is little tolerance for risk in food purchases. When choices have to be made between types of food, many people's economic realities mean that it makes sense to choose foods high in calories that are low in cost, even if they are also low in nutritional value. What looks like a poor choice is actually a reflection of poverty. What looks like an individual preference is in reality shaped by economic and other social factors. Some of these additional factors include public and private research, energy, transportation, and technological and infrastructure investments. These have extensive economic bearing on food production, the food system, and any inequalities that come to bear on these, as noted by the Institute of Medicine and National Research Council. As they also assert, a food system's social and economic success comes as it offers foods that are high in affordability, nutrition, safety, and quality. While this is the case for many, and perhaps most in the United States, there are large swaths of the population who are excluded. Inequalities based on race, class, geography, education, and occupation mean that there are inequalities in the U.S. food system. It also means that the U.S. food system cannot be labeled an unequivocal success.

Some of the contributing factors to this lack of success are rooted in the inextricable linkages of racism, residential segregation, and concentrated poverty. These work with and reinforce each other, creating a set of cumulative disadvantages. The areas of the food system where inequalities exist, as explored in this chapter, show these are structural and institutional rather than individual or cultural. Cultural components are present when it comes to food inequalities, however. These are examined in the next chapter.

CHAPTER 4

Food, Culture, and Inequalities

"You have good taste!" This compliment is handed down when someone sports a new outfit, creates a playlist for a party, chooses a wine for a dinner companion, or prepares a dish for a coworker. What does it mean, though? Like so many things, the answer to that question is, "It depends." Taste is relative, and our—and others'—assessment of what is tasteful and in good taste or what is deemed in poor taste or tasteless is rooted in social characteristics that include race, class, and/or culture rather than some universally defined metrics of good and bad. These concepts are explored in depth in this chapter.

THE CULTURE OF TASTE

Classy or trashy, chic or tacky, everyone has taste. Contrary to popular opinion, especially that of those considered refined, elegant, and sophisticated, all tastes are subjective. Though cast as better, classical music, high fashion, and French dining are objectively as valuable as country music, tie-dyed T-shirts and cutoffs, and Frito pie. It is important to note that tastes in any cultural good—television, visual art, comedy, music, books, fashion, or food—are neither inherent nor neutral. They are powerfully shaped by social forces, with social class being one of the strongest predictors of what is seen as a natural predisposition. While, on its face, no taste is in reality better or worse than another, within a society where statuses are attached to inequalities and where structural disadvantages exist, the cultural tastes associated with those groups with the highest statuses become the norm by which all others are measured—and found to be lacking. This is the logic that supports Karl Marx's often-cited phrase that "the ideas of the ruling class are . . . the ruling ideas." As was the case in 1845 for Marx, this continues to be the case as it legitimizes the low social status of those outside the ruling class and allows cover for their disadvantage and oppression to continue while presenting the ideas, preferences, and privileges of those in power as benign and best for all.

Beginning in the 1970s, Pierre Bourdieu, a French sociologist, wrote a number of influential works on the interrelatedness of social class, culture, and social inequality. As a part of these efforts, he analyzed a related set of interlocking forms of capital: cultural, economic, human, and social. Cultural capital is a collection of resources that allows its possessor to know and show the expected, yet unwritten, social rules in any given social setting. It is about being aware of the way to shake hands, introduce people in social settings, and order lunch in a business setting. Economic capital is the form most familiar to most. It is money, in the form of both liquid assets, such as the cash in one's wallet and the balance in one's savings account, and illiquid assets, such as any properties and stocks and bonds that can be converted (or liquidated) into liquid funds. Human capital is about one's knowledge base. It is a collection of abilities, capacities, formal and informal education, skills, and talents. Social capital is what is inherent in the phrase, "It's not what you know; it's who you know." The "it" refers to how well social relationships can be leveraged to gain a host of personal benefits, especially the kinds that can lead to educational, employment, and financial success. In the United States and similar societies, there is often an individual and collective impetus to amass as much cultural, human, and social capital as possible and then convert these into economic capital. While there is literally more value attached to having higher amounts of income, property, and wealth, cultural capital operates differently. It is an asset that all have. Still, certain expressions of cultural capital are more prized and rewarded than others.

As noted earlier, one way to understand cultural capital is to see it as the rules for action in a given situation. Further, it is important not only to know the rules but to embody and live them in a way that is second nature and effortless. If, for example, you show that you have to think about or are concerned with the rules, you lose. This is because class and the status—in the Weberian sense, discussed in chapter 1—that class confers is something that is part of one's habitus, or the way that one sees, perceives, and acts in the social world, based on the collection of experiences and cultural and social locations, including—especially—their socioeconomic status. As this is an ingrained and embodied process that leads to dispositions, attitudes, habits, practices, and skills, it is as natural and unconscious as breathing. It is also rather fixed such that even as financial resources are lost or gained, habitus and the tastes it engenders will remain static. For example, those who grow up eating white bread in a low-income community will retain a preference for white bread, even if their income significantly rises and they move into an exclusive, wealthy locale. As habitus extends from what people have been socialized to appreciate, notice, dismiss, and revile, tastes and their manifestations become a deeply seated part of who they are. This process is so powerful that it is rarely explored or questioned. Instead, it is taken for granted and as a result, tastes and their manifestations are seen as natural and right. This leads to a justification of the social arrangements that value certain tastes over others. This further leads to a justification of the accompanying social inequalities that occur through individual-level or systemic exclusion of those lacking the supposed correct tastes or habitus. Those who embody dominant cultural capital—the dispositions, attitudes, habits, practices, and skills of those in social, economic, and cultural power—can then more easily enter and maintain membership among this group. When a nondominant form of cultural capital is possessed, the ability to enter and socialize within this group is compromised. Imagine a lunch interview where in addition to technical skills and qualifications, a job candidate's fit within the company culture is also being measured. The ways one dresses, shakes hands, makes conversation, uses utensils, breaks bread, and orders and eats food are all being measured based on how well they reflect the dominant form of cultural capital. This is in addition to their educational attainment, letters of recommendation, and previous experience. When applicants meet all of the stated job requirements but wipe their mouth on their shirt, begin eating before the rest of the table is served, or rip their boneless chicken breast apart with their hands, their likelihood of walking away with a job offer is next to none. Job interviews are stressful enough, but those involving food are often dreaded by recent college graduates who hail from working-class and poor backgrounds where nondominant forms of cultural capital are the norm.

Cultural capital is something learned within families, schools, and neighborhoods, all sites where social class is key. So these are also the sites where status, habitus, and cultural capital are reproduced, as are inequalities. It is important to note that in the United States, race and ethnicity, especially in their interactions with social class, are also components of cultural capital. Since dominant cultural capital is coded as white, elements of other racial and ethnic groups' culture are marked as nondominant, as work by scholars such as Berkeley's Prudence Carter demonstrates. As the cultural capital of whites with middle- and upper-class habitus, tastes, and

preferences in categories such as film, language, music, and food domi-
nates, this is presumed to be what is normal, what is right, and what is
expected of all. Any deviation from that is then regarded as deviant. This
illuminates the links between the forms of capital discussed earlier and
their implications in creating and maintaining systems of deep, and often
invisible, inequality.

FORMS OF CAPITAL AND FOOD

Food allows for a full appreciation of connections between cultural and
food tastes. Just as eating is fundamental to life, food is fundamental for
culture. Still, amid this universality, there is much specificity and vari-
ability as to what, why, and how any particular food is eaten. There is
also much appraisal and judgment attached to this. In his 1979 work on
taste and distinction, Pierre Bourdieu maps what he terms the *food space*
to show the relationships between food practices, economic capital, and
cultural capital. Those with more money in Bourdieu's 1970s France had
preferences for refined, light meals that were prepared raw or grilled, and
those with less money wanted meals that were heavier and more sustain-
ing, such as dishes heavy on meat and carbohydrates.

Pierre Bourdieu asserts that food is one of the key ways that the cultural
and social notion of taste arises and leads to distinctions between social
groups, which are then the basis of hierarchies of inequality. Tastes, then,
are not personal preferences or presentations to the world of sophistication. Rather, they are reflections of the societal boundaries between social
classes and other status groups. They are carefully crafted to delineate distinctions between groups that then reinforce and harden these boundaries,
creating processes of social closure and exclusion. These processes allow
the hierarchies and structural inequalities that result to seem inevitable and
just. They also allow the creation and maintenance of social norms that
increase competition and distance between those who have full knowledge
of the game and access to the resources needed to win and those who do
not. Pierre Bourdieu argues that what people eat, crave, express a desire or
taste for, and how others assess these, are not functions of taste buds but of
social class. Food practices, including etiquette, manners, and consumption patterns, tell the tale of social class, according to this line of thought.
Those who are at the top get to shape the rules, are often deemed tastemakers, and have their interests and reflections represented as desirable,
universal, and objective.

Building on Bourdieu's food spaces, Molly Watson, a food writer, discusses current trends in food. In her typology of food spaces, she asserts

that those with higher levels of economic capital show their class in their penchant for foods that are healthy, refined, and rich in umami—a full, savory taste that means "delicious" or "tasty" in Japanese and has recently been discussed as the fifth taste, in addition to bitter, salty, sour, and sweet—and that incorporate fresh herbs. Those with low amounts of money often have diets described with adjectives such as *sweet*, *white*, *salty*, and *fried*. People with high amounts of the kinds of cultural capital most valued in their society often seek foods labeled as *heritage*, *heirloom*, and *artisan*. Those on the opposite end of this scale eat more items labeled *instant*, *lite*, and *microwavable*. When people have high levels of dominant cultural capital and economic capital, they are likely to eat at highly rated restaurants that are often difficult to secure reservations for. Those with money but nondominant cultural capital typically enjoy dining options available at steakhouses, brunch buffets, and business meals. Those low on both dominant cultural capital and money are likely to eat at fast-food spots, while those with little money and lots of dominant cultural capital are more often found at underground supper clubs and in the long lines in found in front of popular food trucks. One way to understand food inequalities is to understand food culture as a classed culture. People have good manners if they automatically place their napkin in their lap as the food arrives, not if they ask if they should tuck it in their collars. One is seen as having refined tastes when they pair the perfect Burgundy with seared tuna, while eyebrows may rise if a white zinfandel is paired with that entrée. The napkin tucker and the white zin server are met with scorn and other negative judgments that could lead to social exclusion and resultant losses of prestige, opportunities, and access to resources. Other persistently unequal standards and outcomes around food can be seen through a number of social and cultural patterns.

SALES, MARKETING, AND SOCIAL STATUSES

Tufts University's Dariush Mozaffarian and colleagues note that even individual food choices are based on larger social factors such as social statuses, including age, class, gender, and race, culture, health status, and prior knowledge of nutrition and cooking skills. As they are rooted in family, community, and networks, myriad social factors emerge to shape what people eat. Food choices are also psychological, as they are rooted in people's attitudes, motivations, and perceptions. As addressed in chapter 2, social norms, perceptions, and aspirations related to social class and social prestige also influence food choices. In an even larger sense, food choices are deeply shaped by the ways foods are advertised, marketed, and packaged. Most of what is commonly marketed are unhealthy processed and fast foods and sugary drinks. A 2012 Federal Trade Commission food report asserts that the food industry spends less than one-half of 1 percent of all marketing dollars on fruits and vegetables.

Studies suggest that there are more than 200 food decisions made about food every day. These are largely influenced by not just biology and psychology but what is available to eat and messages about food received from various external sources such as parents, teachers, health-care providers, and, certainly, food marketers. This is important because, as prominent food and nutrition activist Marion Nestle notes, "We do not make food choices in a vacuum. . . . We may believe that we make informed decisions about food choice, but we cannot do so if we are oblivious of the ways food companies influence our choices." Marketing often emphasizes quantity. This process, driven by food manufacturers, retailers, and restaurants as well as tableware companies, contributes to overeating. Food packaging and pricing are designed to have shoppers looking to maximize their purchasing power and buy larger sizes of foods that are cheaper than their smaller counterparts. Buying a party-size bag of popcorn or potato chips is more economical than buying the single-serving-size bag of the same product. Since it is unlikely that measuring cups are being used to apportion servings once these items make it inside shoppers' homes, overconsumption ensues. Plates, cutlery, and glasses have also gotten bigger, also leading to distorted notions of what a serving size is.

Some recent researchers are realizing these vast influences as they examine the impact of brand association, food packaging, and other elements of food marketing on food decisions and consumption patterns. Food additives, added sugars, and flavor enhancers have been deployed by food scientists to make many of the foods readily available in stores, restaurants, and other places more appealing and more likely to be purchased. Marketers help convince buyers of this appeal. But measures taken to make food taste better through added fats, salt, and sugars increase its caloric density. In addition, it is available at lower costs but in greater quantities. As such, food marketers contribute to greater consumption and greater weight gain among people in the United States. Consumers often have vague, if any, knowledge of these measures, which serve to change taste preferences as food science taps into pleasure centers of the brain and triggers the same kinds of neural responses that occur with alcohol and drug addiction. Indeed, there are marked similarities in the ways that the regions of the brain associated with rewards—the orbitofrontal cortex, amygdala, insula, striatum, anterior cingulate cortex, and dorsolateral prefrontal cortex—are activated and in what brain chemicals—dopamine, for one—are released in eating, getting drunk, and getting high.

A quick overview of food slogans shows foods that are marketed in ways that create associations between eating, rewards, and happiness, as is the case in McDonald's children-oriented Happy Meals and in its slogans that tell patrons to "Put a Smile On." These associations are also present in IHOP's exhortations to "Come hungry. Leave happy," Kit Kat's claim that "Breaks are Good," Arby's insistence that it sells "Good Mood Food," and Coca-Cola's urging consumers to "Open Happiness." In addition, food has long been associated with celebration. Food marketers exploit this connection as they draw on and create food memories that have consumers feel they should include particular foods—often from particular sellers and companies—to mark momentous occasions such as holidays, weddings, births, deaths, graduations, and promotions. These are also seen in the advent of new occasions such as those Taco Tuesdays, Thirsty Thursdays, and Funday Sundays promoted at restaurants and bars across the United States. These impacts are not equally distributed across populations. As is the case with many social facts, the widespread consequences of food marketing are shaped by social class, gender, race, and ethnicity.

Research published by Dan Jurafsky and several colleagues looks at the ways that Pierre Bourdieu's framework is used in the ways that food is discussed, marketed, and advertised on restaurant menus, in packaging, and in Yelp reviews. There are clear socioeconomic signals attached to food that are revealed in how language—another class marker—is used to describe it. Dan Jurafsky and his colleagues note that glowing Yelp reviews of expensive restaurants use the same kinds of language typically used to talk about sex and other erotic acts. Positive reviews of less expensive restaurants are also classed, as they tend to use language that is associated with drug and alcohol abuse, both of which are commonly associated with poorer members of society, even though alcohol and illicit drug use and addiction exist across class lines.

Furthermore, Dan Jurafsky et al. find that those who review expensive restaurants write longer reviews that use more extensive vocabularies, suggesting higher levels of education, experience with fine dining, and sophistication, trading on their educational capital. Menus at these restaurants as well as more expensive, packaged food items such as gourmet potato chips and fancy chocolate bars also use words that are longer, more complex, and borrowed from French, Italian, and Japanese. At less expensive places and on packaging for cheaper foods, words and sentences are typically shorter and less complex. In lower-income contexts, an emphasis is placed on plenty or (over)abundance, as demonstrated by the presence of heaping plates, large portion sizes, and readily available refills or seconds. Family-style meals, doggie bags, and to-go containers are par for the course for these meals. This is also demonstrated when looking at menu offerings, as there is typically an inverse relationship between restaurant expense and the number of options one can choose from. In other words, an inexpensive restaurant may have six choices for chicken dishes alone while an expensive one may have just six menu options altogether. Likewise, menus at expensive restaurants may emphasize the quality and rarity of the items they serve in contrast to menus at less expensive restaurants, which may emphasize the quantity and variety of their food.

Restaurants commonly engage in the leveraging of cues and signals about economic and cultural capital in what is called menu engineering, in order to manipulate these associations. This also helps status seekers perform the status they want to be perceived as. Font size and type, paper color, and even menu weight are used to tell diners what they should expect from a dining experience and how much it should cost, as work from Vincent P. Magnini and Seontaik Kim in 2016 exemplifies. At more price-sensitive chain restaurants such as those marketed to college students and families, when brand names and mentions of family and tradition are made, sales increase by 27 percent. Diners at these restaurants assess dishes as offering both better quality and values compared with dishes that did not bear these descriptive labels, according to Brian Wansink of Cornell University's Food and Brand Lab. Diners are also willing to pay 10 percent more for the same meal when it is given a more highly descriptive name. Researchers Dan Jurafsky, Bryan R. Routledge, and Noah A. Smith find that at higher-end restaurants, the longer the words used to describe a dish, the more a patron will pay for it. Indeed, for each additional letter in an average word, restaurants were able to increase the cost of a dish by 18 cents. Advertising "grilled fish" on the menu is far less appealing than "a pan-seared halibut" in this setting. There are other distinctions within food marketing that need to be understood in order to recognize and address the ways these lend themselves to food inequalities.

In the case of retail food shopping, amid competition and declining purchasing power for many Americans, analyses reveal a market that is splitting to focus on either upscale or value-oriented food shoppers. As net profit margins for food retailers are low—the industry average is 1.1 percent as of 2016—many stores and chains have gone out of business or consolidated with larger entities. Those that remain are trying to leverage whatever distinct identity they can in order to remain viable. Inequalities are also seen in what is sold, not just marketed. This is apparent as poor neighborhoods have both fewer "good/high-quality" stores and more "bad/poor-quality" stores. Such community residents must rely on less well-stocked grocery stores and convenience stores, where they also are more likely to see shelves stocked with processed foods that are high in sugar, calories, fat, and sodium.

These kinds of variance in food marketing and retailing are not limited to social class but exist around gender as well. A study on food packaging provides evidence for gendered distinctions in how food is sold. When food advertising, marketing, and packaging emphasize masculinity, men and women both show preferences for foods that are unhealthier. Conversely, when food advertising, marketing, and packaging emphasize femininity, men and women both show preferences for healthier foods. Similarly, when there is feminized packaging for a presumed healthier food and masculinized packaging for a presumed unhealthy food, men and women rate the products as more attractive and better tasting and also state that they are more likely to purchase it. These findings are rooted in gender bias and stereotypes.

Another inequality in food marketing occurs in representation in race and ethnicity, especially as these intersect with social class and gender. The racialized and classed origins of food—and their attendant oppressions—in the United States, discussed in chapter 2 continue to have resonance today. Food marketing is a prime avenue where inequalities are enacted and felt. Many of those items deemed as healthier—juices, yogurts, and the like—feature white women in their marketing and advertising. At the same time, many marketing and advertising campaigns for generally less healthy food and specifically fast food feature people of color. University of San Diego School of Business professor Aarti Ivanic has examined this and found that stereotypes and their associated inequalities are maintained when food brands, companies, and the industry itself markets healthier foods to white consumers and junk and fast foods to African Americans and Latinx people. This can have a negative effect in terms of obesity and the food-related chronic diseases that are more prevalent among the latter two groups, both of which also have less access to economic security, food, health care, education, safe and vibrant neighborhoods, and other quality-of-life indicators. Companies target young people of color, as they spend disproportionately more money on marketing to them than to their white counterparts. This occurs despite the fact that children and teens of color have higher rates of obesity and related chronic illnesses, such as diabetes, than white children and teens do.

Other inequalities are seen through a recognition that children are particularly vulnerable to the multibillion-dollar food-marketing industry. Half of the ads that target children are for food. Indeed, children view an average of up to five advertisements for fast food daily. This translates into their preferences and desires for such foods from an early age. Pre-schoolers, for example, rate food as tasting better when it is packaged and advertised with familiar cartoon characters, as a 2010 study by Roberto et al. in *Pediatrics* illuminates. Food and beverage companies spend more than $1.6 billion annually advertising their products to children. While most of this is spent on television ads, other advertising venues include the internet, movies, video games, social media, and text messages, as well as less well recognized ways such as sponsorships and character-licensing agreements. After much pressure from consumers, advocates, and activists, in 2006 Disney agreed to limit many of its character-licensing practices to healthier foods and adopted a set of nutrition guidelines, according to research by V. I. Kraak and M. Story. This meant, with the exceptions of birthday cakes and seasonal candy, Disney would only license its extremely popular characters to foods with smaller portion sizes, fewer calories, and lower amounts of fat and added sugars. In 2016 Disney announced a partnership with Dole Food Company to launch a line of fresh produce and an educational program, both featuring popular characters from their Disney, Pixar, Star Wars, and Marvel brands. Food inequalities exist in not just how consumers are told to buy which foods but in how consumers are actually able to purchase foods and in the kinds of foods they have to choose from.

THE GEOGRAPHY AND GENTRIFICATION OF TASTE

Geography is very much associated with food access—and the lack thereof, as detailed in the previous chapter. It is unsurprising that this is the case in low-income communities. However, those in gentrifying and wealthy communities are also increasingly unable to afford and obtain food. Social inequality occurs here, as increased demand causes prices to climb and makes ingredients that were dietary staples for lower-income residents unaffordable. In a July 2018 interview on the public radio show *The Takeaway*, author Mikki Kendall described the ways her poor grandmother transformed cheap cuts of meat, including offal—animal entrails and organs—into appetizing meals that sustained their family and ensured they ate nutritious meals. When these staples become popular, used in dishes at high-end restaurants and sold at upscale grocery stores, they can become out of reach financially and geographically for people who have been reliant on them. As such, these are replaced with foods that are even cheaper but less nutritionally dense and therefore less healthy. Nevin Cohen, a health policy professor states that this can presage community gentrification, as it is often foodies who spark interest in such foods, which spurs interest in the places where this food is found.

Sharon Zukin and a team of other sociological researchers see this happening in places such as New York's Harlem and Williamsburg communities. Major food and other retailers deserted these places, leaving local entrepreneurs to fill the gap for decades. Currently, they are being "rediscovered" by businesses and newer, wealthier, and often whiter residents. A new economic market is being cultivated and filled with niche and boutique items and experiences, thus changing the character—that is, culture—of the neighborhood. This also increases the social, financial, and cultural distance between low- and middle-income, long-term residents and wealthy newcomers. Social inequality increases as access to both necessary and desired goods, opportunities, and resources improve for those at the highest end of the class spectrum, at the literal and symbolic expense of those on the lower ends. This facilitates the further devaluation of subordinated forms of cultural capital as the ways of life, preferences, and tastes of the privileged come to be representative of the community and its residents, while those who are marginalized become further so, as they feel unwelcome, invisible, and cast aside in their longtime homes.

Furthermore, Pierre Bourdieu's idea of distinction is apparent here, as those more affluent newcomers engage in food shopping and consumption patterns decidedly structured to illuminate cultural capital differences between themselves and those longtime residents. Newcomers are heralded as saviors, tastemakers, and pioneers, ignoring and denigrating those people and practices already present in the community. As neighborhood demographics and culture change, tense clashes also occur. This is especially pronounced when there are racial and ethnic differences between longtime residents and newcomers. The newcomers are often catered to in recently opened cafés, bars, and markets, and they also feel they should be catered to in the rhythm and life of their community and often impose other tastes upon their new environs. This is evident when people who move to a so-called colorful or lively neighborhood use calls to law enforcement or introduce new legislation to tone down what attracted them to the area to begin with. Well before the physical displacement of the poor and otherwise marginalized occurs as a culmination of gentrification, cultural displacement takes root. This, coupled with increasing costs of living, leads to increasing food precarity.

Places where food is bought also reflect and project ideas about the interwovenness of cultural and economic capital. The same is true in terms of how food is discussed. References to eating like locals and peasant meals are in fact markers of what are seen as the foodways of those from lower social classes. Those eating these foods on a regular basis are seen as doing so out of necessity. At the same time, those from more affluent classes "discover" these foods and rave over them as indicators that they are cultural omnivores, or people who switch between elite and nonelite cultural realms of music, film, and food. Individuals who label themselves as foodies are one example of cultural omnivores, priding themselves on the ability to take products from folk and mass culture and turn them into the hottest trends. Sociologists Josée Johnston and Shyon Baumann assert that foodies are in search of foods that cement their distinctive identities, thus their emphasis on items that are local, unique, organic, creative, simple, and high in quality. This allows them to see their dedication to what they consider good food as an egalitarian effort as they choose dives and hole-in-the-wall joints in working-class or remote locales over more elite restaurants. As Johnston and Baumann note, however, they still deploy their food tastes as a form of distinction-making social status that reflects and maintains social inequalities in indirect ways.

This chapter has illuminated the role of culture and the distinction making that accompanies it in the creation of boundaries, perceptions, and realities of class as they relate to food. With a focus on social class and how it structures the desirability, prestige, and other relevant aspects of taste as a symbolic measure, these are macro-level phenomena. Other macro-level phenomena related to food are explored in the next chapter, as attention turns to the health—physical and environmental—impacts of food inequalities.

CHAPTER 5

The Impacts of Food Inequalities

In this chapter, the ways that macro- and micro-level food inequalities affect individuals as well as institutions and other systems is detailed to provide a sense of how pervasive and significant food inequalities are. In particular, the health of both people and the environment as it relates to food inequalities is emphasized. This allows insight into the effects of food inequalities on levels that range from the most intimate to the most global as well as an exploration of how these interconnect.

HEALTH IMPACTS

The Centers for Disease Control (CDC) provides a fact sheet that shows a lengthy list of food-related health conditions, illnesses, and diseases. These include increased risks of the following:

- Overall mortality
- High blood pressure
- High LDL cholesterol, low HDL cholesterol, and high levels of triglycerides
- Type 2 diabetes
- Coronary heart disease
- Stroke
- Gallbladder disease
- Osteoarthritis
- Sleep apnea and breathing problems
- Breast, colon, endometrial, gallbladder, kidney, and liver cancers

- Low quality of life
- Mental illnesses, such as clinical depression and anxiety, among others
- Body pain and difficulty with physical functioning

There are direct and indirect medical costs associated with food inequalities. According to the CDC, some of the direct medical costs include preventive, diagnostic, and treatment services, and some of the indirect costs have to do with morbidity and mortality. Other indirect costs are related to increased unemployment and disability benefits as well as decreased productivity. As employees miss hours and days from work, productivity declines in the form of absenteeism. As employees have decreased activity and focus while at work, productivity declines in the form of presenteeism. With obesity and obesity-related conditions as one of the biggest by-products of food inequalities at the individual level, the costs are high. A report from the National League of Cities illuminates this. The estimated cost of treating obesity-related illness is more than 20 percent of all medical spending, at $190.2 billion annually. This number is predicted to continue growing. In the 10 cities with the highest rates of obesity, the estimated direct costs of obesity and obesity-related illness is $50 million per 100,000 residents.

The What We Eat in America survey, an element of the USDA's National Health and Nutrition Examination, is a nationally representative study that uncovers the paucity of adequate diets among the U.S. population. Called the Healthy Eating Index (HEI), it tracks the types and quantities of foods and beverages consumed in a 24-hour period and issues an overall score. It is also a measure of diet quality. The ideal HEI score, aligned with the USDA dietary guidelines, is 100. The average HEI score in the United States is 59 out of 100, indicating a wide gap between actuality and recommendations. While people over 65 have the highest HEI score, at 66 out of 100, children between 6 and 17 have the lowest HEI score, at 53 out of 100. There are also class differences in dietary adequacy or quality. A Harvard University study points out that these differences are increasing as the gap between the wealthy and the poor in the United States had a twofold increase between 2000 and 2010 and that the nutritional adequacy and quality gains enjoyed in the United States have been largely concentrated in the middle and upper classes.

With more than two-thirds of adults and one-third of children considered overweight or obese, physicians, public-health scholars, policy makers and others see dietary quality as a public-health crisis. Many of the most pressing and most prevalent preventable chronic diseases in the

United States—affecting 117 million people—are linked to poor diets. In addition to health and health-care costs borne by individuals, families, employers and insurance companies, the overall economy is depressed by this. For example, between 2013 and 2018 annual diabetes costs alone rose more than 25 percent to $327 billion, with $90 billion of this coming in decreased productivity. People of color and the poor—who are disproportionately people of color—are acutely impacted by this.

It is hard to find a physician who would not list diet-related illnesses as some of the most pressing health conditions facing the U.S. population. Though doctors often ask patients about their diets and encourage them to eat better, there is little education on how to do so. This is experienced by patients and doctors alike. A research article by Kelly Adams, W. Scott Butsch, and Martin Kohlmeier in the *Journal of Biomedical Education* in 2015 illuminates the paltry nutrition education provided in U.S. medical schools. Only 29 percent of the nation's four-year medical schools offered the minimum recommended 25 hours of nutrition education. Diet-related illnesses are also on the minds of law makers and policy makers, though budget priorities do not reflect this. The federal government spends $1.5 billion annually on nutrition research, a number dwarfed by the $60 billion in spending for research on drugs, biotechnology, and medical devices. Though these spending priorities do not necessarily suggest it, there is a crucial link to be understood between food and health outcomes. One of these is through learning more about the social determinants of health.

A social determinant of health is a resource within a society that has a great deal of influence on the quality and length of one's life. Across the United States, the location of one's home structures how—and how long—one lives. In urban communities in places such as Chicago and New York as well as in rural communities throughout the nation's farm belt, zip codes are correlated with life expectancy. Place—both residential and work—along with access to food, safety, recreation, social support, financial stability, health-care access and quality, and education is a definitive social determinant of health. Social determinants of health are not evenly distributed across U.S. society—members of marginalized groups, especially those who are poor, people of color, LGBTQ+ people, immigrants, and in the overlaps between these categories suffer from decreased emotional, mental, and physical health as a result. Inequalities associated with place, created through prejudice and discrimination rooted in race, ethnicity, and class, lead to inequalities in health. Food is inextricably related here.

The CDC notes that access to foods that support healthy eating habits is vital to health across one's entire life span. It defines healthy eating habits as controlling calories, consuming diverse foods and drinks from across all of the food groups, and restricting one's intake of added sugars, saturated and trans fats, and sodium. Doing so reduces one's risk for risk for chronic disease and conditions that include cancer, cardiovascular disease, diabetes, high blood pressure, obesity, and metabolic syndrome.

Healthy eating—and the ability to do so—is correlated with a number of mental and physical health outcomes. In 2017 a team of researchers from Trinity University reported that there is a correlation between food insecurity, the anxiety this provokes, and disordered eating, including binge eating when food does become available again. Food deprivation can also trigger metabolic changes, including decreased thermogenesis and increased fat stores, that diminish health and facilitate weight gain. When food is available, overeating may ensue. If this becomes cyclical, the risks to physical and mental health increase.

Food insecurity is correlated with increased stress, anxiety, and depression for adults, teens, and children, and with suicidality in teens. Healthy eating and activity patterns, though important in addressing each of these adverse conditions, are difficult to initiate or maintain under such mental distress, which is also often exacerbated when coincident with poverty, racism, sexism, unemployment, underemployment, and lack of access to adequate housing, safe neighborhoods, health care, reliable transportation, and/or other external factors. People who are food insecure are also more likely to develop asthma, cancer, diabetes, eating disorders, heart disease, hypertension, hypoglycemia, kidney disease, and stroke. People without regular access to food also can find themselves in emergency rooms for conditions such as hypoglycemia (which occurs when blood sugar levels are too low), hyperglycemia (which occurs when blood sugar levels are too high), diabetic ketoacidosis (which occurs when one does not produce enough insulin to properly break down glucose and the glucagon needed for insulin to maintain normal glucose levels is high). According to a 2017 study by Sanjay Basu, Seth Berkowitz, and Hilary Seligman, this pattern of hospitalization increases in likelihood toward the end of the month as food budgets run out.

A team of UCLA researchers led by Susan Babey has documented linkages between an inability to access foods that support healthy eating patterns and negative health outcomes, in a study of 40,000 California residents. Among those residents of neighborhoods with fewer fresh produce sources but numerous fast-food restaurants and convenience stores are higher risks of obesity and diabetes. Among those residents of neighborhoods with more fresh produce sources and a greater number of full-service restaurants and grocery stores are lower rates of obesity and diabetes.

Food choices in a neighborhood matter immensely, as the 2013 "State of US Health" report published in the *Journal of the American Medical Association* locates diet as the leading cause of poor health, premature disability, and death among people in the United States. Diet is linked to approximately 700,000 deaths each year and approximately half of all deaths caused by diabetes, heart disease, and stroke. Dariush Mozaffarian of Tufts University offers food as a key indicator in understanding health—and the lack of it—in the United States today, according to a 2017 report. He recommends looking at food as an intervention in order to shrink skyrocketing medical costs and provide better health-care outcomes. By increasing consumption of healthy foods—fruits and vegetables—and decreasing consumption of unhealthy foods—foods high in salt and sugars, processed meats, and red meats—many of the major health concerns can be addressed. This perspective means looking beyond consumer choice and into the social, institutional, and structural influences that have far more power over what is on the dinner table than do tastes for fried chicken, cheesesteaks, and cookies. Food advertising and marketing, food access, structural discrimination, and poverty are the most powerful deciders of food choices.

There are intersections between food, race, racism, and health that also need to be understood. Living in racially segregated places leads to a host of poor health outcomes for African Americans in particular, including access to healthy food options as well as other measures of overall well-being, and opportunities such as better education, more diverse social networks, increased employment options, higher wages, and higher-quality housing stock. In 2017, a group of researchers led by Northwestern University School of Medicine professor Kiarri N. Kershaw found that African Americans who live in neighborhoods with high levels of residential segregation—where there are also fewer and less accessible healthy food choices—also have higher rates of high blood pressure. Conversely, African Americans who move to less segregated neighborhoods—where there are also more accessible healthy food choices—experience drops in their blood pressure.

Poverty must also be explored here. Some researchers, such as a group from Johns Hopkins University, consider the higher rates of obesity for children and adults of color as linked to a lack of access to food options. In communities that lack supermarkets—with their wider range of foods and lower costs—residents tend to eat less healthy diets compared with those living in places that do have supermarkets. In a *San Francisco Chronicle* interview with Tara Duggan, Hilary Seligman, a professor of medicine at the University of California, San Francisco, and the director of UCSF's

Food Policy, Health and Hunger Research Program, says that there are few incentives for people who are food insecure to spend their money on foods considered healthy, given their increased costs. Instead, they use their limited access to food to make sure they have items that are both filling and inexpensive. This means that avoiding and treating illnesses related to diet will not be as easy as just changing what one eats. A focus on access and affordability of foods recommended by doctors and dietitians is also necessary; this is especially important for people who live in food deserts and for those who rely on food banks and pantries. Some food banks now provide not only food but also programs designed to provide specific foods for people at risk for, as well as those already diagnosed with, food-related chronic disease and illness, such as prediabetes and diabetes. These programs have shown success in weight maintenance and glucose stability, both important in preventing and managing these conditions.

At both ends of the spectrum, age is another important factor in explicating the relationship between food and health. Children who are food insecure are more likely to not eat fruits, suffer from headaches, contract colds, and have high cholesterol. The impacts are not just physical but also mental and behavioral, as these children also are more likely to have reported behavioral issues, fall behind in schoolwork, and to fail at least one grade. Senior citizens spend more of their more limited incomes on food. Take, for example, the average 65-year-old with an average annual income around $45,000 who spends 12 percent of it on food, compared with the average 55-year-old with an average annual income around $75,000 who spends 9 percent of it on groceries. Food is the second-highest expense for senior citizens, behind housing costs. As with members of other age cohorts, elderly people forced to choose between food and shelter or food and medicine make choices that limit the amount and types of food they are able to consume. This helps explain why nearly half of this population is at risk of malnutrition and all of the negative health outcomes associated with this. Malnourished elderly people are also less likely to recover from other health conditions. Higher health-care costs are also a factor here.

Food is related to health, not just on consumers' tables but also in employees' work conditions. Some workers within the food system are especially vulnerable to injury, illness, and death. Race and ethnicity are also factors here, as people of color and immigrants from Mexico and Central America are overrepresented at the lower and more dangerous end of the food industry's hierarchy. In 2017 the U.S. Government Accountability Office (GAO) issued a report to Congress in which it cited the meat and poultry slaughtering and processing industry as one of the most dangerous in the United States. Their report also included findings that workers are afraid to complain at work or to the federal Occupational Safety and Health Administration (OSHA) for fear of retaliation by their employers, which though illegal is also a reality. Agricultural workers are also suffering the effects of extreme heat and other effects of climate change. Summer harvesting through the United States, and in the South especially, comes with health risks, as the number of cases of heat-related illnesses and deaths indicate. Given the racial and class marginalization of most farmworkers, their access to health care is greatly decreased, and their likelihood of complications is greatly increased. In the case of undocumented immigrants, this is heightened by fears of deportation. Labor unions, activists, and public advocacy groups are launching efforts to have OSHA create and enforce policies to protect workers from heat-related illnesses, injuries, and deaths, such as adequate breaks, hydration, and shade.

Workplace conditions can lead to a lack of safety in other ways. According to political scientist Adam Sheingate, 48 million Americans are made ill from foodborne microbial pathogens every year. These are mostly minor inconveniences, such as stomachaches and diarrhea, though there are a number of serious illnesses as well. More than 125,000 Americans are hospitalized, and 3,000 die each year from food pathogens. The costs of foodborne illnesses are high, costing more than $75 billion annually, when including health-care costs and lost productivity at work. With more than half of all food-processing facilities in the United States not having a single inspection in five or more years, it is surprising that this number is not even higher. While some foodborne illness is perhaps inevitable, some of this can be associated with the rise of wide-scale industrial food production and insufficient government regulations and enforcement. There are contradictory forces at work here, as some of the failures in the food safety system are due to both duplications and gaps in the actions of governmental agencies that are tasked with food safety. As there are at least 12 distinct federal agencies and departments responsible for food safety—and this is prior to analyzing the state and local level agencies that do this work—efficient and effective coordination of efforts are necessary to assure that public health is maintained. The emphasis within the food industry on maximizing its profits at the expense of the public is a driver of inequality. Government policy plays into this, as the industry is able to use its power to shape laws, policies, and practices. For example, the Food and Drug Administration (FDA) officially agreed with established science when it acknowledged that the food industry practice of routinely giving antibiotics to healthy livestock threatened humans. The food industry's political and financial heft means that the FDA issues voluntary guidelines instead of mandating the regulation or prohibition of such antibiotic use. Allowing the industry to monitor itself allows unequal standards and outcomes to persist.

ENVIRONMENTAL IMPACTS

The success of the U.S. food system is also reliant upon the environment. The University of California, Davis, Sustainable Agriculture Research and Education Program cites the new technological, production, mechanical, and chemical processes that have developed within agriculture since World War II as leading to a number of costs even as efficiency and productivity have increased. In addition to losses in the number of small and family-owned farms, harmful conditions for agricultural workers, and economic and related social collapses in rural communities, chief among these are costs to the environment that have deleterious effects within the food system, for crops, animals, and humans as well as ecologically, on local, national, and global levels. Meanwhile, corporate-owned industrial farms are driven by owners and shareholders to be as profitable and efficient as possible.

Some environmental costs of food production in the United States include air, soil, and water pollution, decreased water supplies, increased greenhouse gas emissions, reduced wildlife habitats and populations, runoff of fertilizers and pesticides, water contamination, and soil degradation and erosion.

With methods in the United States shifting to concentrate much of food production in a declining number of sites, these environmental costs have increased. For example, when livestock production occurs is a relatively constrained geographical area, animal waste contributes to air and water issues as well as odors, pests, and other health and quality of life concerns in those areas. Referred to as concentrated animal feeding operations [CAFOs], they also lead to food safety concerns when waste and other by-products run off into water and nearby fields, contaminating these with pathogens that pose danger to workers and consumers. CAFOs can mitigate these risks by collecting and treating waste in ecologically beneficial and productive ways such as composting and using anaerobic digesters.

Contaminants in the food system come from sources involving emissions of gases and inhalants, such as ammonia, nitrogen oxide, methane, odors, and fine particulate matter as well as antibiotics and growth hormones administered to livestock, pesticides, pathogens, and soil sedimentation. As these are concentrated, they become pollutants and cause a number of harms to the well-being of crops, livestock, plants, wildlife, people, and, indeed, the environment. In their role in increasing productivity in agriculture, pesticides and fertilizers become contaminants that make them among the largest causes of environmental harm in the food system.

When dispersed through the air, soil, and water, pesticides harm not just their target but other living organisms, including humans, as well. Pesticides have incredible range through the environment as they are carried across the air, on the wind, in surface and ground waterways through irrigation and rain, and through runoff to soil and sediment. Pesticides also leach into groundwater and soil. These all mean that pesticides are active at their application sites as well as across geographical spaces. They can also be long lasting in their impacts, as recent studies show the continued presence of pesticides in samples from animals and soil that were taken long after the pesticides' use has been discontinued. It is difficult to assess the full impact of pesticides for a number of reasons, including the fact that there is no comprehensive pesticide-use database and there are few studies that examine pesticide risk to environmental and human health.

Nutrients from fertilizers, such as phosphorus and nitrogen, are also major sources of environmental contaminants and pollutants. The use of fertilizers has been shown to have both immediate, local impacts as well as long-term impacts in communities miles away from where they were initially applied. Rather than creating ideal growing conditions, soil with too much nitrogen can deplete soil quality. Air quality can also be diminished. Rather than lending to crop growth, excessive fertilization can bring about plant loss, invasive species, and an abundance of weeds, leading to increased crop loss or pesticide use, each of which can have negative consequences on yield and the environment, respectively. Plant loss in arid areas can lead to wildfires, which bring with them even more devastation for plants, people, property, and the ecosystem. High nitrogen levels also negatively impact water quality and aquatic life, allowing algae and other invasive organisms to flourish, depleting the water of oxygen, and causing fish and other aquatic plants and animals to die. Nitrogen can permeate local groundwater and well systems after storms or because of irrigation practices. For those with compromised digestive systems, such as infants, the ill, and the elderly, ingesting water with high nitrogen levels causes gastrointestinal distress and interferes with digestion. It can also compromise the body's ability to transport oxygen to its cells, causing methemoglobinemia or blue baby syndrome, as nitrogen compounds mix with iron. This affects marginalized communities of color in particular. As an example, research done in California reveals that places with the worst water quality are more likely to have Latinx people who are more likely to be near or below the poverty line, according to economist Anne Weir Schechinger.

Other issues concern food workers. Food industry workers are also exposed to environmental and other toxins, as they often come into contact with fertilizers, pesticides, poisons, bacteria and other foodborne pathogens, industrial-strength cleaning products, and animal and human bodily fluids and waste. Since these exposures are not systematically monitored, reported, or tracked, the full extent and implications of them are unknown. California, for example, is the only place in the United States that mandates reporting of pesticide-related intoxications. Water and food safety are also environmental issues when exploring the pathogens introduced in the food system through agricultural practices. Foodborne illnesses are often introduced through these means. Bacteria such as *Campylobacter*, *Escherichia coli* (*E. coli*), *Salmonella*, *Staphylococcus* and other pathogens such as *Norovirus* are of concern, as they are found to contaminate crops and waterways and cause serious health concerns among livestock and in humans.

Governmental policies and regulations have a role in rectifying the negative impacts of food production, consumption, and waste. According to their mission, the USDA Economic Research Service (ERS) identifies a number of environmental concerns coincident with food production in the country. It administers and evaluates agricultural practices and policies that are designed to address these in the following areas:

- Soil quality, as compromised by wind and water erosion
- Water quality, as compromised by chemical/pesticide and nutrient runoff
- Air quality, as compromised by soil particulates, farm chemicals, and odor from livestock
- Wildlife habitat, as compromised by fragmentation, monoculture (which reduces landscape diversity), and diverting water for irrigation
- Wetlands, as compromised by conversion to cropland

In this work, the ERS issues a set of best practices for adoption by food producers to limit the environmental harms from their use of nitrogen, phosphate, and potash as food, feed, fiber, and fuel. If best practices are not adopted, these uses can lead to unsafe emissions and pollution, groundwater contamination, and surface water runoff.

One way to reduce these deleterious conditions is agroecology, which hinges on crop diversity, natural ecosystems that rely on native species that will be protected from pests through agricultural practices that draw on natural predators rather than harmful pesticides, and local knowledge of ideal planting conditions. This is a departure from standard corporate farming practices. Agroecology is more efficient and can lead to higher profits for farmers. It is also more sustainable; for example, it provides food to farmers and others nearby that does not have to be shipped in from elsewhere.

Adopting agroecological practices is of particular concern given the prevalence of monocultures—the planting of large, single crops in a plot of land—in contemporary industrial agricultural practices. Unlike in the past, much of contemporary agriculture in the United States is industrial. The number of small and medium-sized farms continually decrease as the number of large, corporate-owned enterprises increase in size and number. Through these interrelated processes, there is increased focus on growing monocultures.

One danger associated with monocultures is their reliance on fertilizers. In growing single crops each year, the soil is more vulnerable to erosion. It also becomes depleted of naturally occurring nutrients. In order to ensure yields, synthetic fertilizers are used. One risk of synthetic fertilizers is that they can lead to hypoxia, or dead zones, where too much oxygen is present in waterways, leading to the development of algae blooms that trigger the depletion and deaths of fish and other sea life in affected waters. This is caused by increased levels of elements such as nitrogen and phosphorus—found in fertilizers—released as runoff that leaches into soil and contaminates water, both nearby and very far away, as is the case when nutrients find their way into tributaries and the rivers they flow into. It is common to have runoff from midwestern farms thousands of miles away in the Gulf of Mexico, the result of it having coursed through the Mississippi River and its tributaries. These elements also are released into the air, causing pollution there too. In all, the human and environmental costs are in the billions annually and the losses garnered by each are incalculable.

Pesticides are another danger associated with monocultures, as these do not have enough biodiversity to ward against noxious weeds and pests that threaten crops. In addition to eliminating some pests, pesticides reduce the presence of desired and beneficial crops and wildlife while increasing the resistance of other weeds and pests, creating the need for even stronger—and more harmful—pesticides. They also harm humans, causing cases of poisoning among workers and those living near industrial farms, and are associated with a host of illnesses, including developmental delays, endocrinal problems, various cancers, respiratory distress, and asthma. Reproductive health is also compromised by pesticides. Incidences of

miscarriages, stillbirths, congenital anomalies, early puberty, and damage
to sperm and ova are associated with pesticide use. Fertilizers and pesticides used in industrial agriculture pose health risks to people, including
farmworkers, local residents, and others. Additionally, a large amount of
industrial agriculture is dedicated not just to monocultures but to monocultures that are not part of the human food system, being used instead
in either industrial applications or for animal feed, both of which are
correlated with various forms of environmental harm. In one example,
as industrial livestock operations often also administer antibiotics, concerns rise about both antibiotic overuse and the rise of antibiotic-resistant
bacteria, which pose significant costs to safety and health. A move from
industrial production and monocultures into more conscious practices and
diverse crops could mean greater yields, greater profits, and greater benefit to human, crop, livestock, wildlife, and environmental health. Proponents of regenerative agriculture contend that this method of growing food
could be used to ensure foods that have greater nutritional value than those
grown with many contemporary conventional agricultural practices such
as monocultures and the use of chemical pesticides. Regenerative agriculture could also improve soil health and air quality while also leading to
greater biodiversity and ecological protection. All of these factors could
support healthy people, healthy food, and a healthy planet.

In one of its missions, the Environmental Protection Agency (EPA)
mediates food-related risks to the environment. Reducing food waste is a
critical issue in this work. More than 39 million tons of food were wasted
in 2015, making this the single largest source of everyday waste. As noted
in a study led by Zach Conrad, people in the United States waste a pound
of food per person per day. This totals 150,000 tons of food daily. This
wasted food uses 30 million acres of land, 4.2 trillion gallons of irrigated
water, 1.8 billion pounds of fertilizer, and 780 million pounds of pesticides. Twenty-two percent of solid waste in municipal landfills is food—
most of which could have been diverted and recovered for other uses,
including feeding the hungry. Estimates are that nearly one-third of all
food produced—some 133 billion pounds—is never eaten. That such large
amounts of edible and safe food are thrown away while so many suffer
from malnutrition and food insecurity is a great irony.

Some food activists and policy makers look at ways to simultaneously
increase access to food and eliminate waste. Food manufacturers, wholesalers, retailers, restaurants, caterers, corporations, hotels, hospitals, colleges and universities, and school dining halls and cafeterias, as well as
farmers and local and community food drives, are important agents in

food recovery. From college campuses to corporate cafeterias to catering companies, uneaten, untouched food that would otherwise be discarded is redistributed to those without enough. In some places, food is picked up from the site and taken to distribution centers or directly to food pantries. In other locales, innovative distribution schemes, such as using food trucks that deliver food directly to those who are food insecure or in need more generally, are utilized. This model is considered more efficient and more effective by people such as Sara Webber, the founder of the Berkeley Food Network, where 40 providers who work with the poor collaborate, leveraging resources, reducing redundancies, coordinating joint efforts, and creating a distribution hub that increases food security. The next chapter delves deeper into the role of institutions and policies as they relate to food inequalities.

CHAPTER 6

The Relationship between Food Practices, Policies, and Inequalities

In this chapter, the relationships between major social institutions and food inequalities are explored. Food inequalities can be addressed—and sometimes created and other times worsened—by the decisions, choices, rules, regulations, and changes made by federal, state, and local governments, corporations, and nonprofit organizations. In some cases, decisions made in one arena can lead to reactions in other arenas, as is the case when nonprofits must shift their spending priorities to make up for the shortfalls that occur in people's ability to obtain food after federal funding cuts in nutrition programs. This is also the case when desires for increased corporate profits result in workers' wages being lowered, such that they would need food assistance from government and nonprofit sources.

GOVERNMENTAL PRACTICES AND POLICIES

Federal Policies

The U.S. Department of Agriculture (USDA) is a federal agency responsible for food. The Healthy Food Financing Initiative (HFFI) was launched during the Obama Administration to provide loans, grants, and tax breaks to retailers addressing food access in underserved communities through coordinated efforts by three federal agencies—the USDA, the Department of the Treasury, and the Department of Health and Human Services. The USDA Community Food Securing Grant Program is an effort to remedy food insecurity by funding community food projects that are focused on increasing the economic vitality of low-income communities. Its Food Safety and Inspection Service ensures the public can safely consume meat, poultry, and processed eggs. In its inspection capacity, it also can protect food workers and consumers through establishing and enforcing policies and regulations. The USDA's Transition Incentives Program provides money to retiring and retired landowners who sell or rent land to marginalized and/or beginning farmers as well as technical and financial assistance to marginalized and/or beginning farmers.

The USDA Food and Nutrition Service (FNS) is tasked to address hunger and obesity. It does so in developing the Dietary Guidelines for Americans, in conjunction with the Department of Health and Human Services (HHS). It also administers 15 federal nutrition assistance programs, including the most well-known and most used Supplemental Nutrition Assistance Program (SNAP), Special Supplemental Nutrition Program for Women, Infants, and Children (WIC), and National School Lunch Program (NSLP). Each of these is addressed in this chapter. SNAP and NSLP are discussed at length in chapters 11 and 13, respectively. In addition, though not discussed at length, there are also the following programs:

- School Breakfast Program
- Special Milk Program
- Summer Food Service Program
- Farmers Market Nutrition Program/Senior Farmers Market Nutrition Program
- Child and Adult Care Food Program, Commodity Supplemental Food Program
- Temporary Emergency Food Assistance Program
- Food Distribution Program on Indian Reservations
- Food Assistance for Disaster Relief
- Nutrition Assistance Block Grants, including Nutrition Assistance for Puerto Rico
- Fresh Fruit and Vegetable Program (FFVP)

SUPPLEMENTAL NUTRITIONAL ASSISTANCE PROGRAM

The largest federal food assistance program, formerly known as the Food Stamps Program, is the Supplemental Nutritional Assistance Program (SNAP). After a successful pilot program initiated during the Kennedy

Administration in 1961, Lyndon Johnson signed the Food Stamp Act into law in 1964. This Act ushered in a program designed to both support the agricultural industry and the nutritional needs of low-income individuals and families. Indeed, the Act clearly stated its intention "to strengthen the agricultural economy; to help to achieve a fuller and more effective use of food abundances; to provide for improved levels of nutrition among low-income households through a cooperative Federal-State program of food assistance to be operated through normal channels of trade; and for other purposes." Though designed to protect growers and create greater food access, the program—and in particular, its food-insecure recipients—was also often the target of scorn, attack, and stigma. Indeed, the 2008 Farm Bill changed the name of the Food Stamps program to the current name as a way of decreasing some of the negative connotations of the program. Other changes in this new law included a name change for the program's educational program, to Supplemental Nutrition Assistance Program Education (SNAP-Ed); increases in the minimum benefit and standard deduction; and elimination of the cap on the deduction for childcare expenses as well as expanded eligibility for recipients. By this time, all states had replaced paper Food Stamps with credit card-like electronic benefit transfer (EBT) systems, something recognized in the new law. Each month, SNAP benefits are transferred onto recipients' EBT cards, which can be used to buy certain food items at one of the 260,000 authorized participating retailers. More on SNAP eligibility requirements and restrictions can be found in chapter 11. The overwhelming majority of SNAP purchases—in excess of 80 percent of all purchases—are made at supermarkets and superstores.

In 2017 the federal government spent $70 billion on SNAP and other food assistance programs. In addition to SNAP and WIC, other programs supported in this allocation are a block grant for food assistance in Puerto Rico and American Samoa, funding for the Emergency Food Assistance Program to provide food to soup kitchens and food pantries, as well as the Food Distribution Program on Indian Reservations. SNAP grants states funds to distribute to recipients. Once states deem applicants eligible, SNAP benefits can be used to buy a limited selection of foods in supermarkets and other stores that sell food staples, which, according to the USDA, are vegetables or fruits; dairy products; meat, poultry, or fish; and breads or cereal. SNAP is considered an important antipoverty program in particular: 92 percent of SNAP benefits went to households with incomes at or below the poverty line, and 56 percent went to households at or below half of the poverty line, which as of 2020 is $26,200 for a family of four. An analysis from the nonpartisan Center on Budget and Policy

Priorities (CBPP) assessed SNAP as keeping 8.4 million people, including 3.8 million children, out of poverty. It is especially vital for children, lifting 2 million children above the poverty line. As it allows individuals and families federally assisted purchasing power, it also allows them to spend money on other basic needs, such as housing, clothing, transportation, and utilities. SNAP has long been the largest U.S. government program designed to decrease food insecurity. Unlike other federal programs that offer food and nutrition assistance, SNAP has had the fewest restrictions and the largest reach, covering people across age, gender, and family status.

SPECIAL SUPPLEMENTAL NUTRITION PROGRAM FOR WOMEN, INFANTS, AND CHILDREN

While SNAP eligibility is open to those who meet the thresholds for income, resources, and housing expenditures, the Special Supplemental Nutrition Program for Women, Infants, and Children (WIC) is a narrower supplemental nutritional program that provides for access to a very limited range of food items and is restricted to low-income pregnant women, breastfeeding women, and children under the age of five who are determined to be at nutritional risk. The USDA describes eligible persons as those who are assessed by a health-care professional to have either medically based risks, including anemia, underweight, maternal age, a history of pregnancy complications, or poor pregnancy outcomes, or diet-based risks that include an inadequate dietary pattern. It is important to note that, though important to increase food access, the receipt of food assistance does not ensure access to adequate nutrition, nor does it completely eliminate food insecurity. In addition, a number of those who are eligible for these and other federal food assistance programs do not receive them. In 2014, though 15 million people were eligible for WIC, just 8 million people actually used the program. In contrast to WIC, more eligible people actually use SNAP. Yet it is still the case that 17 percent of all those eligible, and 28 percent of those eligible who are working poor, do not receive any SNAP benefits, as indicated by the 2018 USDA study *Reaching Those in Need*. Additionally, due to stringent eligibility criteria, many who are food insecure do not qualify for these federal programs. Data provided in a 2014 Feeding America report stress that only 58 percent of food-insecure households participate in at least one of the most common federal food assistance programs: SNAP, WIC, or the National School Lunch Program (NSLP).

NATIONAL SCHOOL LUNCH PROGRAM

Another well-known and better regarded federal food program provides for free and reduced lunches for children in public and private, nonprofit schools under the NSLP. Established as the National School Lunch Act during the Truman Administration in 1946, the NSLP ensures that income-eligible students receive a free or low-cost meal at school. At its inception, the program served just over 7 million children; that number has more than quadrupled, as just over 30 million children at nearly 100,000 schools participated in the NSLP in 2016. The NSLP is administered on the federal level by the FNS and on state level by state agencies through agreements with school food authorities. From the USDA, schools are given food—fruits, vegetables, grains, dairy, and some proteins—and cash subsidies for every meal they serve to an eligible child. Schools must serve lunches that follow the requirements of the program. The NSLP also provides schools with snacks for eligible children participating in approved afterschool programs. Since its launch, the NSLP has provided children at risk for inadequate nutrition with balanced meals that support their educational attainment. Awareness of food insecurity among college students is increasing, as recent calls to expand the NSLP to include colleges and universities and the establishment of campus-based food pantries indicate.

FARM SUBSIDIES

Farmers and other agricultural producers are benefited through federal assistance programs. Indeed, as noted earlier, one component of the Food Stamp Act of 1964 is "to strengthen the agricultural economy." This largely takes place through subsidies. There are more than 60 USDA programs that assist farmers. The largest of these is crop insurance that pays much of farmers' premiums for protection against yield and revenue shortfalls, at an annual cost of approximately $8 billion. As there are no income limits on this program, many beneficiaries are millionaires and billionaires. Twenty farms receive more than $1 million each year in crop insurance claims. Significantly more receive more in claims than they pay in premiums. There are also price-guarantee programs, such as agriculture-risk coverage and price-loss coverage, that pay another $7 billion in annual subsidies. In these, the U.S. federal government supports and subsidizes agricultural policies that produce and distribute maximal amounts of food at minimal costs.

Critics contend that many of these federal programs actually increase income and other forms of inequality; decrease diverse food offerings;

manipulate prices and costs for producers, suppliers, and consumers; and contribute to poor diets. Such efforts may result in improved access to food but also decreased access to important nutrients. Not all growers or all crops are eligible to receive USDA subsidies, which favor sugarcane, soybean, and corn growers rather than fruit and vegetable growers. The former crops have a number of industrial applications, as soybeans are converted into plastics, solvents, cosmetics, and an array of other non-food items, and corn is converted into fuel and animal feed. In their uses for human consumption, corn and soybeans are transformed into sweeteners and oils. These items are among the most identified as foods that contribute to unhealthy food production practices, weight gain, and processed foods. Subsidizing produce would have a number of positive benefits. Research conducted by Dariush Mozaffarian in 2017 asserts that a national program to subsidize the cost of fruits and vegetables by 10 percent would save up to 150,000 lives over 15 years.

Hidden subsidies are apparent when looking at the U.S. tax code, according to public-health professor Nicholas Freudenberg in a 2014 report. He identified the annual $7 billion in social safety-net provisions of federal assistance programs for food, health care, and housing used by fast-food workers as a form of subsidizing the low wages paid in that industry. Grocery store and supermarket owners are other beneficiaries. Census data show that food services, which include restaurants, have the highest rate of workers who receive SNAP of any industry. Some 1.7 million food-service workers received SNAP as of 2015. Grocery stores have the fourth-highest industry rate of workers receiving SNAP, with 472,000 such workers. Freudenberg further identifies the $550 million annual tax deduction for the cost of advertising unhealthy food to children as another federal subsidy.

U.S. IMMIGRATION AND TRADE POLICIES

Immigration policies also reflect, shape, and address food inequalities. In 1986 the Immigration Control and Reform Act (IRCA) allowed for the creation of the H-2A Temporary Agriculture Workers visa. This visa was designed to authorize an immigrant labor pool on farms and other parts of the U.S. agricultural industry. The year 2018 saw some 242,762 H-2A visas certified by the Department of Labor's Office of Foreign Labor Certification. Data from the U.S. Department of Labor's National Agricultural Workers Survey (NAWS) show that the average farmworker is a Latin American immigrant man in his twenties or thirties. Analyses of Department of Labor data show that if current anti-immigrant trends continue and proposed policies are enacted, agriculture-reliant states will suffer economic losses due to the loss of agricultural workers. Agricultural business owners in places most hard-hit have already reported labor shortages impacting their productivity, something that fuels contraction in other parts of the agricultural labor market, as processors, marketers, and retailers are negatively impacted. This ultimately leads to higher prices for consumers, who must then decide whether to spend their money on produce or on other items, such as clothing, transportation, and housing. Indeed, more widespread economic pains can be anticipated as this cycle expands and deepens. To address this, some owners hire attorneys to help them navigate the byzantine process of applying for H-2A visas, designed to allow applications for agricultural guest workers in certain areas for up to one year.

A 2019 article by sociologist Andrew Smolski delineates increasingly punitive immigration policies since the mid-twentieth century Bracero program; they are connected with labor policies that have served to stifle worker complaints and lower their wages through the ever-present threat (and reality) of deportation. These also increase the risks for exploitation and labor rights violations for H-2A workers. Rather than hire workers directly, many major agricultural employers use subcontractors, which enables these employers to avoid legal responsibility and labor costs but increases the workers' vulnerability. This vulnerability is highlighted in Department of Labor data that reveal 93,447 reports of labor law violations between 2000 and 2017—numbers that very well could represent an undercount. There is also wage theft, unsafe work conditions, and minimal enforcement of those rights and regulations that do exist. These H2-A workers are documented migrants who still suffer harm. Employers in year-round agricultural production and processing, such as dairy farms and poultry-processing and meatpacking plants are ineligible for H-2A workers, and many turn to undocumented labor pools instead.

Undocumented agricultural workers are even more exploited and suffer greater inequalities in all aspects of the food labor system, given the risk of deportation if they report harmful and dangerous work practices and conditions. Like all undocumented migrants, agricultural workers are ineligible for such federal government programs as Medicaid, health-care subsidies under the Affordable Care Act (ACA), unsubsidized health coverage on ACA exchanges, or unemployment benefits to blunt the impacts of becoming ill or unable to work.

Smolski endorses decoupling H-2A visas from specific employers to grant workers greater freedom to improve their work conditions. The current system does not allow workers to switch employers, even if they are being denied protections, rights, or pay without risking deportation. Finally, passage of the Agricultural Worker Program Act would ensure undocumented workers have labor rights, autonomy, and a path toward legalized and citizenship status.

Trade policies are another area of concern. U.S. agricultural producers export more food than is imported. Twenty-five percent of all food produced in the United States is sold in other countries. Trade wars, then, are especially of concern in this sector. Assistance during the trade war initiated in 2018 by the United States with China went primarily to farms run by white males. The USDA provided more than $8.5 billion in aid to farms through the Market Facilitation Program (MFP) over the course of two years, and 99.5 percent went to white owners. In Mississippi, a state with a 38 percent Black population and where 14 percent of farms have a Black primary operator, 1.4 percent of the $200 million distributed to farmers through the MFP went to someone Black, according to reporting from Nathan Rosenberg and Bryce W. Stucki for the Farm Bill Law Enterprise. Data also show that 91 percent went to men. Additionally, most of the MFP recipients were members of the upper middle class or were wealthy. Large-scale producers benefited most, demonstrated through the fact that the largest 3 percent of operators received more than 25 percent of MFP funds. Farmers with fewer resources and less affluence were both less likely to receive funds and to successfully come out of the trade war.

There are more local impacts of governments on food inequalities, especially when considering local governments. In addition to the federal government, attention must be paid to state and local government food policies.

STATE AND LOCAL POLICIES

Municipalities have been at the fore of developing food policies, especially in the wake of growing concerns about food deserts, obesity, and diet-related health challenges. Many of these hinge on partnerships with privately owned entities. One popular national trend has been in issuing financial incentives to food retailers. Focused on full-service grocery stores and supermarkets in particular, locales throughout the nation have implemented programs such as New York's Food Retail Expansion to Support Health (FRESH). These subsidize retailers moving into underserved neighborhoods and agree to stipulations such as dedicating space to fresh produce, meats, fish, and poultry. FRESH also offers financial incentives for retailers who own, renovate, or develop retail outlets, including tax freezes and abatements, lower mortgage taxes, and waivers for certain building materials and equipment taxes.

Cities take up this work as well. Baltimore offers its Baltimarket as a form of food justice to improve food access, health, and wellness in their communities through multiple strategies that entail a Virtual Supermarket Program, Healthy Stores Program and a Food Justice Forum. The Virtual Supermarket Program is a system that lets shoppers place online grocery orders that are delivered to local sites, such as libraries, senior centers, and assisted living facilities, where those living under food apartheid conditions and are without cars can pick up their orders. The Healthy Stores Program works with community and religious organizations on community education and promotion of healthy foods. Additionally, it assists corner-store owners with infrastructure, nutrition education, and marketing a variety of healthier foods so patrons can purchase entire healthy meals from one community-based store. They also assist stores in stocking a variety of healthy drinks and fruits and vegetables. Baltimarket's Food Justice Forum is an annual event, planned by the Baltimore Food Justice Committee, a group of grassroots social and food justice leaders. Through the Forum, residents discuss and learn more about food inequalities and the structural inequalities that cause them. They also offer and hear solutions to these.

CORPORATE PRACTICES AND POLICIES

National grocery store chain Whole Foods calls itself "America's Healthiest Grocery Store." It sells organic and, well, whole foods. Whole foods—the category, not the store—are foods that are either in or close to their natural state, as opposed to foods that are heavily refined and processed. Whole Foods—the store—is known for its high-quality items, high food-sourcing standards, high customer service expectations, and high prices. Known also as "Whole Paycheck," as an allusion to its higher prices, Whole Foods stores are often located in high-income neighborhoods and typically service a higher-income clientele. A trip to a Whole Foods store unveils luxuries typically not found at most grocery stores, such as vast selections of expensive, hard-to-find foods from farmers, both local and from more than halfway across the world; upscale, restaurant-quality cuts of meats; full-service bars; in-store restaurants; and coffeehouses, not to mention gelaterias and mochi stations dedicated to selling Italian and Japanese versions of ice cream, respectively. With the 2017 purchase of Whole Foods by online powerhouse Amazon.com, those with Amazon's Prime membership can now order groceries and have them delivered to their homes within two hours in many parts of the countries. Activists and advocates for people with limited access to food, such as those living in food deserts, see this move as a potential way to bridge the grocery gap. Fresh, organic, nutrient-dense foods can be available to those with limited transportation, mobility, and store options, provided they can afford Whole Foods prices. Still, those who cannot or do not participate in the brick-and-mortar experience can reap some of the benefits of the foods and other items sold by Whole Foods. There is, on the other hand, some concern that retailer moves to online food shopping may actually further disadvantage those with already precarious and uncertain access to food. If companies do not deliver or if they charge extra for certain communities, food inequalities increase. The same is true if these food providers do not offer ways to use cash or electronic benefits, SNAP, or WIC. Limited and expensive internet access is also of concern here. If internet connections are spotty, costly, or unavailable, online shopping cannot be used and disparate access will continue.

Whole Foods also has increased its physical presence in areas designated as food deserts. In Chicago, for example, in 2016 a Whole Foods opened in the low-income African American Englewood community on the city's South Side. Prior to Whole Foods having located there, for decades residents were forced to travel to other communities to do any grocery shopping for the many items they were unable to buy at the corner, dollar, drug, and liquor stores that were their only local options for items such as milk and meat. Local media outlets covered the store's grand opening, showing the people who stood in line for upward of four hours to enter the store and the more than 3,000 customers who shopped there that first day, a sure sign of the excitement and need for a full-service grocery store in the neighborhood. Forty percent of the store's employees are Englewood residents, according to a 2017 MarketWatch report. The shelves are stocked with local, African American vendors' food, hair care, and body items. The store regularly has free product demonstrations and workshops on healthy living, food, and cooking. Other grocery stores, restaurants such as Starbucks and Chipotle, and shops have opened, offering even more economic opportunities and development and more shopping options for those who live in Englewood. At the same time, the footprint of stores such as the one in Englewood is smaller, as are the number of items and amenities offered, however, when compared with most other Whole Foods locations. The costs of food are lower at these stores as a reflection of the retailer's commitment to maximize people's access to healthy foods.

Still, longtime community residents point to the prices and the upscale features, such as the popular weekly food and wine pairing demonstrations, and wonder if they are for the current community members or if they and the recently opened Starbucks are instead a harbinger of impending gentrification that will ultimately make not just the grocery items and cups of coffee too expensive but the property taxes and rents as well. This fear is not an unfounded one, as indicated in chapter 3 and as indicated in research provided by Jamie Anderson on the popular real-estate website Zillow. In what is called the Whole Foods effect, homes located near a Whole Foods or a Trader Joe's increase in price and appreciate twice as much as other homes in the country. Research from scholars, including sociologists Nevin Cohen and Daniel Sullivan, discusses what is called supermarket greenlining. This is what occurs when grocery stores and supermarkets perceived as health-conscious and environmentally conscious open outlets in low-income and gentrifying neighborhoods that attract more affluent customers, and less privileged residents remain on the hunt for food they can afford and feel comfortable purchasing.

Greenlining is analogous to what researchers call supermarket redlining to describe larger retailers leaving low-income communities, as both lead to further inequalities. While stores such as Whole Foods state they are opening stores in food deserts to ameliorate decades of supermarket redlining, the economic and social exclusion that lower-income residents face in such stores leads some to discuss them rather as food mirages— places that look like respite from food deserts but create conditions that make food just as inaccessible as before they were opened. In some cases, the presence of supermarkets actually has led to fewer food choices, as their ability to buy in large volume leads to lower prices for customers that smaller retail outlets are not able to match while still turning a profit. This causes them to close down, leaving holes in the retail landscape as well as fewer employment opportunities for residents and less money circulating within local communities. The presence of centrally located grocery stores and supermarkets can also lead to increased travel time for those on the outskirts of their communities, especially if smaller retail food stores are forced out of business. Ending food deserts is vital, but any such efforts must be coupled with another dimension of access to food, and that is the ability to afford what foods are present in one's community to ward off the creation of greenlining and food mirages. Nonprofit organizations are one institutional player working to mitigate these kinds of potentials.

NONPROFIT ORGANIZATIONAL PRACTICES AND POLICIES

According to data reported by Tara Duggan in the *San Francisco Chronicle*, Santa Clara County alone sends 34 million pounds of edible food into landfills annually. Partnerships between state, local, and other environmental planners and policymakers and food banks, for example, mean that this food could be diverted from trash heaps and onto plates. Second Harvest Food Bank serves Santa Clara and San Mateo Counties, where close to 720,000 people are food insecure. Another example is the private-public initiative, the Silicon Valley Food Rescue. In its three-pronged plan, it uses food trucks to pick up food from corporate and college and university partners that is then distributed to people in need; it recovers food from food manufacturers, distributors, wholesalers, and retailers for dispersal to pantries throughout the area they serve, and it forms an organization that allows for efficiencies in communication and education of those rescuing and serving food for food-insecure clients.

Without large-scale shifts across multiple institutions, these efforts are limited in their impact. They may provide important food access to individuals and even to communities; however, they do not, by themselves, dismantle the injustice found throughout the food system. This is why some food activists also focus on developing food policy councils that allow community voices and interests to be advanced into policies, practices, and laws.

Food policy councils started in 1982 in Knoxville, Tennessee, and have grown exponentially. These are collaborations of governmental entities, growers, researchers, advocates, and activists. The Chicago Food Policy Action Council (CFPAC) is one example that focuses on policies to address food, health, and wellness access and disparities. Members offer insights and remedies from their vantage point within the food system to increase food access, affordability, and nutrition to Chicago residents. CFPAC and similar nonprofits facilitate policies that are grounded in residents' cultures are also explicitly designed around culturally appropriate and environmentally sustainable practices that all promote food equity.

Procurement is another place equity can be fostered. Purchasing policies that prioritize local and small growers and producers can be developed to attain this. Nonprofit entities have advocated and created plans that mandate schools, colleges, and universities, hospitals, and workplace cafeterias source foods from marginalized and/or local, independent businesses. One national example is the Good Food Purchasing Program (GFPP). Under the auspices of the GFPP, cities agree to have public institutions such as schools and hospitals purchase food in a way designed to create a transparent and equitable food system built on five core values: local economies, health, valued workforce, animal welfare, and environmental sustainability. The Center for Good Food Purchasing offers tools, technical support, and a verification system to facilitate this. Some of the institutions that use the GFPP include the cities of Boston, Chicago, and Los Angeles; the Los Angeles, San Francisco, and Oakland Unified School Districts;

the Boston, Chicago, Cincinnati and Washington, DC, public schools; the Chicago Park District; Cook County, Illinois; and the Austin, Texas, Independent School District. There are three tiers associated with the GFPP. In the first, employers must comply with international labor standards and domestic labor laws, In the second, employers must be fair-trade-certified or have social responsibility policies that provide safe working conditions, benefits, and living wages to employees. In the third and highest tier, employers must offer workers a union contract, be worker-owned cooperatives, or be certified for their strong labor protections.

Farm-to-school efforts that incorporate learning about farming and food systems into school curricula connect small, local growers to students. Students learn where and how food is grown in ways many urban, suburban, and even rural children and teens are unfamiliar with. These efforts also are ways to offer more investment in local economies. Rather than using large corporations for some or all cafeteria food, buying foods such as dairy, fruits, vegetables, and meats from growers who are relatively close to the school allows for both fresh—and often tastier—foods as well as financial support for small, local farms that then reinvest in their farm and other small, local businesses as well as local tax bases. Such efforts are trending nationally as ways to increase justice and redistribute wealth in local economies and local food systems, according to the National Farm to School Network (NFSN). Groups such as NFSN focus on promoting local foods, supporting school gardens, and providing food and agricultural education in childcare centers, early-childhood education settings, and schools. Organizations such as NSFN seeking to work with small and local growers also can act in ways that promote racial, gender, and financial equity in their work with marginalized people and communities. In providing food to local institutions, small and local growers are key providers of produce, dairy, and other foods. They can also be sources of employment for local residents.

In this chapter was an exploration of ways large institutions—those from government, corporations, and nonprofit organizations—adopt practices and policies that can sometimes work in contradictory ways to both create and remedy food inequalities. Given the complex and bureaucratic array of local, state, and federal policies and agencies, privately owned companies, and a host of nonprofit entities that are part of the food system, this is inevitable. In moving toward greater food equity, collaborations between these entities could be a strong force to reduce and ultimately end food inequalities. Chapter 7 provides a more detailed examination of food activism to force change by those not part of these larger institutions and structures.

Food Activism

This chapter explores ways individuals and groups engage in grassroots, small-scale efforts to address food inequalities. The contemporary food justice movement and its work across various components of the food system, including food access, preserving the cultural significance of food, and pay and rights for workers, are emphasized.

REMEDYING FOOD DESERTS

There are numerous innovative ways being deployed to address the harm of food deserts. Mobile pantries that come to communities and pop-up food pantries at schools, churches, transit centers, and parks represent one way. Many urban farms around the nation have an express mission to reduce the privations associated with food deserts and promote healthy eating and activity as well as social bonding and other important forms of community building. When partnered with local, community-based nonprofit organizations, such as New York City's Teens for Food Justice, food access, cooking classes, and political, science, nutrition, business, and food education are made available in innovative ways to students and community members. In places such as Atlanta, Cleveland, Los Angeles, and Washington, DC, growers have not waited for city officials, state governments, federal plans, or business leaders to offer solutions. Instead, they have started local community efforts on once-vacant and barren lots to train urban farmers, some of whom have not been able to secure employment due to histories of incarceration, inadequate educational and work opportunities, and chronic illnesses. They also stimulate local economies through social entrepreneurship as vendors create food-based businesses that sell fresh fruits, vegetables, herbs, and eggs. Other ventures, such as Cleveland's Rust Belt Riders, are involved in low-cost composting. These collect thousands of pounds of food waste from businesses, organizations, and individuals to compost. The compost is then sold to commercial, community, and urban farmers as organic fertilizers. Chicago's Urban Growers Collective does something similar with vermicomposting and vermiculture, which involve the use of worms to break down waste in the creation of organic fertilizer. The rich products are often referred to as black gold, both for their high nutritive and financial value.

Bakers and chefs are also a part of these efforts. Artist, entrepreneur, and baker Maya-Camille Broussard owns the Chicago-based Justice of the Pies. In addition to running this successful pie shop, she also operates a series of workshops called I KNEAD LOVE, for school-age children in low-income communities. In these, children learn about nutrition, basic cooking skills, and culinary creativity. Justice of the Pies also partners with the Cabrini Green Legal Aid (CGLA), which is a statewide initiative that works with low-income people in navigating the legal and criminal justice system on efforts that use food to grow justice. Noted chef Tunde Wey invests the profits from his applesauce sales to hospitals into ventures designed to increase the economic and physical well-being of African Americans. Using locally grown apples, his aim is to provide sustainable jobs, living wages, healthy foods, and local business and community investment in Kalamazoo, Michigan, while also addressing the racial inequities that have led to these being in short supply. The Nigerian-born Chef Wey is negotiating similar projects in other hospital systems in Michigan as well as in other states.

Smaller efforts include urban farmers and community gardeners who sell honey, meats and fish, and prepared foods, as well as food-based items such as teas, skin and hair products, and candles. Many urban farms, whether established by individuals or collectives, also present ongoing workshop series, educate local children in partnerships with schools, offer cooking classes, act as spaces for various communal gatherings, and work with artists and activists. Community gardens in underresourced and marginalized neighborhoods in places such as Tallahassee, Florida, have been cited as places of transformation, engagement, and empowerment for residents against systemic oppressions of poverty and racism. Indeed, urban farms and smaller-scale community gardens are sites of resistance as well as connectedness and produce.

Another effort to connect vulnerable people with food is the Okra Project, started by Ianne Fields Stewart in late 2018. It provides free, home-cooked, culturally informed healthy meals to Black transgender people. Transgender people of all races and Black transgender people in particular are among the most economically marginalized in the United States. An estimated 34 percent of Black transgender people live in extreme poverty. Even more are food insecure. Despite their needs, transphobia and racism mean that needed emergency food aid, which is often provided by religiously affiliated organizations and government assistance remains unavailable. The name of the Okra Project is derived from kidnapped Africans who carried okra with them to sustain themselves along the Middle Passage and in the United States, where they planted the seeds on the plantations where they were enslaved. In that vein, the Okra Project sustains Black transgender people today while also working to advance their nutritional, health, and economic needs.

PRESERVING CULTURAL FOODWAYS

Foodways shine a light on both history and culture, as they are the behaviors, values, beliefs, stories, traditions, and rituals associated with food that are passed down across generations. Economic practices are also a part of cultural foodways, as are practices around how food is processed, prepared, and consumed. In this, they offer a connection to places, people, time, and ethnic and racial backgrounds. Indeed, foodways are deeply intertwined with how these practices, rituals, beliefs, and values are all lived in intersections with social statuses such as race and ethnicity, gender, and social class. It is easy to see efforts to preserve cultural foodways in thinking about a box of recipes passed down from parent to child or when the same dishes are served at a holiday meal, year in and year out. It is also easy to see how stories about food and purchases of ingredients for meals eaten in childhood do the work of preservation. The fondness and readiness with which Thanksgiving turkey, Hanukkah latkes, African Americans starting the New Year with black-eyed peas and collard greens, and Easter ham are recalled by many people are examples of this as well. These, however, are not the total extent of the ways food customs are preserved and transmitted across generations. Foodways are another example of the cultural and social dimensions of what, why, and how people eat. In a country that advocates, and in many cases, compels, assimilation, retaining food heritage is not a neutral act but can also be a form of resistance and a basis of activism for the marginalized. Kidnapped Africans brought with them seeds and rice braided into their hair as they were transported to the Americas where they were enslaved. These items remain part of African diasporic food cultures today. This is the case as so-called ethnic foods are cast as weird or disgusting or unsafe, often as proxies for the people who make and eat them. This is also the case for those forced to assimilate under colonization, as during enslavement, when people of African descent were made to take Americanized names, people of Mexican descent were made to speak English, and people of Indigenous ancestry were made to leave their land, send their children to American boarding schools, and unlearn their culture. Maintaining a patch of land to grow sweet potatoes outside the enslaved's quarters, retaining burritos as a meal and a name, and planting the same seeds that one's ancestors did even after their land was stolen are forms of activism, even if they are not referred to as such. These examples show some of the work done in the effort to retain some autonomy under oppression. These and other means of preserving cultural foodways are a key component of food sovereignty.

The food sovereignty movement dates back to 1996 and to a presentation by the organization La Vía Campesina at the United Nations Food and Agricultural Organization's World Summit. La Vía Campesina, an international grassroots organization of farmers, Indigenous peoples, and laborers, issued a declaration that states that "each nation must have the right to food sovereignty to achieve the level of food sufficiency and nutritional quality it considers appropriate without suffering retaliation of any kind." This is considered the first use of the term *food sovereignty*, which La Vía Campesina later defined as the right of peoples to healthy and culturally appropriate food produced through sustainable methods and their right to define their own food and agriculture systems. It develops a model of small-scale sustainable production benefiting communities and their environment. Food sovereignty prioritizes local food production and consumption, reinforcing the right to protect local producers from cheap imports and to control production. It includes the struggle for land and genuine agrarian reform to ensure that the right to use and manage lands, territories, water, seeds, livestock, and biodiversity are in the hands of those who produce food and not in the hands of the corporate sector.

Thus those in the food sovereignty movement seek to emphasize local needs, cultural foodways, and health, safety, and environmental concerns in food systems and policies rather than those lobbied for and designed by corporations, developers, and, increasingly, local, state, national, and international policy makers and politicians. Food sovereignty is focused on justice at every level. Some major aims among proponents of food sovereignty include autonomy in all aspects of food-related decision-making, community-defined food systems, an end to oppressive and unequal economic and social conditions related to food, and food practices and policies, including production, processing, distribution, marketing, access, and availability, that sustain communities, health, and the environment.

In the United States, there are considerable overlaps between the struggle to achieve food sovereignty and Native American sovereignty. In their connection to traditional practices, cultural foodways also often offer insight and guidance on sovereignty and sustainability. Heritage, language, community, and the environment can all be preserved through the preservation or sustenance of cultural foodways. Reclaiming Indigenous land and culture is part of the mission of the Traditional Native American Farmers Association (TNAFA). The organization was founded in 1992 as a collective of 17 different Native American communities in the southwestern United States. TNAFA is a stay against the destructive colonialist practices that decimated their communities, ways of life, and foodways. Over the last 26 years, members have worked to restore and sustain traditional agricultural practices as well as their connected spirituality, economic development, health and wellness, and culture. One method of this has been in developing interest among Native American youth in learning about and implementing traditional methods for food growing, cultivating, and cooking. Another has been in seed preservation and conservation. Both are designed to draw connections back to a precolonial past in hopes of shepherding Native communities, traditions, and culture into the future.

Another way this is illustrated is in the lack of federal rules that protect both while also threatening preservation of particular crops and processing methods. Native Americans continue to raise alarms at the loss of sustainable agricultural practices and heirloom crops due to federal food safety rules that threaten traditional foods and production systems. At the same time, most of the 567 federally recognized Native American nations have not adopted their own laws on food production, handling, and processing. As such, their sovereignty will not prevent the enforcement of state and federal laws and policies, which brings into question how much sovereignty they actually have. Advocates and legal experts are at work with nations to develop a comprehensive set of food codes to protect Native sovereignty and practices. Without functioning laws around food, tribes engaged in anything from farming to food handling and animal health are ceding power to state and federal authorities. The First Nations Development Institute, an economic development organization, asserts Native sovereignty as food sovereignty that such food codes can protect.

Advocates for healthier eating often advocate for more traditional diets, as these are focused on whole foods, complex carbohydrates, and complete proteins. A diet based on traditionally grown and prepared nutrient-dense grains, vegetables, and fruits is often better for the environment as well, especially when they are seasonal and local. Other traditional components of diet—preparing foods at home and eating foods communally—are also conserved. Food organizations such as Oldways base their work on these understandings as they endorse and promote old ways of eating through the dissemination of culturally based food pyramids that root people, dietary recommendations, and meal ideas to Africa, Asia, Latin America, and the Middle East and Mediterranean. These are all efforts that support greater justice as it relates to food or, as exemplified in the following section, is related to workers in the food system.

FIGHT FOR $15

The protections, rights, benefits, and pay that union membership offers have been vital to economic stability and upward mobility. However, union membership, on the decline in the private and public sector since the 1970s in the United States, is especially low in the food system. Approximately 12 percent of U.S. workers are union members today. In the food industry, that number is cut in half, at just over 6 percent. There is variation in membership across industry sectors. Currently, 14 percent of food retail workers belong to a union; 13 percent of food-processing workers are union members; 8 percent of distribution workers are unionized; and less than 2 percent of service and farmworkers are union members. Farmworkers are not allowed to unionize under the provisions of the 1935 National Labor Relations Act. Much like that year's Social Security Act, this other component of the New Deal's social safety net explicitly excluded agricultural workers in order to appease racist policy makers, employers, landowners, and voters who did not want to afford the full benefits of the state to African Americans in the Jim Crow South. This continues to be a racially discriminatory policy today, as the majority of farmworkers are now Latinx. Workers covered by a union earn 26 percent more than nonunion workers. They are also far more likely to have employer-provided health insurance and retirement benefits. Unionization has recently been a key pillar of recent demands by fast-food and retail workers and others in the food system for these reasons.

More than a slogan, Fight for $15 is a concerted effort by food workers, in fast-food restaurants in particular, to ensure they earn enough money to maintain a basic standard of living—sometimes referred to as a living wage—in addition to the right to unionize and receive employer-provided benefits. While inflation and costs of living across the United States mean that $15 per hour may still be inadequate to cover housing, utilities, food, and other expenses, it is still more than double the current federal minimum wage of $7.25 per hour, established in 2009. The Fight for $15 movement had its beginning in late 2012, when fast-food workers from chains such as McDonald's, Burger King, and Wendy's started walking off their jobs in concerted efforts across the nation to demand better wages, benefits, and working conditions and to raise public awareness and support. After thousands of fast-food workers participated in several strikes in various cities around the nation between November 2012 and May 2013, a one-day strike occurred in July 2013 in cities that included Chicago, Detroit, Flint (Michigan), Kansas City (Missouri), Memphis, Milwaukee, New York, Seattle, and St. Louis. This was followed by even larger coordinated national strikes in August and December. By 2014 the movement had become a global movement across hundreds of cities and dozens of countries on each continent. Health-care workers, preschool teachers, retail clerks, airport workers, and adjunct college professors have joined in the fight for a living wage. Some organizers and researchers call this the largest labor protest of low-wage workers in the nation's history.

Gains made toward the Fight for $15 benefit food workers in particular. A 2019 Bureau of Labor Statistics report, *Characteristics of Minimum Wage Workers, 2018*, shows that slightly less that 75 percent of employees who earned the minimum wage in 2018 worked in the service industry, and the majority of those worked in food-preparation- and serving-related jobs. As of 2018 approximately 60 percent of minimum-wage earners are employed within the leisure and hospitality industry, which has the highest percentage of employees earning the minimum wage. Almost all of these employees work in restaurants and other food services.

In addition to numbers of supporters, the movement also had gained attention and wins. By 2015 McDonald's increased the wages of 90,000 workers at corporate-owned locations to start at least $1 an hour more than the prevailing minimum, and in 2019 the corporation announced it would cease its lobbying and other efforts against increased minimum wages. By 2020 Amazon and Target had announced increases in their minimum wage to $15 an hour. Walmart announced it would increase to $13 an hour by the year's end. Though this benefits workers at these stores—many of whom are food workers as these retail giants increasingly dominate grocery sales—none of them allows unions, and many fast-food restaurants still are not meeting workers' full demands.

Several states, such as California, Connecticut, Illinois, Maryland, Massachusetts, New Jersey, and New York, and 50 cities and counties have announced raises in their minimum wages to at least $15 an hour as a result of the movement's organizing and activism. The 2016 Democratic National Committee included the Fight for $15 on its platform. In summer of 2019, the U.S. House of Representatives passed the Raise the Wage Act. The bill calls for an increase in the federal minimum wage from $7.25 an hour to $15 an hour by 2025. The bill also calls for a phase-out of the sub-minimum wage of $2.13 for tipped workers. The complementary Senate bill introduced by Senator Bernie Sanders, an Independent from Vermont who caucuses with Senate Democrats, is stalled, as of September 2020, in the Republican-controlled U.S. Senate. If passed, according to David Cooper of the Economic Policy Institute, more than two-thirds of the working poor would receive a pay increase.

CREATING FOOD JUSTICE IN THE FOOD SYSTEM

A just food system does not occur without effort. It also does not occur through the beneficence of owners and employers. The equity and justice within it are the results of agitation, advocacy, and activism that resist the status quo and its maintenance of inequality. This is evident when examining campaigns for higher wages, such as in the Fight for $15 detailed earlier. Indeed, resistance to unfair wages and labor practices takes many shapes. One is labor strikes. Another is unionizing. One of the most notable forms of activism around food since the mid-twentieth century has been through the United Farm Workers (UFW). The UFW was founded by Cesar Chavez and Dolores Huerta in 1962 and continues to work for a safe and just food supply. Its organizing model, initially used to bring national attention to the struggles of Mexican and Filipino workers in California, is still in use by the current UFW and other organizers today.

Organizing has been employed at other points by those seeking to create a more just food system. During the civil rights movement, civil rights leader and organizer Fannie Lou Hamer founded the Freedom Farm Cooperative in Sunflower County, Mississippi. Hamer had been a sharecropper until she was kicked off the land in 1962 by the white owner, who was enraged when Hamer attempted to register to vote. This, other forms of retaliation, and attempts on her life activated Hamer. That trajectory took her from learning about her constitutional rights from Student Nonviolent Coordinating Committee (SNCC) members to becoming one of the movement's most important figures, whose fierce and vocal dedication to freedom made even President Lyndon Johnson fear her power. This was illustrated when he announced an impromptu press conference as a distraction during her impassioned prime-time televised testimony urging the 1964 Democratic National Committee Convention's Credentials Committee to allow the Mississippi Freedom Democratic Party that she cofounded to be allowed as the official delegation from Mississippi. A few years later, Hamer bought 40 acres of rich Mississippi Delta land. This fueled the creation of the Freedom Farm and the ability for poor Black farmers and sharecroppers to gain economic freedom and self-sufficiency. This grassroots effort drew on Hamer's organizing skills and belief in the power and abilities of the people. It had members who planted some cash crops that allowed the cooperative to sustain itself and pay taxes and other expenses. The rest of the land was dedicated to growing produce, such as beans, peas, and greens, that were distributed back to Freedom Farm Cooperative members. Later, Freedom Farm acquired 640 more acres. It also launched a pig bank with 35 female and 5 male pigs, purchased with funds from the National Council of Negro Women. Over the course of three years, the original group reproduced thousands of pigs, creating vital financial and food streams. Though it operated for years, the Freedom Farm Collective did not have the kind of governmental or other institutional support it needed to remain viable. The concept continues, however, to serve as a model for cooperative farming and economics.

Scholar Monica White describes the collective agency of Black farmers who come together to both resist interlocking forms of exclusion and create changes that improve their joint social, economic, and political conditions in places through the Deep South and in urban centers such as Detroit. They do this, much as their predecessors in Fannie Lou Hamer's Jim Crow rural South did, through the formation of cooperatives of independent farmers, tenant farmers, and urban growers who come together to counter, in ways they would not be able to sustain individually, white racism, discrimination from the USDA and lenders, industrial agriculture, and economic struggles. They also offer safety, security, and solidarity. Other examples of cooperatives exist for Black farmers in Chicago and Milwaukee, for members of other racial and ethnic groups, and in multiracial and other kinds of coalitions across the nation. One such group is the National Family Farm Coalition (NFFC). It was founded in 1986, when family farms were in great peril, and is the only Washington, DC–based lobbying group to represent family farmers, fishers, and ranchers. It has 30 member groups in 42 states and advocates for an array of farmer rights, fair pricing structures, air and water quality, strong local economies, the right to sell and buy locally grown and locally processed food, and continued independence from industrial agriculture, as well as for the right to live in vibrant and healthy communities. Their work is also grounded in food sovereignty principles that promote a healthy and regenerative food, farming, and fishing system; vibrant rural communities where all can live with dignity and easy access to foods grown, caught, and harvested locally; fair prices and living wages for all food producers and providers; democratic, community-based control of and responsibility for ecological resources and practices; and social, racial, cultural, and economic and other forms of diversity across all aspects of the food system.

This is a call taken up by other groups, such as those that offer food justice trainings and certifications. Echoing food labeling initiatives that signal to consumers whether foods are grown under cruelty-free practices, organically, without GMOs, in accordance with fair trade policies, and the like, a food-justice certification label has recently been introduced. It is issued by the Florida-based Agricultural Justice Project (AJP) to indicate that all workers across the food chain who created the product in a customer's hand at a grocery store or on their plate at home have been treated fairly. Farms and other food businesses seeking AJP certification must show they ensure workers' safety on the job as well as have workers' compensation, disability, and unemployment insurance and contribute to Social Security on workers' behalf. They must also offer employee leave and employ standards aligned with USDA Organic certification. These policies must be in place for all workers, whether permanent, temporary, seasonal, or migrant. AJP began issuing food justice certifications in 2011 and was followed by the Equitable Food Initiative in 2014 and Fair Trade USA (FTUSA) in 2016. AJP also is an industry advocacy group. It offers consultancy services to farms and food businesses that improve conditions for workers. Its efforts have led to the Regenerative Organic Certification's inclusion of farmers' rights standards, helped shape Whole Foods's Responsibly Grown program, Fair Trade USA's standards, and Ben & Jerry's Caring Dairy Program.

Another example is found through the Coalition of Immokalee Workers' (CIW) Fair Food Program (FFP). This form of food activism has been involved in changing consumers' attitudes and behaviors around purchases. A focus on increasing consumer consciousness and encouraging consumers to demand fairer wages and labor conditions for workers at the stores and restaurants they frequent has been effective. Other efforts aimed at changing consumer practices include urging consumers to request that retailers and restaurants purchase foods with food justice certification. This guarantees that foods are not just certified organic by the USDA but are also produced under just working conditions for workers and fair pricing for farmers. Diners can also patronize members of the Restaurants Advancing Industry Standards in Employment (RAISE) coalition. These 300 restaurant owners pay their staff a living wage, provide benefits and opportunities for advancement, and use sustainable environmental practices.

Environmental justice and food justice are mutually constitutive. Sociologist Robert Bullard describes environmental racism as the product of environmental injustice, supported by an array of institutions such as the economic, government, legal, military, and political systems that meet both private and public policies and practices in ways that bring benefits to whites that people of color bear the costs of. Food inequalities are a result (and a reinforcement) of this form of systemic racism. In addition to a disproportionate share of food inequalities, impoverished communities and communities of color—which often are one and the same—bear a disproportionate share of other facets of environmental inequalities. These communities have more landfills, incinerators, coal plants, and toxic-waste dumps than wealthier, whiter communities do. They also have more exposure to environmental harms caused by the food industry, which are located in areas closer to communities of color and low-income communities, where residents have less political and economic power to halt their placement. The economic argument for these locations is multifaceted. In addition to less political power to stop their location, residents of places with few viable employment options may welcome the jobs these bring. Factory farms and slaughterhouses, rendering plants, and other processing facilities also locate there due to low land costs. Food justice actions recognize environmental concerns in their quests for equity in the food system. A truly equitable food system is one where all benefits and risks, profits and losses, and access and affordability are equitably shared across all people, places, and components involved. Food justice also means that those who produce, process, transport, distribute, sell, serve, and consume food have their interests, needs, concerns, and voices fully and equitably considered in any decisions being made.

The grassroots HEAL Food Alliance represents 50 organizations, which include rural and urban farmers, fishers, food-chain workers, rural and urban community residents, and Indigenous groups, as well as scientists, public-health advocates, and environmentalists. It not only works across the various sectors of the food system but is multiracial as well. In its 10-point platform, it issues what it describes as a call to action and a political compass for transformation that would address systemic food inequalities. The platform includes plans that address health, the economy, and the environment through changes in practices, policies, and laws that would further build upon the forms of activism discussed in this chapter to generate more equity in the food system.

As the problems that cause and result from food inequalities are complex and interrelated, solving food inequalities, their root causes, and consequences must also be complex and interrelated. Many recommended changes focus on individual-level strategies. This focus may result in improved outcomes, but it will be limited without systemic changes that address race, class, gender, and their intersections. As the food system has long tentacles that cross each other as they reach across individuals, interactions, and institutions as well as social structures, radical changes that bring justice, end discrimination, and remedy oppression are needed. Food equality is impossible without immigration, worker, race, class, and gender justice. Food equality is impossible without cultural, economic, political, transit, health-care, legal, educational, housing, and environmental justice. This process will be neither easy nor quick. The strategies employed must come from the grass roots and from positions of power. They must also be sustainable in a multitude of dimensions, culturally rooted, data-based, and community-informed in addition to erasing conceptions of urban-suburban-rural divides.

Food justice activists and workers create and highlight numerous efforts to make the food system more equitable. These include initiatives across the United States to mentor new generations of farmers: to tap into cultural practices and values to encourage more racial diversity among farmers, the development of food policy councils that center on gender and racial inclusion, and programs that focus on introducing children and youth to food equity and sustainability principles and practices. There are also legal efforts designed to help farmers keep their land and sue for redress of past and current harms, and work is being done to change policies, practices, and laws to staunch and remedy structural racism's impact on the food system. The attention paid to reparations to African Americans and Native Americans by Democrats running for the U.S. presidency in 2020 is another example of the ground gained from these calls.

Shifting profits from owners and management to increased wages for workers poses another form of increased equity within the food system. Doing so would come at little to no cost to consumers while greatly benefiting workers, their families, and all taxpayers who would no longer subsidize low wages and high profits. Equity policies in hiring, promotion, pay and other regards are also necessary, as evidenced by the number of lawsuits and settlements against government agencies and employers that call for these and similar remedies. These concerns are further addressed in the next two chapters.

PART II

Controversies and Issues

Is Everyone Treated the Same? Racial and Gender Discrimination in the Food System

In a nation founded on colonization, enslavement, and land expropriation, discrimination in the food system is no surprise. This is evident when looking at all aspects of the food system, including undocumented Mexican and Central American farmworkers' exploitation, poor and African American people's decreased access to food, women's expected roles around food in their homes, and wealthy agribusiness executives' outsized influence on food policy. These are the direct consequences of practices, laws, and other social arrangements created in ways that initiate and further inequality.

This chapter focuses on food workers' experiences of racial and gender discrimination, including during planting and harvesting, at processing plants, and in restaurants. Recent research is analyzed with an eye toward the presence, forms, and outcomes of discrimination rooted in race and gender throughout the food system. These were certainly present prior to COVID-19's presence in the United States and have only been exacerbated since.

RACE AND GENDER DISCRIMINATION IN THE FARMING INDUSTRY

In the United States, the popular image and reality of the average farmer is someone who is white, male, and older. Those who fall outside these categories have a long history of greater difficulties in beginning, maintaining, and keeping farms. Farmers of color, farmers who are women, and farmers who are immigrants not only have smaller farms but are less likely to receive government supports and subsidies. In addition, they are often subjected to fraudulent or deceptive lending practices and are denied loans or given higher interest rates than white men are given. Marginalized farmers also grow more specialized and labor-intensive crops, which means an overall result of an expenditure of more effort for less financial payoff. Land foreclosures occur at disproportionate rates for marginalized farmers as well. These realities are rooted in a long history of racist and sexist practices, policies, and ideologies.

During the Civil War, white farmers were granted land expropriated from Native Americans, who were forced onto reservations, through the 1862 Homestead Act, a path not available to the formerly enslaved African Americans. Most African Americans in the Jim Crow South who did not work as domestics or in other kinds of service for whites were relegated to sharecropping. As such, many African Americans were locked into a peonage system built to make sure they never left it. Indeed, white property owners, legislators, lenders, and government officials worked on individual and systemic levels to deny African Americans the ability to obtain and retain farmland and operations. Those who did own land have been systematically dispossessed of it.

Historian Pete Daniel documents this in his work on African American farmers. In 1940, at the height of Jim Crow, there were nearly 700,000 African American farmers. By 1970 there were fewer than 46,000, a decline of 93 percent. In 1997, 20,000 African Americans farmers owned just 2 million acres of land. This is down from 16 million acres of farmland. Much of this farm loss has been facilitated by the USDA. After a series of lawsuits against the USDA for discrimination against African American farmers, the 1999 *Pigford v. Glickman* case provided a settlement of more than $1 billion to 16,000 African American farmers for the racist loan denials that occurred between 1983 and 1997. Congress approved a second settlement of another $1.2 billion in 2011. The USDA has similarly been ordered to pay a group of Native American farmers and ranchers a $680 million settlement and provide $80 million in loan forgiveness. Subsequently, Latinx and women farmers have also filed claims against the USDA for civil rights violations.

New forms of inequality have also developed and have even further disadvantaged African American farmers. One example of this is found in numerous lawsuits alleging African Americans have been defrauded, had contracts canceled without cause, or have been excluded from contracts on the basis of their race by Koch Foods, an Illinois-based food processor and distributor with a large share of the U.S. poultry market. The USDA has substantiated those claims, finding that a number of Koch Foods practices toward Black suppliers were discriminatory. A 2017 lawsuit against Koch Foods found that the company practiced unjust discrimination and violated the law with regard to African American farmers they had contracts with, according to a 700-page case file obtained by Isaac Arnsdorf, an investigative journalist for ProPublica. Despite this finding, Koch Foods was not penalized. The company was also sued by the Equal Employment Opportunity Commission (EEOC) on behalf of Mississippi-based Latinx employees claiming they experienced sexual harassment, retaliation, and discrimination. The company, which denied wrongdoing, was ordered to pay nearly $4 million in a 2018 settlement. Marginalization and disparate treatment are not limited to Black and Latinx farmers nor to Koch Foods as a perpetrator.

Inequalities in Farm Ownership

Other historically derived inequalities become evident upon looking at the discrepancies between who owns farmland and who works it. Work from scholars Megan Horst and Amy Marion determines that white people own more than 97 percent of leased farmland—a category referred to nonfarming ownership—and are 96 percent of farm owner-operators and 86 percent of tenant farmers. In addition to a near-monopoly on land, whites also possess 98 percent of all landowning farm-related income and 97 percent of operating farm income. Whites also have more access to national and international markets, receive the overwhelming majority of federal subsidies, are more likely to receive cash infusions through loans and investments, and hold more trademarks and patents on plant, animal, and technological advances. All of this furthers racial and ethnic income and wealth gaps and other inequalities. Farm owner-operators of color have smaller farms, less land, and lower earnings and wealth than whites do. On the whole, it is more likely that farmers of color will be tenants rather than owners, with the lowered incomes, security, and autonomy that accompany this status. Racial and ethnic disparities are especially vivid for Latinx people, who are 2 percent of nonfarming owners, 6 percent of owner-operators and tenant operators, and more than 80 percent of farm laborers. While the majority of farm owners are white, a Department of Labor's National Agriculture Worker Survey finds that approximately 70 percent of farmworkers in the United States are immigrants from Mexico.

A November 2019 USDA report finds that 41 percent of farmers are from marginalized backgrounds. Thirty percent are primary producers, those with final decision-making power. As they hold 21 percent of all agricultural land and account for 13 percent of market value in production, their operations are typically smaller and generate less in revenues than those owned and operated by white men. According to an analysis by researchers at Portland State, men comprise 63 percent of nonfarming landowners, 86 percent of farm operators, and 87 percent of tenant farmers. Those women who do farm earn less than their men counterparts do. This is seen as women earn close to 40 percent of all farm-related income but women farm owner-operators and tenants earn only 3 percent of farm-related income.

Women account for more than one-third of farmers, a 27 percent increase in the five-year period between 2012 and 2017. The number of farms operated by women increased by 23 percent during this time frame. While 91 percent of all U.S. farms have at least one man as a farmer, 58 percent have at least one woman in that capacity. Thirty-eight percent have a woman at the helm of the farm as the primary producer. Only 9 percent of U.S. farms are operated solely by a woman. Women who are primary producers are more likely to be on beginning and limited-resource farms than men are. Women are primary producers of 19 percent of beginning farms and 11 percent of established farms. Similarly, they make up 27 percent of limited-resource farms and 11.5 percent of non-limited-resource farms. Some 38 percent of U.S. agricultural sales and 43 percent of U.S. agricultural land belong to women. Women, however, are more economically vulnerable than men. This is seen when 28 percent of women primary producers fall outside the paid labor force. USDA data reveal that there are almost twice as many women who are second or third producers compared with primary producers on farms. Their roles are often more concerned with business management rather than the farm production concerns of the primary producer. Second and third producers provide added focus on farm business management relative to production management skills that the principal producer possesses. Most of the women referred to here are white, at 95 percent of the population of women farmers, followed by Latinas at 3 percent, Native Americans at 2.2 percent, African Americans at 1.1 percent, and Asian American and Pacific Islanders (AAPIs) with just under 1 percent of the share of women farmers in the United States.

USDA data find African Americans are 1.4 percent of the country's farmers. Their farms are smaller compared with those of other farmers. They are concentrated in the southeastern and mid-Atlantic United States, though the largest number of African American farmers is found in Texas, where they make up 3 percent of that state's farmers. Between 2012 and 2017, there was a 5 percent increase in the number of African American farmers and a 3 percent decrease in the total number of farms they operated. This percentage is the same as the decrease in the total number of U.S. farms during this period. African American primary producer farms account for 0.4 percent of agricultural sales and 0.5 percent of agricultural land in the United States; 71 percent are men and 29 percent are women.

USDA data also show that slightly more than 3.3 percent of the U.S. farmers are Latinx. They are concentrated in California, Florida, New Mexico, and Texas. Between 2012 and 2017, the number of Latinx farmers increased by 13 percent, and the number of Latinx-operated farms grew by 8 percent. Latinx primary operator farms account for almost 6 percent of U.S. agriculture sales and almost 4 percent of U.S. agricultural land. Latinx farmers are typically younger than other U.S. farmers, at 55 years old, compared with 57.5 years old on average. They are also more likely to be beginning farmers. Similar to overall gender patterns among farmers, 65 percent are men and 35 percent are women.

USDA data also show that AAPIs constitute 0.7 percent of the country's farmers. They are concentrated in California and Hawaii, where they are 6 percent and 35 percent of the respective state's farmers. Between 2012 and 2017, the number of AAPI farmers increased by 5 percent, and the number of farms they operated increased by 2 percent. AAPI-operated farms account for just under 2 percent of total U.S. agriculture sales and 0.3 percent of agricultural land. As with Latinx farmers, AAPI farmers are typically younger than others. With 40 percent of all AAPI farmers having fewer than 10 years of experience, they are also more likely to be beginning farmers. There is greater gender parity among AAPIs as 55 percent of operators are men and 45 percent are women.

Native Americans, according to USDA data, are 2.3 percent of the nation's farmers. They are concentrated in the western and Plains states, specifically in Arizona, New Mexico, and Oklahoma. Between 2012 and 2017, they saw a 10 percent increase in the number of farmers and a 7 percent increase in the number of farms they operated. Their farms accounted for less than 1 percent of agricultural sales and more than 6 percent of agricultural land in the United States. Native Americans farmers are more likely to demonstrate gender balance, as 56 percent are men and 44 percent are women. These data and patterns reveal the need for greater progress with regard to gender, race, and ethnicity.

Through targeted employment practices at the Farm Service Agency and the establishment of programs from their relatively recently created Office of Advocacy and Outreach, the USDA has made attempts at greater inclusivity. Federal Farm Act programs have been in place since the 1990s to assist farmers from marginalized backgrounds, such as women of all races and people of color of all genders, in an attempt to ameliorate past harms and exclusion. Indeed the 2018 Farm Act targets funding to members of these groups to provide increased cost share, loss compensation, and loan assistance. It also includes funding for research related to their status and concerns. Still, these efforts have been more piecemeal than systemic. In addition, according to a *Pacific Standard* report by Emily Moon in 2019, women farmers remain subjected to numerous forms of exclusion and discrimination. African American and other farmers of color experience this too. The experience of discrimination on farms is not limited to farm producers and owners. Farmworkers are highly vulnerable to discrimination.

Inequalities and Farmworkers

Unlike farmers, farmworkers are hired agricultural workers. There are racial, nationality, and citizenship distinctions in the ranks of the work done on farms beyond those detailed earlier. Farmworkers—those who are laborers, graders, and sorters—are more likely to have been born in Mexico. Farm management—those who manage, inspect, and supervise—are more likely to be white, U.S.-born citizens. Forty-five percent of farmworkers are born in the U.S, and 54 percent are U.S. citizens. Sixty-four percent of farm managers, inspectors, and supervisors are white, 3 percent are African American, 27 percent are of Mexican descent, and 3 percent have other Latinx ancestry. Seventy-six percent of those in management have been born in the United States, and 84 percent are U.S. citizens. There are also educational distinctions: 48 percent of farmworkers have less than a high school education, 32 percent have a high school diploma or its equivalent, and 20 percent have at least some college education. In comparison, among those in farm management, 24 percent have less than a high school education, 31 percent have a high school diploma or its equivalent, and 45 percent have at least some college education. This is reflected in pay distinctions. Among farmworkers, though whites are in fewer of these positions, their pay is higher than comparable farmworkers of color. For every dollar in income earned by white farmworkers, people of color earn 78 cents. Among agricultural inspectors, 35 percent are white. They have a median income of $32,079. People of color account for 65 percent of agricultural inspectors, and with a median income of $17,353, they earn slightly more than half of what their white counterparts do. The reality is even more stark for the 60 percent of agricultural inspectors who are Latinx, who earn a median income of $15,619, according to Yvonne Yen Liu and Dominique Apollon.

RACE AND GENDER DISCRIMINATION IN THE PROCESSING INDUSTRY

As shown earlier, marginalized farmers experience racism and sexism in their dealings with processing companies. This is also the case for processing workers. Racial, ethnic, and gender discrimination is common in food processing and production. White people are 55 percent of workers in food processing and earn slightly more than $40,000. Food processors who are people of color earn $24,400. Among poultry-, meat-, and fish-processing workers, white people have a median income of $23,645, compared with Asian Americans' $24,285, Latinx people's $21,386, and African Americans' $17,949. Similar patterns of whites outearning people of color are found in other food-processing jobs.

A series of recent lawsuits further illuminate some of the discrimination in this sector. California's Marquez Brothers, a producer of Mexican foods, settled a discrimination suit for $2 million in 2019 after allegations that it reserved so-called unskilled positions for Latinx workers. The settlement came two years after the EEOC filed suit because of numerous cases of non-Latinx job applicants being denied work in favor of Latinx applicants with fewer qualifications. In conjunction with the financial damages, Marquez Brothers agreed to hire an external monitor, set hiring goals, and adopt plans for hiring transparency and diversity, discrimination reporting, and antidiscrimination training, a common set of remedies in such cases.

Tyson Foods, one of the world's largest food processors, agreed to pay $1.6 million in back wages and benefits to nearly 6,000 job applicants who were rejected employment at plants across three states between 2007 and 2010. This 2019 settlement with the U.S. Department of Labor centered on allegations of systemic hiring discrimination. Though Tyson did not admit to any liability, in addition to the financial settlement, the company agreed to hire some of the applicants as well as change its hiring and training processes.

In 2018 Illinois-based Koch Foods, one of the world's largest poultry processors, settled a 2011 class action lawsuit brought by Latinx workers. The settlement included EEOC monitoring; implementation of antidiscrimination policies, training, and a 24-hour bilingual hotline for reporting discrimination; and $3.75 million in financial relief for the victims of widespread patterns of sexual harassment, racial and ethnic discrimination,

and physical abuse, and for victims of retaliation against Latinx employees of the company's Morton, Mississippi, chicken-processing operations.

Soon after the $3.75 million Koch Foods settlement was announced,
Koch's seven Mississippi plants were raided by Immigration and Customs Enforcement (ICE), and nearly 700 workers were arrested at Koch's
seven plants there. Threats and actual calls to ICE are common practices
used by employers to enforce control over and instill fear in workers
who would otherwise demand better labor conditions. Union representatives and workers' rights advocates cite examples of ICE raids occurring
in the days after wage, health, or safety violations are reported. After an
employee was killed in an Ohio meatpacking plant, the Occupational
Safety and Health Administration (OSHA) fined his employer more than
$200,000 for three separate instances of lack of safety guards that resulted
in the employee's death. A week later, there was an ICE raid that led to
the arrests of 140 workers. Many suspect this arose from retaliation by the
company's owners.

Latinx workers predominate in the meatpacking industry, making up
44 percent of workers. Another 25 percent are African American. In animal slaughtering and processing more generally, 35 percent are Latinx and
23 percent are African American. Indeed, African American and Latinx
people are overrepresented in some of the most dangerous, low-paying
occupations within the industry.

RACE AND GENDER DISCRIMINATION IN THE RESTAURANT INDUSTRY

In the last ten years, employment in the restaurant industry has been
both the fastest growing and among the worst paying. It is also rife with
racial and gender inequalities in both work and wages. In the United States,
the paid labor force is 53 percent men and 47 percent women and 66 percent white, 11 percent African American, 16 percent Latinx, 6 percent
AAPI, and 1 percent Native American. In an equal society, these demographics would be reflected in all occupations and share of wages. The
United States, certainly, is not an equal society. In the restaurant industry, 48 percent of restaurant workers are men and 52 percent are women.
Fifty-five percent are white, 11 percent are African American, 25 percent
are Latinx, and 8 percent are AAPI. When looking specifically at fast-food
restaurants, men make up 35 percent of the worker population, compared
with women's 65 percent. In terms of race, 64 percent of fast-food restaurant workers are white, 14 percent are African American, 16 percent
are Latinx, and 3 percent are AAPI. The share of Native Americans in

restaurants in general and in fast food specifically is so small that research-ers do not include it in their data.

In 2015 the nonprofit organization, Restaurant Opportunities Cen-ters (ROC) United issued a report on the restaurant industry's ongoing race- and gender-based occupational segregation and wage inequality. It illustrates that even more than a half century after Jim Crow laws were deemed illegal by the U.S. federal government, there remain stark patterns of racial exclusion in restaurants throughout the United States—both in the South and the North. This has marked implications for financial secu-rity. Work by Heidi Shierholz of the Economic Policy Institute reveals that restaurant workers have a poverty rate that is close to three times that for all workers. Racial discrimination means that people of color who work in restaurants are almost twice as likely to experience poverty as their white counterparts are.

In some markets, fine-dining servers and bartenders can see annual earnings in fine-dining restaurants that are between $50,000 and $150,000. A six-year paired audit study—consisting of applicants who are evenly matched on all characteristics except for race—of fine-dining restaurants conducted by ROC in 2015 finds white applicants are more likely to be interviewed and twice as likely to be hired when compared with equally or better-qualified applicants of color at the same restaurants, a finding consistent with other studies. Racial discrimination is also present when people of color are hired in restaurants. When compared with their equally qualified white peers, workers of color earn 56 percent less. ROC data fur-ther demonstrate that nearly 30 percent of workers attribute denied promo-tions to racial discrimination.

Race and gender combine such that white men are placed in the more prestigious and more lucrative jobs. In one study, 81 percent of manage-ment positions and 78 percent of positions such as captain, manager, and bartender are occupied by white workers. Within these positions, most were white men. At the same time, women are more likely to work as servers, but as they are overrepresented in casual dining establishments with their lower price points, their tips are lower, making it more difficult to survive on those and their guaranteed federal minimum wage of $2.13 an hour. There are also indicators that white men garner the highest tips, even in the same or comparable dining establishments. This is seen as women working in the "front of -the house" earn 76 cents for each dollar that men do. There is some more equity in the "back of the house," where the gap decreases, as women working there earn 88 cents for each dol-lar that men do. Overall, women working in restaurants earn 11 percent less than men do.

People of color are more likely to work in restaurants' back of the house as cooks, dishwashers, cleaners, and food preparers, in positions where their low wages are not augmented by tips. When they work in the front of the house—typically consisting of those restaurant workers with high levels of interaction with customers—people of color are overrepresented in the lower echelons of these positions as bussers and runners rather than hosts and waitstaff with their higher wages and share of tips. Whites are 60 percent of front-of-the-house workers, African Americans are 11 percent, and Latinx people are 20 percent. In the back of the house, whites are 47 percent, African Americans are 12 percent, and Latinx people are 34 percent of workers. Even when people of color and white women are in more lucrative and higher status positions, they earn less than white men in those same positions.

This is true across all facets of restaurant work and particularly so at the top. When picturing a home kitchen, most see a woman preparing meals. When actually going out to eat, this is far from the case. As with many other degree programs, women make up half of culinary graduates. They make up 40 percent of cooks but fewer than 20 percent of chefs and fewer than 7 percent of executive chefs—the most prestigious and highest-paying position in a restaurant—in the United States. Women chefs also earn nearly 30 percent less than men chefs, according to data from the "Sharpen Your Skills" report from Women Chefs and Restaurateurs. This pay disparity is the highest among restaurant work. In addition to having fewer opportunities and less money, women chefs and restaurateurs, like women in other parts of the restaurant and food industry, are often subjected to sexist taunts, pregnancy discrimination, sexual harassment, and sexual abuse from male customers, colleagues, and employers. Indeed, restaurants account for the largest number of sexual harassment claims in the United States. Sustained efforts are needed to combat the violations, discrimination, and the barriers to entry that mark the restaurant industry.

RACE AND GENDER INEQUALITY IN THE FOOD INDUSTRY

A McKinsey & Company report by Alexis Krivkovich and Marie-Claude Nadeau from November 2017 notes that even as the food industry is one of the largest and fastest-growing industries in the United States, women do not benefit from this when it comes to earnings, power, and representation. While women make most of the decisions about what foods are purchased in their homes, they do not make decisions within the industry, where they are relegated to entry-level positions. They constitute approximately half of entry-level employees. When women are hired, it is typically in support roles rather than those that have clear routes to raises and promotions that put them in line for moves up the corporate ladder. Their presence declines at each level above this, however, showing a persistent glass ceiling at best. By the time corporate executive level positions are analyzed, women account for fewer than 25 percent of these positions. Those women who are present are overwhelmingly white, as women of color barely are hired into these positions. Indeed, women of color make up 14 percent of entry-level food industry employees and only 3 percent of food industry corporate executive roles. In comparison, men of color represent 14 percent of entry-level positions and 7 percent of executive positions. Likewise, white men make up 37 percent of entry-level and 70 percent of corporate executive positions. Even as companies with racial and/or gender diversity in their management and executive ranks outperform and show more innovation than those dominated by white men, inclusive workplaces remain exceptions rather than rules, as these data portray. Systemic barriers, rather than personal choice or a lack of skill or ambition, are at the root of this. The McKinsey & Company report explains that some 20 percent fewer women in the food industry obtain an initial promotion. The realities are even more stark for both women and men of color in this industry. All the while, across gender and race, food industry employees cite similar loyalty and attrition rates. What vary are opportunities and equality. Though women are underrepresented across the food industry, when looking at entry-level positions, they are most likely to be represented in operations, followed by manufacturing, and then distribution. In operations, women represent 58 percent of entry-level employees and also have higher rates of promotion. They account for 32 percent of executive positions. Operations employees are also more racially diverse, across gender, when compared with other subsectors in the food industry. Women account for 48 percent of entry-level positions among food manufacturers, and they make up 20 percent of executive roles. Women are least represented among entry-level distributor jobs, at 35 percent. When looking at executive ranks, women make up only 9 percent of those positions.

Across the board, white people are overrepresented in management positions within the food system. Eighty-five percent of CEOs, 78 percent of industrial production managers, 81 percent of transport managers, and 68 percent of food-service managers are white. Whites account for 56 percent of nonmanagerial positions within the food system. Almost half of management positions are held by white men, and another 25 percent are held by white women. Of white managers, 65 percent are men and 35 percent are women. Thirteen percent of food industry managers are

Latinx. Some 66 percent are men, and 35 percent are women. Seven percent of food industry managers are African American. Of these, 52 percent are men, and 48 percent are women. Six percent of food industry managers are Asian American; 65 percent of this population are men, and 35 percent are women. There are also pay inequities here.

A study by Liu and Appolon highlights the race- and gender-based earnings disparities among food workers. For every dollar of income white men earn, Asian American men earn 83 cents, African American men earn 71 cents, and Latino men earn 66 cents. Women are even more disadvantaged. Asian American women earn 68 cents, white women earn 63 cents, African American women earn 53 cents, and Latina women earn 50 cents for every dollar white men earn. These disparities are also reflected in the positions occupied within food work.

White managers have an annual median income of $38,433, compared with $33,787 for people of color. In nonmanagerial roles, whites have a median income of $22,913, and people of color have a median income of $18,738. The median income of white CEOs is $116,144. The median income of CEOs of color is notably lower, at $76,379. White industrial production managers have a median income of $66,195, and people of color in these roles have a median income of $61,103. White transport managers have a median income of $52,792, and people of color have a median income of $46.845 in the same positions. Food-service managers have a median income of $32,731 if they are white and $31,675 if they are people of color. The pay gaps by race are lowest in food-service management and among nonmanagerial positions.

In addition to pay discrimination, sexual harassment and assault are ubiquitous for women in the food system. Most of the sexual harassment, abuse, and assault is perpetrated by men against women. Harassment, abuse, and assault by members of one's gender and by women against men also occur, though these patterns are less common. More than 80 percent of women farmworkers report being harassed or assaulted at work, for example. Employers and coworkers deploy a number of tactics in sexually harassing and assaulting workers. Sexual harassment occurs through sexual staring and leering, sexual gestures, sexual jokes, requests for dates and sex as well as in quid pro quo offers that may entail more pay, more overtime, special treatment, or the granting of time off or bathroom breaks in exchange for sex. In addition to forcible and coercive rape, other forms of sexual assault and abuse include unwanted kissing, unwanted touching, exposing genitals, and rubbing against workers as they pass by.

As this chapter details, there remains deep and persistent structural inequities faced by people employed across the food system. In the wake of rights movements for workers, people of color, and women that have changed laws, policies, and practices, why has this stayed the case? One answer is that the continued marginalization of people is aligned with stereotypes about work that have been historically associated with the people who have provided it. Growing, making, and serving food have long been areas that women of all races and people of color of all genders have been relegated to in the United States. Compared with other industries, the work done in fields and kitchens is undervalued culturally and symbolically, leading to its continuous undervaluation financially. These histories and association make it easy to perpetuate practices of inequality. More inequalities in the food system are explored in the following chapter.

CHAPTER 9

Fair Wages for Fair Work? Equity in the Food System

The current U.S. food system consists of several interrelated components. The first is production, which includes farmers, ranchers, fishers, and farmworkers, hired workers who plant, cultivate, grow, harvest, and care for crops and livestock. The next is processing, which takes foods in their most natural state and transforms them through refining, slaughtering, pasteurizing, fortifying, freezing, fermenting, preserving, and packaging. Distribution occurs across several parts of the food system. Here, foods are transported from production to processing sites and again from processing sites to warehouses and then on to distribution centers. From there, foods move to wholesalers and then to the next part of the food system: the market, where they are purchased by retailers and restaurants, which then sell to consumers. The food system has the largest share of workers in the current U.S. economy, with 14 percent of all U.S. workers employed across its five sectors. More than half are in food service, 15 percent in distribution, 14 percent in retail, 12 percent in production, and 8 percent in processing. Inequalities in opportunities, prestige, and pay in positions through these components of the food system are analyzed in this chapter. Particular attention is paid to the contrasts between income earned by frontline workers at the bottom of the scale and CEOs at the top of the scale.

THE IMPACTS OF WAGE INEQUALITY ON FOOD WORKERS

Data from USDA's "Ag and Food Sectors and the Economy" show that 11 percent of U.S. workers are employed in the agricultural and food sectors. This accounts for 22 million full- and part-time workers. Another

19.4 million U.S. workers are employed in agriculture- and food-related industries. Food workers account for approximately $2 trillion, or more than 13 percent of the U.S. Gross Domestic Product (GDP). Even as the economy has grown and worker productivity has increased, there has been a stagnation in food workers' wages. It has also seen more growth, expanding by 19 percent between 2003 and 2016, compared with the 10 percent growth in other industries. This growth has not, however, been seen in wages in the industry. Through the food system, it is apparent that the majority of food workers are in low-wage jobs.

An analysis from the Food Chain Workers Alliance (FCWA), from which many of the data in this chapter are drawn, shows frontline food workers, with their median hourly wage of $10.00, are the lowest paid of all U.S. workers. In comparison, the median hourly wage for all other U.S. industries is $17.53. As this is the fastest-growing economic sector in the nation, an increasing number of U.S. workers in the lowest-paid jobs is of deep concern for workers, their families, and the economy. Data from Bureau of Labor Statistics' *Characteristics of Minimum Wage Workers* show that eight of the ten lowest-paying occupations in the United States are food-system jobs, and of those eight, women are overrepresented in five occupations in 2019. Jobs within the food system have lower earnings than their comparable nonfood jobs. Within retailing and manufacturing, for example, those in food jobs earn less than those in nonfood jobs in the same industry.

Survey data from the FCWA show that 23 percent of all food workers earn subminimum wages, 40 percent earn poverty wages, 26 percent earn low wages, and 14 percent earn living wages. When the data are disaggregated by race and gender, further bases for inequality are elucidated. Overall, only 14 percent of food workers earn a living wage. Most food workers never are promoted or given raises, despite the duration of their employment or quality of their work. Research from the FCWA also indicates wage theft, which could be in the form of employers keeping employees' tips and other minimum-wage violations, failures to pay overtime, denying paid breaks, forcing workers to work off the clock, and otherwise denying employees their full earnings, is widespread. This is particularly the case in restaurants, as Sylvia Allegretto and David Cooper use Department of Labor data to show 84 percent of restaurants illegally failed to make sure tipped workers earn at least the minimum wage in combined salary and tips. Labor data claim that more than one-third of food workers—many of whom are in the lower echelons of the food industry, such as hired farm-workers, retail workers, and restaurant workers—face wage theft in an average week. This all has serious repercussions for workers' abilities to secure needs such as housing, health, and safety.

Food Workers' Housing

Housing is an issue for many food workers. Farmworkers, especially in areas in the United States with high costs of living, increasingly face work that is insufficient for their survival. People harvesting grapes for wine in Napa Valley, as one example, have commutes that last for hours each way because they cannot afford to live any closer to their jobs. Their low pay means increased transportation and time costs. Some larger growers provide housing to migrant farmworkers, who live in dorms that have rules and restrictions more reminiscent of halfway houses than colleges. Food workers in other sectors, especially fast-food workers in expensive cities such as Chicago, Los Angeles, Miami, New York, Seattle, and Washington, DC, also find it difficult to afford housing and other necessities on the low wages.

Food Workers' Health and Safety

Jobs within the food system are decidedly more dangerous than non-food-related jobs, even within the same and similar occupational categories, as an analysis of U.S. Bureau of Labor Statistics data from the 2016 National Census of Fatal Occupational Injuries makes clear. With low pay, few benefits, poor work conditions, high rates of turnover, and worker shortages in areas affected by decreased immigration flows and deportation of undocumented immigrants, workers can be placed in harmful conditions. FCWA research finds that one-fifth of food workers surveyed do not receive paid sick days, which leads many to show up to work sick or face missed pay and job loss. This has serious public-health consequences, as numerous contagious foodborne illnesses, such as hepatitis A, norovirus, *Shigella*, and *Staphylococcus aureus*, have been traced to ill food workers, as have other contagious diseases, such as the seasonal flu. Though the FDA Food Code issues recommendations that ill workers not work while sick, these recommendations are often not followed, nor are most workplaces monitored for compliance. A 2015 CDC study found that most restaurants fail to follow FDA recommendations. One key finding in the study is that some 12 percent of food workers report coming to work while experiencing vomiting or diarrhea. This is a critical issue, as Americans eat in restaurants on average five times a week; between 1998 and 2013, there were close to 10,000 foodborne illness outbreaks involving restaurant food, causing 124,608 reported illnesses, 4,427 reported hospitalizations, and 32 reported deaths. Nearly half of these outbreaks are attributable to worker health, as sick employees handle food, drinks, and other surfaces that they contaminate.

Additionally, food workers may be pushed to work harder and less safely, leading, for example, to increased risks and injuries. Other increased risks occur because food-related industries have higher rates of severe injuries caused by objects or equipment compared with non-food-industry workplaces doing the same kinds of jobs. Food retail workers have higher rates of injuries than other retail workers do. The number of work injuries for people in food preparation and serving-related occupations increased by 64 percent in 2016, the largest increase for all occupations. Production workers, that is, farmers, fishers, and ranchers, also face risks from animals, which are not present in other production workplaces. There are also more slips, trips, and falls resulting in serious injury, due to the slippery conditions that abound in the food industry. Other health and safety risks include burns and cuts, especially for food preparation workers, and the chronic pain and repetitive-motion injuries workers in production, processing, and distribution often suffer from the strains of their physical labor. Indeed, FCWA data show that more than half of food workers are injured or otherwise face health problems while at work.

Conditions in meatpacking and poultry-processing plants are among the most hazardous for all workers. They are no longer associated with the good pay and benefits they had at one point. Today they are some of the worst jobs available in the food system. A single plant can contain areas that vary from blazing hot and humid to freezing cold. They are also loud, smelly, and slippery from water, condensation, viscera, and blood. Workers regularly experience high rates of respiratory and skin infections and slips and falls. Workers on processing lines also engage in a lot of repetitive motions that lead to injury. Since the late 1970s, line speed at poultry plants, for example, have increased by 200 percent as lines have gone from processing 70 birds per minute to 140 per minute. This speed leads to not just repetitive-motion injuries but injury from sharp knives and dangerous machines as well. A National Employment Law Project report finds that an average of 27 poultry workers suffer work-related amputations or hospitalizations in the United States daily. Of the 14 companies with the most Occupational Safety and Health Administration (OHSA) severe injury reports, 4 are in the food-processing business.

Food workers are also more likely to be killed on the job when compared with almost all other U.S. workers. Among the industries with the highest OSHA reports of severe injuries involving amputation or hospitalization, the 5th highest is supermarkets/grocery stores, and the 12th is poultry processing. On average, the occupational fatality rate in the United States is 3.6 deaths per 100,000 workers. This number is much lower than the average for many employed in the food industry. Fishers have the second-highest occupational fatality rates, with 86 deaths per 100,000 workers. Farmers, ranchers, and other agricultural managers rank

8th, with 23.1 deaths per 100,000 workers. When looking at sheer numbers, this occupational group has the second-highest number of fatalities, at 260 in 2016.

Food workers have one of the highest suicide rates among U.S. workers, according to Centers for Disease Control (CDC) data from 2018. The suicide rate for women across all occupations is 7.7 per 100,000 workers. Women who are employed as waitresses have a suicide rate of 11.3 percent per 100,000 workers, making this the occupation with the fifth-highest suicide rate for women. Though no other women in the food industry are among the occupations at highest risk for suicide, women employed in food preparation and service saw the largest increase—54 percent—in suicide rates among women, according to the CDC report. There is even greater risk for men in the general population and certainly those employed within the food industry. The suicide rate for men across all occupations is 27.4 per 100,000 workers. Fishers and hunters currently have the highest suicide rates of men in any occupation, with a rate of 119.9 per 100,000 workers. Men chefs and head cooks have a suicide rate of 47.8 per 100,000, and men farmers, ranchers, and other agricultural managers have a suicide rate of 43.2 per 100,000 workers. For farmers in particular, the current farm crisis, with 750,000 farms having gone out of business since 1981, has fueled poverty and despair and a massive increase in suicide rates. Farmers work long hours, have high debt and little disposable income, and live in isolated, rural communities, where others face similar struggles amid a culture of individualism, pride, and few mental health and other important supports.

INEQUALITIES IN THE PRODUCTION, PROCESSING, AND DISTRIBUTION OF FOOD

Food production includes those who are farmers, ranchers, fishers, and hired workers. Food processors are those who take raw food goods and transform them in processing facilities. When these are shipped to warehouses, they move into the realm of distribution.

Inequalities in Food Production: Farmers

There are 2.5 million workers in food production. Median wages for frontline workers in this sector are $11 per hour. Many of these workers do not work a full year, however, pointing to the seasonality of much of the work that occurs in this sector. An FCWA report shows that 40 percent of food production workers report fewer than 180 days of work annually.

According to the USDA, 40 percent of the land area of the United States is used for farming. The nation's farms generate nearly $400 billion in sales, with about one-quarter of that amount in net farm income. Fifty-five percent of sales derive from crops and 45 percent derive from livestock. In decline from pre–Dust Bowl heights of 6.8 million farms in the 1930s, there are now a little more than 2 million farm operations and 3.2 million operators. Despite this and the importance of food from a health, nutritional, cultural, and social perspective, farmers and ranchers receive only 15 cents out of every dollar spent on food at home and away from home. This is half of the 1980 level, when farmers and ranchers received 31 cents.

The distribution of income generated in production is unequally distributed among this population. USDA data on Farm Labor from 2018 show that the largest farms in the United States—those with gross sales in excess of $1 million—constitute 4 percent of all operations. Though a small amount of the overall number of farms, these largest outfits account for 66 percent of the total market sales of U.S. farm products and an even larger share of the aggregate total net U.S. farm income. On the other end of the spectrum, 51 percent of U.S. farm operations have gross farm sales of less than $10,000. Furthermore, these tend to operate at a deficit. Many farmers, across age, race, and gender, are being pushed into financial harm or completely out of business by rising costs and debts and flat market prices, growth in large-scale factory farms, and moves in the industry toward consolidation. USDA data detail a decline in the number of farms being passed on from generation to generation that dates back more than 40 years.

Another example of the inequity among farmers is that on farms with gross sales greater than $350,000, the average farm household income is more than $200,000 in total income, with nearly 75 percent of this coming from farm income. This is in comparison to farms with less than $250,000 in gross sales where the average farm household income is $70,000. 20 percent of this income derives from farm income, 60 percent from wages and salary from off-farm employment, and 20 percent from unearned income, such as Social Security and other benefits or investment income.

Inequalities in food production also exist as farmers attempt to take their products to market. The meat and poultry industries, for instance, are powerful enough to set the prices of both what they pay for supplies and what they charge for their products. Even among owner-operator farmers, there is a move toward more contract work. In this practice, a large agricultural producer apportions work to multiple small farmers. Such contracts now make up approximately 40 percent of all U.S. production and the majority of beef, pork, and poultry production. These realities pose difficulties for small, independent farmers trying to bring their products to market.

The market value of goods in the food system rises with each phase between the grower and the consumer. Caught between the push and pull of making a profit and selling goods at competitive prices, small farm operators are at a disadvantage. One way to address this is to encourage consumers to buy food directly from growers, whether through the farm, farmers markets, farm-to-school and farm-to-table initiatives, or community-supported agriculture programs that allow consumers to buy shares of farmers' produce, eggs, dairy, and meat. There is much room for growth in this area, as currently only 8 percent of farm sales fall under this category. Though there is more focus on creating more local, sustainable, and equitable ways of making and disseminating food, many barriers remain. It is difficult, for example, for small farms to obtain loans in general and even more difficult to obtain loans for sustainable farming. Without specific programs for sustainable practices, the costs of entry—and sustainability—may prove too daunting. Even as small-farm owners, especially people of color, women, and other marginalized groups, experience deep inequalities compared with industrial and large producers, farmworkers who are hired by small and large owners are even more vulnerable.

Inequalities in Food Production: Farmworkers

Recent data from the Department of Labor's National Agricultural Workers Survey estimate there are approximately 2.4 million total farmworkers in the farm sector. An estimated 60 percent of total full-time equivalent labor on U.S. farms is hired. Farmworkers earn an average of $10.60 per hour. Some 75 percent of U.S. farmworkers are immigrants. Half are undocumented migrants, and 20 percent have legal authorization, such as a work visa—either the H-2A or a green card—according to a 2019 analysis by sociologist Andrew Smolski.

As a result of their immigration status, low wages, and poverty, many hired farmworkers are multiply marginalized and vulnerable to further inequalities, including chronic underemployment and spells of unemployment. Farmworkers have poverty rates that are among the highest of any occupation in the United States. Furthermore, for non–U.S. citizen farmworkers, poverty rates are approximately three times as high as those for citizen farmworkers. They have median weekly incomes that are two-thirds less than U.S.-born employees.

Farmworkers experience few markers of success and much social exclusion. They tend to live in inadequate housing. They have little autonomy in their workplace, and those who live in housing owned by their employ-ers also have little autonomy outside of their workplace, as the boundaries between work and personal life are blurred. They also have few avenues for recourse, given their lack of economic and political power. This is of particular concern given the immigrant, and often undocumented, sta-tus of many. This group does not have access to federal protection, such as workers' compensation and unemployment insurance, because of its occupational classification, as most state governments disallow seasonal and migrant workers' participation. Farmworkers' immigration status excludes many from these programs as well. Farmworkers have extremely limited access to health insurance, health care, and social services. In addi-tion to a lack of health insurance, rural farmworkers, like other rural resi-dents, must travel miles to the nearest provider. This is a definite barrier, especially given farmworkers' limited access to private transportation and the absence of public transportation. Language barriers, experiences of discriminatory treatment, and fears of deportation also pose significant obstacles to medical treatment for farmworkers.

Farmworkers are often paid piece rate rather than an hourly wage. This is profoundly financially exploitative. Florida orange pickers earn 85 cents per 90-pound box of oranges, according to a National Farm Worker Min-istry analysis. The average worker picks eight boxes in an hour, so in an eight-hour workday, a worker produces 64 boxes of oranges and in turn receives $6.80 an hour, an amount lower than both state and federal mini-mum wage. For Florida's tomato pickers, the average piece rate is 50 cents for every 32-pound bucket of tomatoes, a rate that has remained flat for the past 30 years. It can take an entire 10-hour day for a tomato harvester to earn the equivalent of the minimum wage. This is not just a long day but an arduous one. Under this system, pay is determined by the quan-tity picked, pruned, or harvested. There are disincentives for farmwork-ers to take breaks—assuming they are offered—for water, shade, or the bathroom, as any time away from the harvest is money lost. Farmworkers who are paid by piece rate are often exempted from minimum wage and other government policies and protections. While industrial farms must make up the difference between piece rate and minimum wage for their employers, contractors and independent farm owners are exempted from this requirement.

Perhaps even more exploited are incarcerated people who are forced to work in agriculture on prison farms. Recent work from Ashanté Reese and Randolph Carr shows there are more than 30,000 incarcerated people working in the food system. Many of these workers are paid less than one dollar a day, which is reminiscent of enslavement, especially when the disparate incarceration of African Americans is considered. In places such as Texas, where the state's Department of Criminal Justice holds 130,000 acres of farmland, some prison farms are located on what had been plantations. Prison farms in Texas produced nearly 12 million pounds of food, harvested more than 120 million pounds of cotton, grains, and grasses, produced approximately 5 million eggs, canned close to 300,000 cases of vegetables, and processed more than 22 million pounds of meat in 2017 alone.

Inequalities in Food Processing and Distribution

There are 1.75 million workers employed in the food-processing sector. Fourteen percent of U.S. manufacturing workers are employed in food processing and manufacturing. Of these, 32 percent are in meat processing, 17 percent are in baking, 11 percent work in processing fruits and vegetables, and 9 percent work in dairy processing. Pay in this sector varies greatly, with poultry processors averaging $29,000, fruit and vegetable processors averaging $57,000, and grains processors averaging $73,000 annually.

Workers at processing plants tend to be members of marginalized and particularly vulnerable groups with few other economic options, including single parents, people of color, undocumented migrants, and people with histories of incarceration and few of the skills valued in today's economy. Maximizing plant production is a goal with serious consequences—and inequalities—for employees who are often exploited in their workplaces. One example comes in bathroom breaks. Though company officials may deny that employees are denied bathroom access and state that any supervisors denying bathroom access would be immediately terminated, line workers, some former supervisory staff, and union representatives tell a different story. They describe supervisors who are instructed to leave the floor to avoid line workers asking for bathroom breaks and employees who face sanctions, such as being yelled at, fined, or fired when their bodies' schedules do not comply with their bosses' schedules. At some food-processing plants, workers are allowed only scheduled bathroom breaks, despite OSHA regulations that allow for reasonable breaks whenever an employee needs one. Still, when they need to relieve themselves outside of their scheduled 12-minute bathroom or 30-minute lunch window, some employees must sneak to bathrooms while coworkers cover for them. When this is not feasible, some employees urinate on themselves or wear adult diapers rather than risk going to the bathroom. There are health risks that come with this. Employees who avoiding consuming liquids during their shifts can become dehydrated, and those who suppress urination can develop painful urinary tract infections, both quite serious situations when experienced over an extended amount of time. People who are pregnant, elderly, or have medical conditions can be especially harmed by such practices. Women are disproportionately impacted by lack of access to bathrooms at work as they experience pregnancy, menstruation, and urinary tract infections, leading to some employees filing sex discrimination claims such as ones that were filed in 2018 against plants in North Carolina and Georgia, according to reporting from Milli Legrain in *The Guardian*.

The FCWA estimates there are 3.2 million workers in distribution, which includes transportation, warehousing, refrigeration, and logistics and comprises 15 percent of food workers. The median wage for frontline distribution workers is $14 per hour or $35,000 per year. Transportation and warehousing have an even higher hourly median wage of $19.31. Distribution workers have higher incomes than many others in the food system. Still, pay gaps are present, and people of color are overrepresented both in jobs at the lowest end of this sector and in positions not covered by unions.

Large food retailers increasingly are able to develop and maintain their own distribution networks, which reduces their costs but also reduces worker pay as well as opportunities for other distributors. At the same time, other food retailers are compelled to also reduce their costs in order to remain competitive. This also means that producers, processors, and distributors are obligated to adapt to the demands of large retailers. For example, roughly one-third of all food products sold by major manufacturers are sold through Walmart, the largest retail company in the United States and the second largest publicly traded company in the world. This gives them great power and control over others in the food system.

Inequalities in Food Retailing and Service

From warehouses, food goes to retailers and restaurants before making its way to consumers, who make purchases from retail workers or restaurant and other food-service workers. The majority of food industry workers are concentrated in retail and food-service jobs at the bottom of the prestige and pay scales; 12.4 percent of U.S. workers are in food retail sales. There are just over 3 million retail workers at supermarkets, grocery stores, and convenience stores. These workers sell food, do such in-house processing as cooking, baking, and preparing foods for purchase, stock shelves, and do other maintenance. Frontline retail workers have median annual earnings of almost $20,000, which is less than half of the average annual earnings of all U.S. workers. The majority work less than full-time. When looking across retail workers, variances in earnings come to light. Recent Bureau of Labor Statistics data show that butchers have a median hourly wage of $15.39. Cashiers earn $11.53 an hour. First-line supervisory workers earn $19.95 an hour. Food preparation workers earn $12.19 an hour. Stockers and order fillers earn $12.37 an hour. Women are overrepresented in the categories with lower earnings just as men are overrepresented in the categories with higher earnings. Retail workers in unionized workplaces fare better than those who do not work in such places. As more retail grocers become big-box superstores, driving out smaller chains with more labor unions and worker protections, retail workers experience more inequalities at work. Walmart, the nation's largest food retailer; Whole Foods, the nation's 10th-largest food retailer; and Target, a rapidly growing food retailer, are known for their hostility to union organizing. These kinds of stores also do not allow for the type of specialization and career progression that food retailers have offered in the past.

The bulk of food workers are in food service. These nearly 11 million workers prepare, cook, and serve food as well as tend bar and wash dishes in full-service restaurants, casual dining and fast-food venues, catering companies, food trucks, and institutional food services such as cafeterias and dining halls. Frontline food-service workers have median hourly wages of $9.30, for a median annual wage of $12,000. In restaurants, 49 percent of front-of-the-house and 70 percent of back-of-the-house workers earn less than the poverty level, and only 25 percent and 11 percent of each, respectively, earn a living wage as Restaurant Opportunities Centers United's data show.

Recent trends in scheduling practices among retail and food-service employers disadvantage workers. In addition to limiting employee hours to ensure that they will not qualify for employer-provided benefits, employees do not receive much notice about their schedules, making it difficult to plan and balance work with other aspects of their lives. Employers often compel workers to be on call, or they cancel shifts at the last minute. While touted as workplace flexibility during the recruiting and interview processes, this benefits employers and not employees, as it reduces workers' ability to work and earn as much as they would prefer. Another inequality exists when looking at the ratios of executive pay to frontline workers.

INEQUALITIES IN CEO VERSUS WORKER PAY

Workers make up the overwhelming majority of people employed in the food system. They are vital for its success. This is not reflected in their wages or through benefits. Eight percent of the nation's Fortune

100 companies hail from the food industry. Their CEOs' combined eight incomes are equal to those of some approximately 10,300 food-service workers. Food service has the greatest number of frontline workers for each CEO. There are approximately 4,000 workers to one CEO. Food retail is next, with approximately 2,000 workers for every CEO. There are more than 1,200 workers for every CEO in food production. Food processing and distribution have the fewest number of workers to CEOs, with approximately 500 workers for each CEO in both of these sectors. White men are a higher share of CEOs in the food industry than overall, as they represent 72 percent of food industry CEOs compared with 62 percent of the total private sector CEOs. Approximately 15 percent of food industry CEOs are white women, 5 percent are Latino men, and fewer than 2 percent are African American men and Latinas. African American women, Asian American women, and Native American men and women represent 1 or less percent of food industry CEOs. There are also stark differentials in pay for CEOs compared with their employees.

A 2016 Food Chain Workers Alliance analysis illustrates the stark disparities between the earnings of food company CEOs and food workers. CEOs have a base salary that is on average 6 times more than the average frontline employee's is. This comparison greatly underestimates the gap, as it does not consider CEOs' sizable bonuses, stock options, and other forms of compensation. Matt Krantz provides a 2019 *Investor's Business Daily* data analysis that shows the CEOs of the 11 most popular fast-food outlets earn a median wage of $6,617 an hour. Workers at these 11 chains have a median wage of $13 an hour. At the top of this list is Chipotle Mexican Grill's Brian Niccol, whose earnings are $33.5 million or $17,458 an hour. This is more than 2,400 times the annual earnings of a Chipotle worker: $13,779. For the CEO of Restaurant Brands, the Canada-based holding company that owns Burger King, Popeyes, and Tim Hortons, compensation is $18,782,877 or $9,783 an hour. Workers there earn $10 an hour or 978 times less than their CEO. Stephen Easterbrook, the CEO of McDonald's, earns $15,876,116, while his average employee earns $7,473 annually. This means that Easterbrook earns more in an hour than the average employee does in a year. These disparities are emblematic across the food system. In an exploration of pay inequality between CEOs of S&P 500 companies and workers, Sarah Anderson and Sam Pizzigati, writing for the Institute for Policy Studies, find that approximately 80 percent of S&P 500 companies pay their CEO more than 100 times the salary of their median worker. This inequality is even more apparent among the approximately 10 percent of companies that pay their median worker wages that are below the poverty line for a family of four. Of the 50 companies with the highest CEO-to-worker pay gaps, 5 are in fast food. Three other food companies are included in this list: consumer food companies Del Monte and Coca-Cola and retailer Walmart. At each of these companies, CEOs earn more than 1,000 times the wages of the median worker.

This and the previous chapter show the depths of food inequalities for those closest to it—food workers. Food workers experience high rates of food insecurity globally and in the United States. One report estimates that 2.5 million of food workers' households are food insecure. Another way to understand this is that more than a quarter of food-insecure people are food workers. The irony of so many food workers being unable to afford products they harvest, make, or sell is a striking one. Their inability to buy healthy, fresh, and/or local foods has even greater implications for health, economics, and sustainability. Higher wages, upward mobility opportunities, safe work conditions, and such benefits as employer-provided health care, paid sick leave, paid holidays, and retirement plans are also important resources that many fast-food workers do not have access to. These disadvantages contribute to a lack of access and availability of food in communities that have become known as food deserts, the subject of the next chapter.

CHAPTER 10

Do Food Deserts Really Exist? Community Access to Food

In his *Good Food Revolution*, MacArthur Foundation "genius grant" awardee and food justice activist Will Allen calls attention to the intersecting realities of race, class, gender, and geography in ways people access and consume food. This is influenced by his years as an urban farmer in Milwaukee. Drawing on his experiences as the son of sharecroppers, a professional basketball player, a corporate executive, and an internationally renowned farmer, Allen details the history of labor, housing, and racist exploitation that continue to delimit African Americans' and other marginalized groups' life chances. Allen and his daughter, Erika Allen, of the Chicago farm and nonprofit organization Urban Growers Collective, also advocate for policy shifts to address pressing and interrelated food inequality issues that disproportionately affect marginalized groups. These include poverty, hunger, institutional and environmental racism, food insecurity, and food deserts. A major emphasis of this work is ameliorating both the conditions that cause and that are caused by food deserts through growing good food—foods that are healthy, whole, and local.

Still, there are some who question whether food deserts and food apartheid exist, some who question their prevalence, and still others who question whether the foods readily available in low-income areas and communities of color reflect consumer preferences rather than external structural, institutional, and policy choices that limit the availability of good foods. In building off previous chapters, what follows is an in-depth look at access to food in marginalized communities. This includes rural areas that are far from grocery stores; communities of color, where across class lines, grocery stores are less available than in comparable white communities; and poor communities in urban areas, where there is more access to fast food and processed foods and where the most foods are also the most unhealthy.

Rather than discuss food deserts, farmer and food activist Karen Washington, in an article by Anna Brones, uses the term *food apartheid* to discuss and illuminate the conscious policy and other decisions that lead to the systematic inequality that make food in general and healthy food in particular a scarcity in communities inhabited by African Americans and other targets of social exclusion in the United States. Among the health costs of life under food apartheid are increased rates of diabetes, depression, and hypertension. For infants and children, developmental delays and negative effects on behavior and academic achievement can occur. Researcher Angela Odoms-Young tallies the annual social costs of food insecurity at more than $167.5 billion. This entails losses in worker productivity and increases in the price of health care and public education, as well as the costs of emergency food aid from places such as food pantries and soup kitchens. She further notes that there is an inextricable link between race and ethnicity with the experience of disability, incarceration, poverty, and unemployment, statuses that also contribute to food insecurity. When combined, access to food is even more compromised, and the harmful consequences of its lack are deepened. These are very much rooted in entrenched systems of social exclusion. Housing policies and practices fuel this exclusion.

REDLINING AND FOOD DESERTS

Across the United States, food access can be mapped onto various historical and contemporary patterns of social exclusion rooted in class and race. Today's food deserts and food apartheid hew closely to yesterday's creation of racially segregated neighborhoods, even after the end of legal segregation. Redlining was a U.S. federal and banking policy wherein a red line would delineate Black and integrating neighborhoods, rendering them ineligible for FHA and other loans. This created segregated urban and then suburban communities that have fueled interconnected forms of racial inequality for generations, including disparate access to affordable healthy foods. These maps also reveal the continuation of racially segregated access to employment, income, wealth, quality education, and health care, as well as morbidity and mortality rates, creating the food apartheid Washington describes. An overlay of Federal Housing Authority (FHA) redlining maps, initially drawn in the 1940s and used until the Fair Housing Act of 1968, and maps of urban communities that lack full-service grocery stores and supermarkets and access to fresh foods show considerable overlap. Indeed, the practice of large grocery store and supermarket chains closing existing stores and not opening new stores is known as supermarket redlining. An absence of full-service grocery stores is a fairly new phenomenon.

Through most of the twentieth century, an array of food was readily available in people's local stores. It was not until white flight and its accompanying suburbanization that this started to change. The racist exclusionary policies that overwhelming favored whites as home buyers and prioritized highways and suburbs over public transportation and cities have and continue to deeply shape food access. As whites left urban communities, many full-service grocery stores did as well. The suburban job and supermarket creation that these spurred also cut urban dwellers off from employment and shopping opportunities. The remaining stores lost access to credit and financing from municipalities, states, and banks while seeing drops in their consumer bases, leading to financial distress and eventual closings for some stores, and higher prices, lower quality, and fewer options for others. This led to a spiral of more people and jobs leaving and more stores declining or closing. The racism that fueled white flight continues to reverberate and deepen inequalities. Stereotypes and discrimination add to this, as supermarket and grocery chain-store owners and developers rely on these in their decisions to not open stores in predominantly African American neighborhoods. Perceptions of places and their inhabitants as dangerous, unreliable, and incapable mean lack of food access, of healthy foods, of employment opportunities, and of contributions to the local tax base.

The case of Detroit is instructive here. Three chain supermarkets service the entire city of Detroit. This is 3 more than were present in 2009. A 2017 Detroit Food Policy Council report asserts that approximately 30,000 Detroiters do not have access to a full-scale supermarket. Most residents shop at the city's 70 less-resourced, independent grocery stores. Detroit with its 79 percent African American population has far less food access than neighboring, predominantly white suburbs. The 74 percent white Washtenaw County has 8 supermarkets, and the 81 percent white Macomb County has 27 supermarkets. Recently, the Food Industry Association, a grocery trade group, announced plans by grocers to address this. A spokesperson says that its members are conducting listening tours and meeting with local community stakeholders to address community needs, bias, and discrimination.

There is a demonstrable link shown between rates of neighborhood poverty and supermarket presence. When compared to affluent white communities, high-poverty communities, across race and ethnicity, have roughly between 2 and 3 times more grocery stores and approximately 1.5 times more convenience stores than supermarkets in their community. A team of public-health researchers from Johns Hopkins University, headed by Kelly Bower, finds that in poor communities, across racial and ethnic lines, there are more small grocery and convenience stores. Taking an intersectional perspective that considers the interlocking effects of race and class demonstrates that there is differential access to food for communities of poor whites, poor Latinx people, and poor African Americans: the most supermarkets are present in poor white communities, followed by poor racially diverse ones, and the fewest are found in poor Black communities, even when there are the same rates of poverty in the each of the communities studied. Similarly, studies point to the presence of higher-quality grocery stores in Latinx neighborhoods relative to African American ones. Food environments are important considerations when exploring food apartheid and deserts.

FOOD ENVIRONMENTS

Food justice is a key component of environmental justice. Certainly this is the case because the environment—access to land, soil and air; water quality; and sustainability—shapes how food is produced. Food production in the United States and globally is a major contributor to environmental degradation in its production of not just food but also methane, nitrous oxide, carbon dioxide, and other greenhouse gas emissions, toxic runoff, and waste. Another connection comes through understanding people's food environment. This involves looking at what kinds of foods are available to them through their local communities. Are there farmers markets and entire sections of supermarkets with abundant amounts of fresh produce? Are there more fast-food joints than supermarkets? Are gas stations, liquor stores, and dollar stores the only places to buy milk and other food staples? Are bananas, oranges, and apples the only fresh produce available at the nearest store? The answers to these questions provide a picture of one's food environment. According to some working to end food inequalities, there are areas referred to food deserts that may more accurately be described as food swamps. They contend this is a more accurate way to frame the food environments and the low-quality food options readily available through the overabundance of fast-food restaurants, dollar stores, and convenience markets. As seen in other chapters, food access is about more than proximity to a grocery store or supermarket. Quality and variety of food at available retail outlets are also factors in the ability to purchase healthy, nutritious, and safe foods.

Food Quality

Researcher Jerry Shannon finds that poor residents living in urban food deserts were more likely to bypass stores in their local communities in favor of ones that were more distant. When shopping close to home, they spend their SNAP benefits in more costly convenience stores, discount markets, and specialty stores, where culturally specific items are available. When shopping in local stores, residents recounted feeling mistreated, condescended to, and that they were given poorer customer service compared with when they shopped in more affluent communities. This was the case even when they shopped at stores within the same chain, where presumably corporate training procedures and expectations would be the same. This was also the case with fast-food outlets such as McDonald's, which prides itself on replicating the same experience for customers no matter where or what they are eating. Food quality, choices, and prices; crowded shelves and aisles; store appearance, amenities, and even carts were seen as inferior in the local stores compared to those in the suburbs. Residents also discussed negative experiences and a lack of safety from fellow customers and in the area around their nearest stores, which led those who could afford the transportation and time costs to seek shopping opportunities outside the community.

A team of researchers helmed by the University of Chicago's Marynia Kolak provided evidence for similar patterns in low-income African American communities in Chicago. This also contributes to further inequalities. As money is spent on food, little of it stays in the community, where it might otherwise be reinvested to benefit those who are spending it. Data reveal that in some communities, it is not uncommon for residents to spend more than $10 million each year in grocery stores and supermarkets outside of the community. In another way that supermarket redlining occurs, food choices, quality, and variety vary from neighborhood to neighborhood, even among stores within the same retail chain. Thus food quality is also an issue when it comes to those places where it is purchased. Indeed, in a study of Chicago and an adjacent suburb by Daniel Block and Joanne Kouba, stores in the predominantly African American lower-middle-class Chicago community offer food items at competitive prices but poor quality, whereas the upper-middle-class, racially diverse suburb it borders offered food items that are both competitively priced and high in quality. There are more stores in the African American community than in the suburbs, but most of those stores are independent grocers. Those chains that are present are convenience stores and discount supermarkets. They also find that though there were fresh produce items, such as onions, potatoes, lettuce and peppers, available in the vast majority of the stores in the African American community they examined, more than half of the stores that had fresh produce were selling items determined to be of poor quality. Stores were also more likely to stock items that were more shelf-stable due to the added preservatives, salt, and sugar that diminish the healthy qualities of food. Food deserts are part of the food environment for far too many in the United States. As more attention has been paid to the lack of food access in urban and rural settings, dollar stores have entered to fill the void.

Dollar Stores in Food Deserts

More U.S. consumers get food from dollar stores than from, for example, Whole Foods. Another sign of their ubiquity is that there are about 6 dollar stores for each Walmart. In the last decade, the number of dollar stores in the United States increased by more than 50 percent, from approximately 20,000 to more than 30,000. As dollar stores are overrepresented in African American and other communities of color, there are racial and ethnic inequalities that these map onto and exacerbate. Rural towns, isolated from any nearby grocery stores and supermarkets after local stores closed in the wake of the rise of big-box retailers, also have seen a boom in the number of dollar stores. Critics discuss the harm to full-service and small grocery stores when dollar stores open up. Whether in rural communities or large cities, dollar stores decrease existing stores sales and profits and have caused some to close their doors. In small towns through rural America in particular, the presence of dollar stores drives grocery stores out of business, limiting both food choices and employment opportunities. An Institute for Local Self-Reliance analysis by Marie Donahue reports that the presence of dollar stores causes sales declines of 30 percent at local independent supermarkets in small towns. When stores cannot sustain such a drastic sales loss, they are forced to close. This causes depressed employment opportunities, as local independent supermarkets employ an average of 14 people compared with dollar stores that employ an average of 9 people. Given that dollar stores do not sell fresh produce and that the bulk of the foods that they do sell are highly processed, there are negative consequences for consumers in places where dollar stores are the only nearby place to purchase groceries; dollar-store shelves of processed, sugary, and fatty foods become the only option for many. Responding to this, Dollar General recently started selling fruit and vegetables at some of its stores. Critics, however, note that as only 500 of the chain's more than 15,000 stores do so, this is an insufficient effort.

Dollar stores pose harm to consumers financially as well. Dollar stores often sell smaller-sized packages or quantities of items than those available in other food retailers, and the price per unit or ounce at the dollar store is actually higher. Additionally, dollar stores do not contribute to local tax bases in the ways that locally owned stores do. When cities and towns use tax incentives to attract dollar stores, they further drain resources away from communities. These chains' presence also chills investors and retailers on the idea of opening new grocery stores and supermarkets. Even as city councils halt permits and issue ordinances against them, and politicians run on campaigns promising to end dollar stores' presence in their communities, the nation's two largest dollar stores, Dollar General and Dollar Tree, plan to open another 50,000 stores in the near future.

Social and Cultural Impacts of Food Apartheid

For many, food is a coping mechanism and a source of comfort. When neighborhood and other external factors both increase stress and limit healthy food access, this can be quite harmful, especially when other coping mechanisms are not available. Physical activity and spending time outside have positive mental and physical health outcomes that are hampered for those living in places with a lack of parks, green spaces, and gyms and/or high rates of unsafe conditions and neighborhood distrust, crime, and violence. There are inextricably complex systematic barriers for many in the United States. Since the 1970s, processes of deindustrialization mean those employment options that had been there for people with a high school degree (or less) have all but disappeared, especially when it comes to jobs that pay enough to support oneself, not to mention a partner and children. Jobs that lead to the achievement of the American dream—a home in a safe neighborhood where one can raise a family with all the trappings of a middle-class life—are largely available to only those with college degrees and are becoming more difficult for even these people to attain, as they are strapped with the costs of affording those degrees.

These barriers and their associated inequalities are worsened when the overall context of life for those who are food insecure is further analyzed. Erin Drucker headed a team of University of South Carolina researchers that found that the children in their study were members of families where their parents had their own physical and mental health struggles, experiences of intimate partner violence, housing instability, inconsistent work and insufficient incomes, spells of unemployment, a lack of reliable transportation, and social and other forms of isolation that equated to limited social networks and limited social support to mitigate the myriad challenges they faced in addition—and related—to their lack of food. Attention to these and other sociocultural issues can reduce food inequalities. Many communities, especially those in rural environments and in cities inhabited by people of color, have seen a massive exodus of not just employment options and state, regional, municipal, and other local services that a healthy and vibrant tax base support, such as schools, health care, and recreational avenues, but also businesses that include full-service grocery stores, leaving residents who live in such areas with few local places to buy food besides liquor stores, convenience stores, drug stores, dollar stores, and gas stations.

Transportation is a major social issue that contributes to food inequalities, as those who are food insecure, receive SNAP, and receive WIC are more likely to rely on rides from others, public transportation, biking, and walking when shopping for food. This restricts freedom in shopping, as they must adapt to others' and public transit schedules or limit shopping to daytime hours—which may be further hampered by inflexible work schedules—to avoid walking home in the dark. Purchases are also limited to what can be easily transported home, making cost-effective bulk purchases unlikely if they must be carried home by hand, on a bus, or while riding a bike. Indeed, older adults living in rural communities are particularly impacted. For many in such environs, lack of access to a car means that either or both the time and financial costs of finding healthy food options is too high to be affordable.

In addition to an absence of food when there are few, if any, supermarkets, there is also an absence of employment. An analysis presented by Sarah Treuhaft and Allison Karpyn for the Food Trust show that food retailers are often key providers of not just employment but also economic revitalization in communities bereft of jobs. They offer work and contributions to the tax base, and they allow money spent on food to remain and circulate within the community, all vital for a community's economic health. Indeed, as estimates in this analysis show, a large grocery store in a community can lead to somewhere between 150 and 200 jobs, explaining the excitement seen by local politicians and residents when a major grocery chain announces it is moving into an underresourced neighborhood. Communities that are economically healthy are less likely to abound in the kinds of structural inequalities found in poor neighborhoods, as discussed earlier in chapter 3. In this way, the presence and abundance of fresh and healthy foods are thought to act as anchors for other investments in housing, education, health care, recreation, and other institutions desirable for individuals, communities, and societies.

Sarah Treuhaft and Allison Karpyn's study in Philadelphia noted that when a supermarket was introduced into a food desert, residents' diets became healthier. There were also positive changes in residents' perceptions of access to healthy food and neighborhood satisfaction. These changes, while much higher for regular supermarket users, were present for sporadic supermarket users as well. The residents were directly involved in bringing the supermarket to their community, another factor in their increased positive perceptions and neighborhood satisfaction. This indicates the need for development and policies that are inclusive of a population's self-determined interests, needs, and concerns. Policies are discussed in the next three chapters in a look at SNAP, corporate policies, and the School Lunch Program.

CHAPTER 11

What Can I Use SNAP For? What the Supplemental Nutrition Assistance Program Provides

Among the most known, used, and vilified government food policies in the United States are those need-based programs designed to assist people with cash and the ability to purchase food for themselves and their families. The largest federal food program is SNAP. This chapter builds on the discussion of SNAP in chapter 6 and focuses on public perceptions and debates over SNAP, what it provides, and who receives it.

WHAT DOES SNAP DO?

Though it is a federal program, SNAP is administered by states. Each state uses federal guidelines to establish its own application process. Applicants must undergo an eligibility interview and provide various forms of documentation to verify their eligibility, including identity, residency, immigration status, household composition, income and resources, and deductible expense documentation. Once they are approved, SNAP recipients receive an Electronic Benefits Card, which they can use, much like a debit or credit card, to purchase food at eligible retail outlets.

SNAP can be used to purchase the following:

- Fruits and vegetables
- Meat, poultry, and fish
- Dairy products

- Breads and cereals
- Other foods, such as snack foods and nonalcoholic beverages
- Seeds and plants, which produce food

SNAP cannot be used to purchase the following:

- Beer, wine, liquor, cigarettes, or tobacco
- Vitamins, medicines, and supplements
- Live animals
- Prepared foods fit for immediate consumption
- Hot foods
- Any nonfood items

SNAP is particularly adept at responding to economic shifts, allowing individuals, families, and households key nutritional assistance that allows them to weather decreased wages, underemployment and unemployment, and other personal and social crises without experiencing major nutritional deficiencies or starvation. Research by Hilary Hoynes and Diane Schanzenbach shows that SNAP enrollment and expenditures track with the U.S. unemployment rate. During the Great Recession that started in 2008, for example, those states with large increases in their unemployment rate also had large increases in the program. With its state-level administration, SNAP has shown more responsivity than other federal antipoverty programs that receive block grants. Such programs, like Temporary Aid to Needy Families (TANF), do not show corresponding increases, even as families experienced more unemployment. Proposed changes to SNAP that would reduce this responsiveness are particularly worrisome for many, especially as a growing number of U.S. economy observers were predicting another recession even before the COVID-19 crisis began.

Researchers from the Center on Budget and Policy Priorities (CBPP) find that rates of food insecurity decrease by a third among children who are SNAP recipients. They also find that children who are SNAP recipients have better health outcomes and are less likely to be underweight relative to low-income children who do not receive SNAP. These positive outcomes carry into adulthood, as adults who received SNAP as children have better health outcomes and lower incidence of metabolic syndrome. There are also indicators that children who receive SNAP show gains in math and reading skills and have a higher likelihood of completing high school. As adults, women in particular have increased rates of employment, higher income, and lower rates of poverty.

Following the USDA recommendation of eating 2 cups of fruit and 2.5 cups of vegetables daily would cost a person between $2.10 and $2.60 every day. This amounts to half of the daily allowance of $4.20 for SNAP benefits, which are intended to be distributed across three meals and to suffice the most recent Dietary Guidelines for Americans, which include protein, grains, dairy, oils, and produce.

SNAP also has an education component. In 1992 the federal government began funding Food Stamp Nutrition Education (FSNE) state plans. These optional plans were established to help states pay for programs that do nutritional education designed to create linkages between food security and healthy diets. Eligible participants received nutrition training, information, and materials to facilitate healthy food choices and increased physical activity. The 2008 Farm Bill changed the name of this program to its current Supplemental Nutrition Assistance Program Education (SNAP-Ed).

In some states, SNAP-Ed offers nutrition classes as well as what is called FVRx, that is, prescriptions from health-care providers for fruits and vegetables, for enrollees. These prescriptions are written to cover free, fresh, and sometimes locally grown produce. In addition to providing food and nutrition education and lowering weight, mortality and health risks as well as direct and indirect health costs, such programs also increase the economic health of communities when they incorporate local growers and retailers. Indeed, policies that subsidize produce on a wider basis would have a number of positive benefits. Research conducted by Dariush Mozaffarian and posted on the Conversation website finds that a national program to subsidize the cost of fruits and vegetables by 10 percent would save up to 150,000 lives over 15 years.

WHO RECEIVES SNAP?

Currently, in any given month, some 40 million low-income Americans receive SNAP benefits that help them obtain a nutritionally adequate diet. On average these amount to about $126 a month, which is $4.20 a day, and $1.40 a meal, per recipient. Assuming that families spend 30 percent of their income for food, the formula used to determine SNAP amounts is designed to cover the shortfall between that 30 percent family contribution and the cost of the USDA's Thrifty Food Plan, a low-cost, nutritionally adequate diet plan. Since 2013, due to an improving economy and decreased costs of food in the Thrifty Food Plan, almost all SNAP beneficiaries have seen some declines in their monthly SNAP allotment.

Federal rules dictate three tests that must be met in determining an individual's or household's eligibility for SNAP:

1. Gross monthly income—defined as income before any taxes or deductions are taken out—must be at or below 130 percent of the federal poverty line.
2. Net monthly income—defined as income after taxes or deductions are taken out—must be at or below the poverty line.
3. Assets must fall below the following limits:

    a. those individuals or households without a member who is elderly or has a disability must have assets of $2,250 or less
    b. those individuals or households with such a member must have assets of $3,500 or less.

SNAP is one of the largest and most important antipoverty programs for U.S. households and families with children. It is also vital for households with people who have disabilities or are elderly. A 2015 report by Hilary Hoynes and Diane Schanzenbach and published by the NBER illuminates this, as nearly 50 percent of all SNAP households include a child, and nearly 75 percent include a child, a person with a disability, or an elderly person. Most unemployed adults without children are limited to three months of benefits, unless they are working at least 20 hours per week or participating in a qualifying program. States may seek temporary waivers from this time limit for areas with high unemployment, as was the case during and immediately after the Great Recession. States can and do exert their authority to create and enforce work requirements for adult SNAP recipients.

There are a number of vulnerable populations that are ineligible for SNAP. Groups completely ineligible for SNAP include strikers, certain legal immigrants, all undocumented immigrants, and most college students. There are calls to expand SNAP's reach to include college and university students. In recognition of the economic burdens of the cost of college, decreased buying power, and increased housing and other costs, urgency around their food security is increasing. A 2018 Government Accountability Office (GAO) study reports that a third of all college students cannot afford food and basic nutrition. Students living off campus, students of color, and students on urban campuses are at particular risk of food insecurity. The work of Temple University sociologist Sara Goldrick-Rab is often cited as one of the initial calls to pay attention to this growing need. She and her colleagues write that as many as half of college and university students experience food insecurity, which is at a rate higher than the national average. As higher-education costs rise, financial aid declines, incomes stagnate for many, and more low-income students enroll in undergraduate and graduate programs, hunger on college campus has become more of a pressing concern. Students have called for colleges and universities and legislatures to address this issue. Students without sufficient access to affordable foods suffer the consequences of diminished health and grades and increased stress, depression, and anxiety. Some campuses have subsidized food purchases for students and opened food pantries in response. In California 2019 legislation allowed college students to qualify more easily for CalFresh, the state's food assistance program. On the federal level, a group of six Senate Democrats, including Elizabeth Warren (MA), Kamala Harris (CA), and Richard Durbin (IL) proposed the College Student Hunger Act of 2019. If passed, the measure would allow more college students to qualify for SNAP.

WHERE IS SNAP USED?

Recent changes in the SNAP program mean that a number of food outlets are no longer allowed to receive SNAP payments. In 2017 the USDA redefined rules and declared that all outlets with more than half of their sales from prepared foods—any foods not intended for home preparation or home consumption; foods cooked or heated by the retailer, whether before or after purchase; and baked goods—to be restaurants and thus ineligible for SNAP payments. These include bakeries and delis where SNAP recipients were able to buy breads, meats, and cheeses, for example. As deli meats are precooked, they are now deemed ineligible under the new rules. Public food markets are especially vulnerable to this. Public food markets, where individual vendors set up stalls and sell the wares they specialize in, differ from supermarkets and other types of grocery stores in that they consist of multiple vendors selling food—much of which is fresh and locally sourced—separately. Some well-known examples of these in the United States are Baltimore's Lexington Market, Philadelphia's Reading Terminal, and Seattle's Pike Place Market. These are permanent installations, open year-round, and can operate as not just places to obtain food but also offer employment opportunities, public safety, and spaces where community members can come together. There are particular repercussions for public food markets located in low-income neighborhoods where food and transportation options are scarce. In communities with high levels of SNAP recipients, removing these outlets' ability to receive SNAP payments leads to food outlets losing revenue and their employees losing hours, if not jobs. In June 2019, members of Congress began efforts to have the USDA's Food and Nutrition Service (FNS) reconsider their rules about SNAP retailer eligibility in order to address this issue.

The 2014 Farm Bill authorized a two-year pilot program that allows SNAP recipients to buy food online. The pilot program launched in April 2019 in New York and will expand from there to Alabama, Iowa, Maryland, Nebraska, New Jersey, Oregon, and Washington. It allows SNAP benefits to be used at national retailers including Amazon, FreshDirect, Safeway, and Walmart as well as regional retailers Hy-Vee and ShopRite and local outlets Dash's Market and Hart's Local Grocers. SNAP benefits will only pay for food, and any fees will have to be covered by the consumer.

SUPPLEMENTING SNAP

SNAP provides critical though insufficient amounts of food support to its recipients. This is seen when exploring the shortfalls between benefits and dietary necessities. As noted by researcher Parke Wilde, many of those receiving SNAP remain food insecure. As of 2015, for example, 53 percent of low-income SNAP recipients were food insecure, compared with 25 percent of low-income people who did not receive SNAP. There are advocacy and policy efforts to bolster the program, even amid threats to it, to provide even more nutrition and food security.

Federal and other food assistance programs can be transformed through more efforts like the Food Insecurity and Nutrition Incentive program, which provides greater value for SNAP benefits by turning $1 of SNAP into $1.50 to $2 when fruits and vegetables are purchased. In an effort led by nonprofit organizations, 24 states across the nation allow SNAP recipients to double their purchasing power at farmers markets by matching each SNAP dollar they spend. Called the Double Up Food Bucks program, it started at Detroit farmers markets in 2009 and became standard in Michigan and spread across the nation, due to the work of food activists, farmers, and policy makers, who recognized the good in such efforts for SNAP recipients, farmers, and the public in general. Some grocery stores are following suit. The Fair Food Network, the nonprofit group that advocated for and launched Double Up Food Bucks, estimates that since 2009, the program has benefited more than 300,000 low-income families and more than 1,000 farmers. They describe this program as one that is both unique and multifaceted, as it is aimed to provide important supports to individuals and families, small farmers, and local economies in urban, suburban, and rural locales. There is evidence of these programs' effectiveness.

For SNAP recipients, programs such as the San Francisco–based EatSF and the Los Angeles–based Vouchers for Veggies offer vouchers for fruits and vegetables that can be used to supplement their scant access to produce. Those who receive the $10 to $20 monthly vouchers show positive health outcomes such as decreases in blood pressure, glucose levels, and weight. Still, SNAP is increasingly under attack.

THREATS TO SNAP

In addition to unemployment insurance, SNAP has been one of the quickest-activated parts of the federal social safety net when there is falling economic insecurity. In July 2019 the USDA proposed a policy change that threatened this responsiveness. It would end the automatic eligibility of benefits for those receiving broadly defined, means-tested federal benefits, such as TANF. Analysts of the proposal contend that more than 3 million people will lose access to SNAP if the proposal is adopted. Opponents of the proposed changes have raised concern that this loss of SNAP benefits may also lead to the loss of free and reduced-price school lunches. This policy change is constructed in such a way that it would also bypass congressional approval.

In contrast to other federal subsidy programs such as the Supplemental Nutrition Assistance Program for Women, Infants and Children, SNAP does not require food purchases to meet any nutritional requirements. Numerous proposals have been made to institute basic nutritional requirements as part of SNAP, but each has been rejected by Congress and the Department of Agriculture, with many opposing the proposal as an infringement on recipients' freedom to make their own dietary choices. This is one of the most heated debates in policy and public discourses on SNAP.

Data from USDA's "Food Prices and Spending" show that approximately 10 percent of SNAP dollars are spent on sugary drinks such as soda and fruit drinks. This is slightly higher than the 7 percent of food dollars spent on sugary drinks by non-SNAP recipients. Critics of the SNAP program point to these data illustrating that some of the most commonly purchased items by recipients are sugary drinks. This perspective does not allow for parents buying soda and fruit drinks as a treat for their children to possibly help ameliorate some of the lack that children living in poverty face daily. Most in the United States do not meet federal guidelines for produce consumption. All U.S. households purchase many foods with empty calories. SNAP households purchase only 6 percent more empty calories than other groups do. This leads some advocates for the poor to note that some criticisms of the program are rooted in the idea that people who are poor are either incapable of making their own decisions or do not deserve anything considered a nonessential item. Data from USDA's "Food Prices and Spending" show that SNAP households maximize their food budgets with calories that cost less than households that do not receive SNAP. SNAP households purchase fewer vegetables, greens and beans, fruit, whole grains, seafood, and plant proteins than do non-SNAP low-income and higher-income households. This is logical, given their lower incomes and ability to purchase food. Children in households that receive SNAP acquire approximately 500 more calories from schools than other households do.

One proposal that recognizes SNAP recipients' autonomy and con-strained food budgets calls for a provision in the Farm Bill to incentivize SNAP recipients' purchase of fruits and vegetables, nuts, whole grains, and fish by offering a 30 percent premium on these healthier foods. Less healthy foods could still be purchased, but consumers would literally get less for their SNAP dollar when buying these. This plan retains consumer choice while rewarding what scholars consider the healthiest choices. Pre-vious pilot programs using a similar model illustrate its benefit. When SNAP recipients received a 30 cents incentive for every SNAP dollar they spent on fruits and vegetables, they ate 26 percent more fruits and vegetables, bought greater quantities and a greater variety of fruits and veg-etables, and stated that fruits and vegetables were more affordable due to the incentives. So far, recent attempts to impose new limits on what SNAP recipients can use the program to purchase have been denied by the USDA.

In the current political climate, even the stringent guidelines pro-vided by the program are seen as too liberal by critics and some poli-ticians. Vocal fiscally conservative politicians and their supporters call for the funding for SNAP and similar programs to be curtailed, if not eradicated. This is the impetus for such legislation as in early 2018 when the U.S. House and Senate each passed separate bills that would signifi-cantly reduce federal spending on food assistance for working-class and poor people, families, and children. These proposals came at a time when SNAP caseloads, applications, and spending had been in decline since 2014.

An analysis by Laura Wheaton, a researcher at the Urban Institute, reveals that changes proposed to take effect for SNAP in April 2020 would mean that nearly 4 million fewer people would receive SNAP benefits each month. Many of those who remained eligible would see a decrease in the size of their benefits. More than 3 million individuals would experience an average reduction in monthly benefits of nearly \$40, and 2.2 million families would experience an average reduction in monthly benefits of \$127. Wheaton forecasts a 9.4 percent reduction in the number of people participating in SNAP and an approximately 8 percent total reduction in benefits. As these changes would mean changes in the ways in which families are automatically enrolled in other forms of federal assistance programs, other access to food would also be jeopardized. Utility allowances for SNAP recipients would also be reduced, leading recipients to spend more money on heating, communication, and other utility costs and reducing the amount of money they have available for food. Furthermore, students receiving free or reduced lunches would also be affected. The Urban Institute study projects 982,000 public school students would lose access to this nutritional assistance under the proposed changes. On the whole, these changes would cause further food insecurity and its attendant consequences among a population with already limited access to food and nutrition.

On March 13, 2020, Chief Judge Beryl Howell, a federal judge of the U.S. District Court in Washington, DC, temporarily blocked one new SNAP rule from taking effect amid the coronavirus epidemic. This rule called for a work requirement for the nearly 700,000 adult SNAP recipients who do not have eligible disabilities or children. This population, referred to as to able-bodied adult without dependents (ABAWD), would only be able to receive SNAP for three months in a 36-month period unless they were working 20 hours a week or enrolled in an employment or training program. The new rule also was designed to limit states' abilities to provide waivers to this rule. Given this and the vagaries in finding part-time, let alone full-time employment prior to the coronavirus outbreak and the related layoffs that started in the low-wage, service sector, 19 state attorneys general, New York City, the District of Columbia, and several private plaintiffs sought an injunction to stay the implementation of this rule, which had been set to take effect April 1, 2020. In her opinion, Howell wrote that food access was vital "especially now, as a global pandemic poses widespread health risks, guaranteeing that government officials at both the federal and state levels have flexibility to address the nutritional needs of residents and ensure their well-being through programs like SNAP, is essential." She also deemed parts of that rule "likely unlawful because they are arbitrary and capricious." The USDA cited its intention to appeal the ruling. This legal battle—taking place during an emerging global health, economic, political, and social crisis that most alive today have never seen the likes of—underscores the importance of SNAP for many in the United States.

Even before the emerging complications caused by the COVID-19 crisis, this would also have ripple effects beyond SNAP-reliant individuals and households. SNAP benefits not only its recipients but retailers, processors, and producers. As the USDA Economic Research Service illustrates, $1 billion in SNAP retail food expenditures amounts to $267 million in farm production, $87 million in processing, and 3,000 food industry jobs.

CHAPTER 12

What and How Do We Eat Now? How Large Agriculture Businesses Shape Food Availability and Tastes

This chapter looks at the role of large agriculture corporations in lobbying for food practices and policies. Major food companies use their sway over local, state, and federal governments to enact policies that increase profitability and decrease worker safety and health. The use of food science to enhance taste perceptions and cravings are also addressed in this chapter.

CORPORATE POWER AND POLICY MAKING

Lobbying

Corporate and government relationships may create inequities as the food industry, whether in the case of individual companies or industry lobbyists, seeks to leverage its financial and marketing power into favorable policies and laws. Its access to policy makers and politicians might mean that public health and the public interest take a back seat to corporate interests. One example of this was apparent as the Obama administration planned to implement voluntary guidelines that would limit advertising unhealthy foods to children. The food industry paid their lobbyists millions to ensure Congress would fail to enact these guidelines. Lobbyists have similarly been able to use their financial clout to ensure Congress would not enact wage increases for fast-food and other food workers. The Arkansas-based Tyson Foods has used its influence in states it has plants in to reduce workers compensation eligibility. Across the industry and in a number of states, industrial agriculture has used its political power to repeal or block local minimum-wage laws in cities and towns in Alabama, Florida, Iowa, Kentucky, and Missouri and to strip away collective bargaining rights. This occurs amid years of federal, state, and local defunding and deregulation efforts that could have protected workers' rights and health.

The Institute for Food and Development Policy lists numerous special interest and lobbying groups that help write U.S. farm bills in their favor. Some of these are such major food retailers as Walmart, Target, and other national chains; food manufacturers such as Coca-Cola and Nestle; agricultural conglomerates such as Cargill, DuPont, and Monsanto; such government and special-interest groups as the American Farm Bureau Federation, the National Corn Growers Association, and the International Dairy Foods Association; and advocacy organizations such as the Center for Rural Affairs, the Environmental Working Group, and the Food Research and Action Center. They go on to state that it is corporate actors who have the greatest role in the policies and language included in farm bills. They do so in ways that preserve their interests in food production, processing, distribution, and service. Corporations also have outsized influence as they fund private, public, and academic research, education, and development and as they lobby Congress and other legislative bodies.

A single company—North Carolina's Smithfield Foods—has been ordered by five juries to compensate its neighbors more than $600 million in damages due to waste, pestilence, and odors from its pork production operations. Another North Carolina jury awarded $473.5 million to neighbors of industrial hog farms in that state, which houses 2,400 swine operations and 9 million hogs. Even though the award was later reduced to $94 million due to state limitations on claims, industrial agriculture operations organized a massive lobbying effort to protect their interests even more strongly. In response, industrial agriculture companies in North Carolina and across the nation have successfully lobbied state legislatures to create laws that shield them or cap financial liability from suits over the noxious smells, noises, and water they produce.

Consolidation

Corporate consolidation limits choice, reduces workers' mobility, hampers competition, increases costs, and creates other forms of inequality. An example of this is in seed choices for planting. What had been referred to as the Big Six in 2008, comprising Monsanto, DuPont, Syngenta, Dow,

Bayer, and BASF, is now the Big Four, with the mergers of industry giants Bayer and Monsanto into Bayer, and DuPont and Dow into Corteva. The Big Four, now comprising Bayer, Corteva, ChemChina (which bought out Syngenta), and BASF control more than 60 percent of the global seed market. After a $66 billion merger between Monsanto and Bayer was approved by the Department of Justice, 77 percent of all seed corn, 69 percent of all seed traits, and more than 90 percent of the cotton and soy markets in the United States were all controlled by Bayer. As the majority of these and the other Big Four companies' products are genetically modified, companies hold all rights to the seeds. These are rights that they ardently guard, as the copyright lawsuits they pursue against small farms show.

With increasing consolidation of seed companies, the costs to farmers who are increasingly compelled to purchase seeds from the Big Four increase. At the same time, the ability of researchers and smaller and industrial farmers to innovate is compromised. Seed diversity is also compromised. The latter two points raise particular concern for food security. Even as these GMO seeds are created to be resilient against pests, diseases, and other threats, if they manage to be infected, a major source of the food supply will be affected.

In addition to limiting the wages and rights of workers, the industrialization and corporatization of the food system increase inequalities for smaller employers. The presence of major corporations—especially those that are vertically integrated in ways that cross multiple sectors of the food system—hampers the viability of small and independent farms, processors, distributors, retailers, restaurants, and others in the food system.

Small, independent farmers find that corporate ownership deeply impacts their ability to farm. This is because nearly 75 percent of all the seeds on the market are owned by only 10 companies. This monopoly reduces seed choice and diversity, hampers sustainability practices, and increases costs. These seeds are patented and the patent owners, powerful agricultural corporations, limit if not prevent seed reuse from one year to the next. As such, farmers are forced to buy new seeds or face costly halts in their production, or to fight expensive, potentially bankrupting lawsuits. Stories abound about industry giant Monsanto, for example, and the tens of millions of dollars it has been awarded in hundreds of patent infringement lawsuits against hundreds of small farmers and businesses.

Corporate consolidation has impacts off the farm as well. Distribution networks, fueled by the desires and demands of large retailers, favor large-scale food producers, processors, and manufacturers. Those able to access large-scale, continuous production, storage, and transportation practices are best positioned in the contemporary food marketplace. This is an example of vertical integration within the industry. This happens as a single corporation controls farmland, labor, and then food production and distribution as well. This emergent move toward efficiency and consolidation reduces worker autonomy and consumer choice as major industrial agricultural businesses now account for more than 80 percent of the foods in the marketplace. Suppliers are obligated to adapt to the demands of large retailers. For example, roughly one-third of all food products sold by major manufacturers are sold through Walmart, the largest retail company in the United States and second largest publicly traded company in the world. Walmart's size, influence, and purchasing power mean that the corporation can keep its costs low by forcing its suppliers to sell to it at lower costs. This forces suppliers to seek lower costs from those they do business with, depressing costs and wages throughout the food system. Walmart's hostility to unions and record of poor work conditions and labor practices also cause spiraling effects that negatively affect workers through the food system. These impacts are felt by Walmart's suppliers as well as its competitors.

Subsidizing Low Wages

Another form of government subsidy is revealed when examining the number of food workers with wages so low that they qualify for government antipoverty assistance programs. National outrage is sparked each time workers at Walmart, McDonald's, and other companies in the food industry reveal that their workers are advised by their corporate offices to apply for social service assistance to augment their low wages. Walmart is the largest grocer in the United States. Groceries make up more than half of all sales at the retail giant. With their low wages, largely part-time hours, and inability to unionize, many of the millions of Walmart employees sorting, stocking, and selling these groceries are receiving SNAP benefits. Walmart and other, similar retailers benefit from both the SNAP payments their customers bring into the stores and the SNAP payments their employees get to subsidize their low wages. In this, experts claim Walmart and Amazon are among the biggest SNAP beneficiaries. McDonald's workers alone receive $1.2 billion in taxpayer-funded public assistance. Employees of corporate giants and small food companies rely heavily on federally and state-funded assistance programs that offset their low wages. This is especially the case in fast food: 40 percent of fast-food workers live in poverty. Many others live close to the poverty line. This affects not just workers but also their families: 25 percent of families with a member with a fast-food job earn below the poverty line; 43 percent earn less than two times the federal poverty line; 87 percent of fast-food workers receive no health benefits from their employers. This is not limited to part-time work; the families of more than half of fast-food workers who work at least 40 hours each week are enrolled in at least one public assistance programs. Other occupations within the food industry are similarly subsidized. For example, 35 percent of agricultural workers have family members enrolled in at least one public assistance program.

A closer data analysis shows the rate of SNAP use is 1.5 times higher for food workers than for other U.S. workers. Food workers also use Medicaid at higher rates than other workers. A lack of employer-provided health care means that food workers rely on emergency room visits, since they cannot access or afford primary care. Nearly 35 percent report using the emergency room for this reason. An analysis of census data by Brynne Keith-Jennings and Vincent Palacios reveals that 26 percent of dishwashers, agricultural grader and sorters, and food preparation and serving workers, 23 percent of cooks, nearly 20 percent of restaurant and food-service workers, approximately 17 percent of both animal slaughtering and processing workers and commercial bakery workers, and approximately 16 percent of grocery store workers, retail bakery workers, and crop production workers receive SNAP. A Berkeley study shows that 52 percent of fast-food workers receive at least one federal assistance program, whether Medicaid or the Child Health Insurance Program (CHIP), the income assistance program Temporary Aid to Needy Families (TANF), the Earned Income Tax Credit (EITC), or SNAP. This is more than double the average number of all workers who receive such assistance. Some fast-food workers receive combinations of these programs. The study includes only the cash assistance portion of TANF, and it does not include receipt of state EITC programs, childcare assistance, or other state-funded assistance programs for low-income workers. Fast-food work is the occupational category with the highest reliance on federal public assistance programs. Indeed, fast-food workers receive nearly $7 billion in publicly funded assistance each year. It is important to note that this total, though high, underrepresents the total needs of workers and their families.

CORPORATE POWER IN SHAPING HOW AND WHAT WE EAT

Research indicates that U.S. consumers are faced with more than 200 food-based decisions daily. These include decisions about what to eat, where to eat, how much to eat, how much to spend to eat, and whether to eat in a restaurant or buy groceries for meals at a store. Decisions abound at the store as well. For those who do not face food insecurity or live in a food desert, there are choices about what kind and which store to visit. The questions continue inside the store. Consumers today spend more time in stores making purchasing decisions due to the number of products available, confusing or unclear labels, and a lack of comparable sizes, costs, and claims across products. Amid the decision overload, shoppers can quickly revert to habits and perceptions that are not in the interest of optimal health. Convenience foods, those known from one's childhood, store displays, and ubiquitous marketing and advertising become even more appealing under this constellation of circumstances. Six of the 10 most profitable food production categories in the United States are related to convenience foods: snack foods; cookies, crackers, and pasta; chocolate; sugar processing; ice cream; and candy, all foods low in nutritional value and high in fat, sodium, and sugar. This illustrates the power that food corporations have in what U.S. consumers have available to eat. When coupled with food advertising and marketing, this also illustrates their power over how U.S. consumers eat.

In 1970 the U.S. fast-food industry generated $6 billion annually. By 2015 that number ballooned to $200 billion. The industry's power affects the economy in the ways consumers eat and in farming practices. Some food justice advocates hold the industry responsible for rises in factory farming and for the increase in government subsidies for animal feed crops such as corn and soy.

The amounts of sugar, sodium, and fat that U.S. consumers eat continue to grow. This is not a matter of willpower or gluttony, as individual-level recommendations to eat fewer sugary sodas, salty chips, and fatty cheeseburgers imply. Calorie counts on menus, simpler nutrition facts on food labels, and public-health campaigns emphasize providing people with information on what they eat and drink to compel them to make healthier choices, but these measures neglect the structural barriers to doing so. Far less attention is paid to the food industry's use of food marketing, science, engineering, and neurogastronomy in shaping consumers' tastes and choices. According to Harvard researcher Jessleen Kanwal, this emerging science, involves the nexus of neuroscience, food science, psychology, biochemistry, and culinary arts to understand the role of the senses in our perceptions of what we eat.

Neuroscience can be used to trick our brains' taste and pleasure centers. What we taste—a food's flavor—is not just a function of taste but relies on a combination of all our senses. Neurogastronomy is also used to shape our perceptions of what and how we eat. This is related to comments that we might hear about "eating with our eyes" and the way our stomachs growl when we smell something we like. Taste sensations are most associated with flavor. As salty, sweet, bitter, sour, and umami taste bud receptors are engaged, particular areas in the taste center of the brain, called the gustatory cortex, are activated. Smell is related to taste in two ways. Those smells we get from faraway food are associated with orthonasal smelling. Those smells we get as we swallow are associated with retronasal smelling. The latter activates olfactory receptor cells that signal the brain, creating an image of sorts of the smell of food. Sound is also at play in taste perceptions. Different foods produce different sound frequencies, and emerging research finds that these frequencies can change how taste is perceived. For example, low-frequency sounds can make foods taste more bitter and high-frequency sounds can make foods taste sweeter. The ways that foods feel—their textures—also are correlated with their flavor, as is the case in studies showing that flavor intensity increases as food hardness decreases. As the senses combine, foods maximize flavor in the higher-order cortical region of the brain. Restaurateurs are aware of this, as is reflected in their extensive choices not just in menus and flavor profiles but in food service. Research-driven decisions about serveware colors, utensil materials, and plate shapes reflect this. The perception of salt can be increased through the use of rougher flatware just as the perception of sweetness can be increased by using a rounded plate without adding a grain of salt or sugar during food preparation. These principles are also considered in music and ambient noise, paint colors, and furniture choices at restaurants. Neurogastronomy is also used by food companies that seek to enhance flavor in ways that activate the brain's pleasure center. The added sugar, salt, and fat in fast, packaged, and processed foods do this at low financial and high health costs.

Some positive applications of neurogastronomy are its use in enhancing flavor for those with damage to their taste buds. Cancer treatments that involve chemotherapy are known for suppressing patients' appetites. Neurogastronomy can heighten taste perceptions in ways that make food more appealing during chemotherapy. Dieticians and parents see neurogastronomical possibilities that may make vegetables more palatable to picky children as well. In these cases, manipulating and combining colors, textures, sounds, and smells can prove promising for flavors and tastes. These positive possibilities account for a small amount of the work done in neurogastronomy.

Food engineers work to perfect products before they go to market. They are also used to optimize or enhance a product that fails to meet a food company's expectations after it has gone to market. They recruit participants to taste variant after variant of foods and drinks as they engineer foods and beverages that the participants rate highest in taste, smell, texture, mouth feel, sound, and other variables. Tasters are also asked numerous questions about their perceptions of the products in terms of value and quality, as well as the emotional states tasters experience during and after sampling. In addition to human testers, statistical, computer, and other forms of modeling are employed. This is all part of the research-and-development process at food companies, where each ingredient, fresh and natural or processed and artificial, as well as each decision about food packaging, branding, and marketing is carefully tested, analyzed, and formulated to maximize taste and taste perceptions rather than nutrition or satiety. The ingredients that are most commonly used to maximize taste are also those that are heavily subsidized and thus cheaply available, such as sugars and plant-based oils.

Food companies specialize in determining consumers' sensory-specific satiety level. This is also known as the bliss point and refers to the reaction that bold flavors create and that cause the brain to become overwhelmed to the point of reducing the appetite for more. Popular foods in the soda, cookies, and chips aisles of stores rely on this effect to introduce complex tastes without pushing consumers past the point at which their brain tells them to cease their consumption. Foods are engineered to invoke cravings for the product; they are designed to hit consumers' bliss points and keep them reaching for more. A related concept is that of vanishing caloric density. Foods that melt in consumers' mouths are perceived as much lower in calories than they really are. Snack companies in particular work to enhance this. A single company like the Texas-based Frito-Lay can employ a research team that includes 500 chemists, psychologists, and food technicians conducting research at an annual cost of $30 million. One product can undergo thousands of tests, as was the case when Dr. Pepper introduced a new flavor in 2004. The extremely popular cherry vanilla flavor introduced to consumers underwent 61 formulations and nearly 4,000 taste tests in addition to statistical modeling before its eventual release.

Labels and marketing are also important tools in food companies' arsenals. Labels that declare foods and drinks as 100 percent fruit, low fat, or all natural are accurate yet deceptive in their implied healthiness. Fruit juice is a better choice than soda but lacks the nutritional value of a piece of fruit. One-hundred-percent fruit juices and smoothies often contain a lot of cheaper, filler juices such as grape or apple. Foods that have lowered fat contents often have sugar and salt added to compensate for the taste lost with the fat. Foods that are all natural can still have be processed and have high amounts of natural additives.

Understanding food-related chemical, biological, neurological, and psychological aspects as well as the social and cultural power of food and how food companies draw on these in creating and marketing products is key for efforts to change how, why, and what people eat. A study by Jennifer Falbe and colleagues demonstrates that sugary drinks have addictive properties. Researchers observed that a group of adolescents 13 and 18 years old who were deprived of sugary drinks for three days started to report headaches, cravings, and decreased feelings of well-being, contentment, motivation, and concentration. These are symptoms associated with withdrawal. Avoidance of these symptoms may outweigh health promotion messages calling for the cessation or reduced consumption of these beverages. A clearer understanding of the mechanisms involved in sugar and other food addictions is needed in any public-health campaign, including those for obesity reduction. The next chapter, in an exploration of recent changes in the National School Lunch Program, takes up the intersection of policy change and public-health campaigns.

CHAPTER 13

Healthy Lunch, Hungry Kids? Lunch at School

As public-health concerns over rising childhood obesity rates grew, a response by parents, policy makers, food activists, chefs such as Alice Waters and Jamie Oliver, and former First Lady of the United States Michelle Obama was to change guidelines on lunches in public schools to include lower fat, sugar, sodium, and caloric counts. A backlash ensued by those claiming this was governmental overreach and/or that the foods were no longer as tasty as they had been. This chapter takes up this concern and other related school-based food concerns.

WHAT IS THE NATIONAL SCHOOL LUNCH PROGRAM?

School lunches are vitally important, providing the only meal some children will have in a day. School administrators and teachers are aware of this, as those who stock their offices and desks with extra snacks and send their students home with enough food to last over the course of a long weekend could attest. This is also the impetus for larger-scale actions, such as the move by school districts around the nation to offer year-round lunch programs to ensure that children are fed even when school has been dismissed for the summer. Outside of schools, those who offer afterschool programs are aware of the food insecurity that many children experience. This is evident in the number of programs that offer dinner, rather than snacks, to those in attendance.

Funded by the federal government, the National School Lunch Program (NSLP) benefits families whose children can eat reduced and free meals at schools. It also benefits food corporations that provide meals and generate profits. Health and nutritional gains for children and financial gains for small, local farms and producers could mean significant losses for large food management, manufacturers, and services companies. As more calls to rid schools of premade, processed food were made and instituted, more pushback ensued. This was fueled by political and cultural rhetoric of urban elitism and big government. It is important to note that despite some reports and beliefs, though the USDA establishes guidelines for what must be included in school lunches, the menus are established by local school districts, just as before the changes in guidelines were issued. This was also heightened by antipathy toward President Barack Obama and First Lady Michelle Obama that was rooted in racism. Conservative activists and media and food companies shared messages designed to turn public support against proposals, funding, and implementation of Michelle Obama's signature programs during her role as First Lady of the United States.

Schools with large numbers of students who live in poverty can offer free lunches to all students enrolled at the school under a recently introduced federal program, the Community Eligibility Provision (CEP). The CEP allows schools and districts with the nation's highest poverty rates to serve lunch at no cost to all enrolled students without collecting individual household applications. These schools are then reimbursed for meals using a formula based on the percentage of students categorically eligible for free meals based on their participation in other specific means-tested programs, such as the Supplemental Nutrition Assistance Program (SNAP) and Temporary Assistance for Needy Families (TANF). The introduction of this program has been accompanied by rising student test scores and falling disciplinary cases, suggesting correlations between hunger, student performance, and student behavior.

What Do Students Eat at School?

The NSLP requires meals to provide one-third of the daily calorie, protein, calcium, iron, vitamin A, and vitamin E needs. These meals score significantly higher on health scores than most meals U.S. children eat. As the NSLP requirements changed to require fresher and healthier foods, school meal costs increased. Some children, used to fried and processed meals and foods with higher sugar, fat, and sodium content, complained about the changes as well. As a support, the Healthy, Hunger-Free Kids Act of 2010 authorized an additional six-cent payment for each meal when schools could show they were following the new requirements. The act also authorized the CEP.

Still, the meals provided are typically not made from scratch on school premises. In her research on the NSLP, Dr. Jennifer E. Gaddis finds that the job of cafeteria worker has vastly changed. As food services companies placed bids for school district contracts, the focus has shifted to companies providing the cheapest meals allowable. These are often foods filled with preservatives and fillers that are trucked in from all over rather than whole, nutritious foods that are sourced from local growers. In previous generations, lunch ladies preparing meals for children from scratch were seen sweating over pots in hot school kitchens. Today, the cafeteria workers Gaddis studied are more likely to be found reheating and microwaving premade food. As school funding has decreased, a number of schools are unable to establish kitchens that meet federal guidelines. This facilitates the kinds of "reheat and eat" school meals Gaddis describes. These meals are not only frozen but also highly processed and rarely contain fresh or locally procured foods. Schools with larger budgets and more affluence can augment the federal lunch reimbursement rate, whereas poorer schools cannot. As such, some schools are unable to ensure that each child they feed will have meals that are fresh and healthy, let alone local in origin.

Who Does (and Doesn't) the NSLP Serve?

According to the USDA website, "National School Lunch Program," in 2018 school cafeterias served nearly 5 billion lunches. Approximately 75 percent of these were served to students who qualified for free or reduced-price lunches. Approximately half of public school students receive lunches under the NSLP. More than 30 million U.S. schoolchildren receive reduced or free meals through their schools. Snacks for children in approved afterschool programs that have educational or enrichment activities can also be reimbursed through the NSLP. Students of color are much more likely to use NSLP than white students. Children from food-insecure and marginally secure households are more likely to eat school meals and receive more of their food and nutrient intake from school meals than children from food-secure households do.

Federal law caps all school lunches at $2.90 per lunch. A family of four that earns up to 185 percent of the poverty line, currently about $48,000 per year, pays a maximum of 40 cents for each child's lunch. A family of four that earns less than 130 percent of the poverty line, currently $32,630, qualifies for free lunches.

Children whose families who earn too much to qualify for free and reduced-price school lunches through the federal NSLP can accumulate school lunch debt quickly. According to reporting from Jessica Fu, schools surveyed note an average lunch debt of $2,500 per school. Washington, DC, area school districts saw $500,000 in accumulated lunch debt, and there has been a rise in lunch debt from $13,000 in 2016 to $356,000 in 2018 in Denver school districts. In recent years local newscasts, cable reporters, and Twitter feeds have recounted stories of regular people paying off schoolchildren's lunch debt. Though the federal lunch program spends nearly $14 billion in reimbursements to schools annually, rules prohibit them from using those funds to eliminate their students' meal debts. Individual and collective fundraising efforts are used to fill the gap instead. In December 2019 Katelynn Hardee, a kindergarten student in California, set up a stand to sell hot cocoa, apple cider, and cookies and used the $80 in proceeds to pay off the negative lunch account balances of 123 students at her school. While often shared as a feel-good, heartwarming story, it illustrates the food inequality and injustice many children face. In the last few years, social media have periodically exploded with stories of children having hot lunches thrown away by cafeteria workers who realize the children they are ringing up have insufficient funds in their school lunch accounts. Examples of lunch shaming, where students in schools are stigmatized when they have insufficient funds in their food accounts, are rampant across the nation. The agency that administers the NSLP finds that 60 percent of schools have engaged in some form of lunch shaming. This is evidenced each time there has been collective outrage over learning that students have their hands stamped to indicate they have unpaid meal balances, are forced to sit in special sections of cafeterias, are given cold cheese sandwiches at school even as their fellow students throw away full trays of food, are given demeaning notes to take home to their parents, and are otherwise mocked by school authorities when they cannot afford a school lunch. In addition, 35 percent of schools sanction students with meal balances. This includes prohibiting them from extracurricular activities, including homecoming and prom, and withholding grades and diplomas. To date, 6 percent of debts have been sent to collection agencies.

Feel-good stories of fundraising campaigns by children to pay off their classmates' school lunch debts are regular occurrences on the evening news even as many question the very idea of school lunch debt in a nation of such wealth and food waste as the United States. Recalling Karen Washington's work on the system of food apartheid (as reported on by Anna Brones), school lunch debt has overlapped with another major axis of inequality in the United States—police brutality. A 2018 lunch debt drive was launched in the name of African American Minnesota school nutrition supervisor Philando Castile, who was the victim of an extrajudicial killing by a suburban Minneapolis police officer. As Castile was beloved for his efforts to make sure all children in his school could eat at his own expense, "Philando Feeds the Children" was launched and raised more than $150,000, enough money to eliminate all the outstanding student lunch debt at all 56 schools in the St. Paul, Minnesota, public school system that employed him until his killing. A year later, his mother presented a check eliminating another $8,000 of debt at a Minnesota high school in her son's name. Sometimes not even fundraising is enough to ensure that children can have their lunch debt paid off so that they can eat healthy, nutritious meals.

In 2019 reports of a Pennsylvania school district that threatened to recommend that children with school lunch debt be removed from their parents' custody and placed into foster care raced across the nation. Even after many, including Todd Carmichael, CEO of Pennsylvania-headquartered La Colombe Coffee Roasters offered to pay off the more than $22,000 worth of debt, the school board repeatedly refused to clear the debts before ultimately accepting his offer and issuing an apology to the approximately 1,000 families affected. In 2017 bipartisan bills to end the embarrassing and harmful practices of lunch shaming were introduced in both chambers of the U.S. Congress. After being referred to various committees, no action has been taken on either proposed bill.

Let's Move!

Michelle Obama's efforts were designed to solve the obesity crisis in ways that were good for children and businesses, as she noted in speeches and writings on her Let's Move! campaign. Let's Move! is a comprehensive initiative, now under the auspices of the nonprofit Partnership for a Healthier America, began in 2010 as the signature program of former First Lady Michelle Obama. Its focus is the creation of a healthy lifestyle around food and movement in service of its stated goal to end obesity for children within a generation. One metric of the program's success would be meeting its target of reducing U.S. childhood obesity rates to 5 percent by 2030, a rate not seen since the late 1970s. Former president Barack Obama established the nation's first Task Force on Childhood Obesity to both develop and implement a comprehensive plan, across the federal government, to coordinate strategy, identify benchmarks, and create an action plan to accomplish said goal. The report presents a series of

70 specific recommendations that started with prenatal care and spanned across childhood, ranging from decreasing screen time; limiting chemical exposure; providing better and more accessible nutritional information to parents and guardians; boosting children's physical activity at school, home, and elsewhere; increasing food access and affordability; and promoting whole fruit and vegetable consumption, as seen in Michelle Obama's 2016 "Turnip for What" (a take on the then popular rap song, "Turn Down for What") viral video. As children spend much of their time and eat many of their meals in their schools, educational settings are a particular focus.

The Partnership for a Healthier America (PHA) was formed to reverse the increased rates of childhood obesity and the health challenges and chronic diseases associated with these. Another, interconnected focus is the production of healthy, sustainable food by food companies. The PHA website establishes its goal that "all children—especially those disproportionately affected—will live healthier lives, growing up to be adults free from obesity, diabetes, heart disease, and other chronic conditions." This fuels their mission "to leverage the power of the private sector to bring lasting, sustainable change that improves the food supply and increases physical activity." They do so in efforts to improve the healthiness and nutritional value of food and drinks. They also work with corporations and institutions to improve food choices and increase physical activity for children and young adults in such places as schools, afterschool and other local community programs, and other environments where children and young adults spend time outside the home.

Sociologist Ivy Ken asserts that such public-private partnerships and alliances allow food corporations to retain lucrative income streams and avert condemnation for their role in providing unhealthy foods and increasing obesity, because they laud their involvement in efforts such as PHA and Alliance for a Healthier Generation, established during Presidents Obama's and Clinton's respective administrations. Both programs tasked schools to reduce unhealthy and processed foods from school cafeterias, vending machines, and other meals. At the same time, as Ken illustrates, the Alliance for a Healthier Generation has 120 corporate partners such as the Dr. Pepper Snapple Group, and Domino's Pizza. PHA's corporate partners include Coca-Cola, Hershey, Nestle, and PepsiCo. These companies, purveyors of foods and drinks with empty calories, excess sugars, and unnecessary fats, can use their involvement in campaigns that profess to keep children healthy in ways that allow them cover and continued profits. While ceding to demands for fewer calories and less fat in creating new foods that meet guidelines established through these and related programs, their corporate partners lobby against restrictions on sugar, antibiotics, hormones, pesticides, and artificial dyes, flavors, and additives. In addition, the USDA launched the Smart Snacks Product Calculator and Product Navigator as interrelated tools that all state food-service directors could use to make informed decisions on purchasing foods in line with federal regulations. Packaged and processed foods are available as options through these tools, while fresh fruits and vegetables are not.

Experts recommend schools and governments rethink corporate partnerships in favor of local ones with community-based alliances. These can be accomplished through linkages with organizations such as the Farm to School Network or the Edible Schoolyard Project. These offer fresh food, better health and nutrition, infusions into local economies, and employment opportunities, and they also increase students' science, food, and environmental literacies.

USDA's Farm to School Census uses data to show that 42 percent of school districts—that is, more than 42,000 U.S. schools—have some form of farm-to-school activity. Their report finds that more than 7,100 school gardens have been planted. These initiatives start as soon as prekindergarten, as more than 1,500 school districts have this kind of programming. Across the board, these can range from efforts as simple as giving students packets of seeds or seedlings planted in disposable cups, which they can take home to grow, to programs where students grow the foods they eat for lunch and snacks to social enterprises that allow students to take veggies, fruits, and food-based products to market. Some of these are done in conjunction with larger public and nonprofit farms and gardens, as part of college and university programs and classes, in small patches of land next to a community center, on a school's rooftop garden, or even indoors using hydroponics and aquaponics, which allows for fruits, vegetables, and fish to be grown symbiotically in a closed system that circulates the nutrient-rich water from fish tanks to plants. In some cases, there are schools with salad bars in their cafeterias that are supplied with food grown on the premises. Let's Move! funding for school-based farm programs supplied the food in the salad bar in some instances.

Schools that have gardens have children who eat more fruits and vegetables. This is also the case when schools incorporate food-based curricula and activities that involve gardening, nutrition, and cooking. This is something that children carry back to their homes and communities, so the benefits of these programs are spread to others in their households and networks.

OTHER FEDERAL SCHOOL AND COMMUNITY FOOD PROGRAMS

Nearly 15 million children utilize the School Breakfast Program. Students in schools eligible for the CEP can eat breakfast for free as well. Schools that participate in school lunch and breakfast programs receive reimbursements for milk through the USDA's Special Milk Program (SMP). The SMP is also available to children in half-day prekindergarten and kindergarten programs as well as childcare institutions and eligible camps that do not have access to school meal programs.

The Child and Adult Care Food Program (CACFP) reimburses for food in afterschool programs, childcare centers, day-care homes, and adult day-care centers. CACFP also provides reimbursements for meals for children residing in emergency shelters and for adults over the age of 60 or living with a disability and enrolled in day-care facilities. In 2018 the Summer Food Service Program (SFSP) provided meals to 2.7 million children each day at nearly 48,000 locations across the nation. SFSP reimburses participating programs that serve free, healthy meals and snacks to children under 18 in low-income areas.

In the previous chapters, a thorough look at food inequalities throughout the U.S. food system has shown their interconnectedness, pervasiveness, and malignancy across social statuses, place, institutions, and structures. Indeed, there are a number of powerful influences—and barriers—surrounding the ability to make healthy food choices. These can create, continue, and calcify social, health, and economic inequalities. They can also be improved through policy efforts. In part IV, real-world examples bring these into even sharper focus.

PART III

Scenarios

CHAPTER 14

Case Studies

CASE 1: I WILL (NOT) DRINK TO THAT

Synclaire is watching the nightly news when she sees that her city council has introduced a new tax on the purchase of all sweetened beverages. The anchor cuts to a clip from the press conference where the mayor, head of the city council, and a physician from the local hospital discuss the rationale for the tax. They say the tax will discourage consumers from buying sweetened beverages, such as soda, sports drinks, bottled teas and coffees, and the like. Consuming fewer of these will lead to lower obesity rates as well as lower rates of food-related illnesses and chronic health conditions. The physician says that the associated health costs of these conditions will decrease, and the mayor adds that this will reduce the city's burden of paying for these costs by the public. A reporter asks what the tax will fund, and the city council head responds that the proceeds will go to fund public-health initiatives, universal prekindergarten, employment, and community development programs in the city.

The next morning, Synclaire goes to her local corner store and asks the owner what she thinks of the new tax. The owner is extremely upset and adamant that it will harm her business. She talks about declines in profits, probable layoffs of employees, and the potential need to close her business after the tax goes into effect. At work, Synclaire hears her colleague talking to their manager. They say that the tax will impose burdens on those least able to afford it while doing little for actual health outcomes. Their manager agrees and starts derisively referring to the head of the city council—the woman who introduced the tax proposal—with the nickname "Queen Sugar." Soon this nickname is being used by her political opponents, media pundits, and angry constituents. Driving home from work three nights later, Synclaire hears an ad on one of her favorite local radio stations that is highly critical of the tax and urges listeners to bombard city hall, the mayor, and the city council with phone calls, emails, and tweets to voice their dissatisfaction with the measure. On her commute into work the next morning, Synclaire hears a report on the local public radio station that is discussing the potential health benefits of the tax. If the consumption of drinks with added sugars is limited, the risks of cardiovascular disease, dental decay, hypertension, fatty-liver disease, insulin resistance, and type 2, or adult-onset, diabetes in children, adolescents, and adults should also decline.

Synclaire sees both sides of the argument. On the one hand, she thinks all possible steps should be taken to improve health, reduce costs, and fund these important programs. On the other, she believes that people who can will just travel to the surrounding suburbs, enriching their tax base rather than the city's, and that people without cars or with less money will end up paying higher costs. She also feels that there is too much concern on the part of the city over what she chooses to drink. At the end of the week, Synclaire wonders who is correct.

Analysis

In cities and other locales with taxes on sweetened beverages, the breadth of products covered by these taxes varies. Some include beverages with added sugar, and others include beverages with any added sweetener, whether natural or artificial and whether the sweeteners add calories or are calorie-free. Some are limited to store purchases, while others cover drinks sold in bars, cafés, and restaurants. Whether they only include soda or expand across juices, fruit drinks, coffee, and tea, they are commonly referred to as soda taxes. Revenues generated from the tax are used in public-health campaigns, increases in food access and affordability, school funding, nutrition education, community and school gardens, playgrounds, and community programming.

Berkeley, California, was the first municipality to impose a tax on sweetened beverages. The municipality taxed the distributors of drinks with added sugars.

Philadelphia was the next U.S. city to introduce a soda tax. After a citywide vote approving the tax, the Philadelphia City Council approved a 1.5-cents-per-ounce tax on sugar and artificially sweetened beverages. The Cook County, Illinois, Board of Commissioners passed a 1-cent-per-ounce tax on the retail sale of all sweetened beverages sold in Cook County in

November 2016. Sugar and soda industry lobbyists were both vocal and covert in their opposition to the tax. There was an immediate appeal and a restraining order issued that delayed the tax, to be paid directly by consumers, until August 2017. The ordinance was repealed two months later in a vote supported by 15 of the county's 17 commissioners—several of whom had voted to institute it the previous year.

The International Council of Beverages Associations and the American Beverage Association (ABA) strongly resist soda tax proposals and implementation. For example, more than $4 million in advertising and a total of more than $10 million were spent to encourage the failure of the Philadelphia soda tax proposal. Food and beverage companies join this fight, as seen through the millions spent by Coca-Cola and PepsiCo between 2011 and 2015 alone to lobby against 29 separate public-health bills designed to increase nutrition or decrease soda consumption. In 2018 the food and beverage industry spent more than $23 million on such lobbying—$5.4 million was spent by Coca-Cola and another $2.8 million was spent by PepsiCo. The hostility to soda taxes is not limited to the beverage industry, however. Some opponents resist the taxes and refer to them as a tax on the poor. A soda tax is regressive, as it disproportionately impacts the poor, causing more economic harm to the group least able to afford it.

While sales and consumption do decline in the wake of soda taxes, Cook County, Philadelphia, and other localities do see geographic shifts in where sugary beverages are purchased. In Chicago, for example, residents who had access to transportation and time shopped for sugar-sweetened and artificially sweetened drinks in the surrounding five counties that make up metropolitan Chicago. Low-income residents of localities with soda taxes are least able to travel to adjoining communities without these taxes, as they have less access to cars. Still, in those locations with soda taxes, research is emerging that suggests that they are effective in decreasing sugar consumption and promoting health without the dire consequences feared by businesses and the food and beverage industry.

CASE 2: I'M NOT EATING THAT

Brett and Jett are 11-year-old twin boys. They live in Missouri, where they are fifth-grade students in a public school. Their parents have noticed that they seemed more moody, tired, and out of sorts than in the past. Initially, they attributed these changes to puberty, moving to a new school after attending private schools, and the fact that they were still getting used to the increased academic workload expected of fifth graders. This changed one day at the beginning of October, when they learned of the difficulties their sons seemed to be experiencing at lunchtime each day. Brett came home from school and went immediately to bed for a late-afternoon nap. When he woke up a couple hours later, he went into the kitchen, where his mother was working on a project with Jett and his father was preparing a lasagna dinner.

Brett ate an apple, then some yogurt, followed by a bag of pretzels, and a couple of cookies. As he reached for the milk, his father asked why he was eating so much. Brett playfully rolled his eyes and said, "Cause I'm hungry?!" His mother followed up and asked what he had eaten for lunch at school. Brett replied, "Mom, I didn't eat. We never eat at this stupid school. I hate all the lunches they try to make us eat at this stupid school. We used to have pizza and nachos and cheeseburgers and fries at our old school." Jett added, "And cookies and pudding for dessert." The twins exchanged a look before they simultaneously yelled out, "The nugs. We love the nugs. We miss the nugs," in reference to their beloved chicken nuggets. Brett continued, "Now, it's just disgusting. The food doesn't even taste like anything. It's just bleh." Jett jumped in to tell their parents, "Yeah, today, they gave us broccoli. You know I hate that stuff. It's gross." Brett followed up, saying, "I'm not eating that, that, that cr—." A look from his mom made him change that to "I'm not eating that stuff anymore." Jett concurred and asked his father if they could both just take their lunch to school for the rest of the school year. Their parents were shocked both by how upset their sons were and by the fact that they were not eating much at school. The boys settled down, and the family enjoyed their dinner. After packing away leftovers for the boys to take to school the next day, the parents went to the family computer to learn about food policies in their new school district. In looking at the monthly menu posted to the website, they saw a note indicating that the school follows USDA guidelines that include balanced meals with a protein, grains, fruits, vegetables, and milk. The note further explained that all the protein is lean and low in sodium, all the grains used are whole grain, and that the fruit and vegetables are also whole. Their mother responded, "I understand why the boys are so upset. I wouldn't want to eat that crap either," while their father said, "At least it's healthy?"

Analysis

With the passage of the 2010 Healthy Hunger-Free Kids Act, school lunch guidelines were updated after national calls for healthier options. As public-health concerns over rising childhood obesity rates grew, a response by parents, policy makers, food activists, chefs such as Alice Waters and

Jamie Oliver, and former first lady of the United States Michelle Obama called for changes in lunches in public schools to include lower fat, sugar, sodium, and caloric counts. The 2010 Act requires that students are served a fruit and vegetable every day, and it calls for increases in the number of whole-grain foods and limits on the amount of fats and sodium in meals. Implementation of this Act has not been as smooth as proponents had hoped, however. As noted in chapter 13, this has been a very controversial effort. Most schools have to achieve these mandates on $1.30 for each student. They also have to account for students such as Brett and Jett, whose palates lead them to reject foods that taste less appealing than those with higher amounts of fat, salt, sugar—all components in giving foods more satisfying mouth feel and brains more satisfaction as they trigger its pleasure center. They also have to reassure parents who do not want their children missing meals and the nutritional needs these supply. Parents such as Brett and Jett's can also become dismayed at the financial and time costs of preparing lunches for their children every day. This is of particular concern for low-income parents who rely on free and reduced lunches and cannot easily afford to buy or make these additional meals for their picky eaters.

Schools with salad bars, food-based curricula and school gardens, for example, are more successful in convincing students to eat more produce. These, however, are expensive programs, and not all schools or school districts can afford their cost. Though there are some grants available to fund these, writing successful grants takes knowledge, skills, and time that are not equally available to all who need the grants. Parents and some school staff reported increased amounts of food waste and complaints of hunger after new school lunch mandates went into effect. There are some programs that address this through working with school nutrition staff to create meals that are both nutritious and tasty.

In addition to healthier and more nutritious meals, since the passage of the 2010 Healthy Hunger-Free Kids Act, there has been research showing a corresponding increase in student test scores and a decrease in disciplinary cases, suggesting correlations between nutrition, student performance, and student behavior.

Case 3: Why They Come

Yesenia and Josué are a married couple from El Salvador. After living under economic and political crises there, they decided to come to the United States to seek work and more safety. They wanted to apply for refugee status, as there was a lot of violence in their town and their teen son and daughter were constantly being threatened. They knew this would not be successful, though, after seeing other people from their town having their applications denied again and again. After taking an arduous trip by foot and on top of trains with their 13-year-old son and 15-year-old daughter to Mexico, Yesenia and Josué traveled to the United States with the help of a coyote, a person paid handsomely to transport people without legal status through the dangerous mountainous and desert terrain between the two countries. While some who make this perilous journey are apprehended by Border Patrol agents who actively surveil the areas between the United States and Mexico, fall ill and must return, or are killed by disease, injury, or others, Yesenia and Josué make it to the United States along with their two children. They have family in the United States, and they spend their first few weeks in New Mexico with Josué's sister. They must eat and find their own home soon, however. Without legal status to work, they must take whatever jobs they can to support themselves and their children. Yesenia and Josué also send money back home to El Salvador to help their family members who remain there. They both come from a long line of agricultural workers. Because of their experience working in fields in El Salvador and their limited job opportunities, they, like many other Central American migrants, find employment as migrant farmworkers. They hear from Josué's brother-in-law that there are more opportunities for work in California, so they make their way there. Though they want to settle down and establish a home, they must follow the work. In order to allow their children to make friends and attend school, they let them stay with Josué's sister and her family, and the children enroll in school in New Mexico. In March Yesenia and Josué are in Ventura County, California, where they harvest strawberries. By June they have moved on to Santa Cruz County, where they harvest avocados. By the fall, they are harvesting kale in Salinas, Monterey County, and in winter, Yesenia and Josué are in Orange County, back in Southern California, to harvest citrus. In the course of a year, the couple move across the vast state of California. They do not see their children for much of the year, as they have no paid time off and their earnings are too low to miss work for long enough to travel to New Mexico. The children stay with Yesenia and Josué for a few weeks in the summer, but as that is prime harvest season, they have little opportunity to spend much time with them. Though their situation is not what they would prefer, they endure it to make a better life for their two children and to help their relatives back in El Salvador.

Analysis

Pew Research Center data presented by Jeffrey S. Passel and D'vera Cohn note that undocumented workers such as Yesenia and Josué constitute 5 percent of the civilian workforce, 24 percent of the farming industry, 8 percent of production (which includes food processing), and 8 percent of the service industry (which includes restaurant work). Of the 18 industries with the highest shares of undocumented workers, 9 are wholly within the food system. The U.S. Department of Labor National Agricultural Workers Survey (NAWS) indicates that half of all farmworkers are undocumented.

For migrant farmworkers such as the couple here, as they move from field to field and from farm to farm, there is little stability. This disrupts their family life and social relationships. Children who accompany their parents can experience numerous disruptions to their education and social relationships. For families such as Yesenia and Josue's, children are in stable housing and educational situations but at the expense of living together as a family. For undocumented migrant workers who do not speak English, who do not have transportation, who are transitory, and who do not have legal status in the United States, these issues are critical. They coexist with significant economic inequality. Farmworkers in general are among the least well-paid workers in the food system, and undocumented workers with the same skill sets as immigrants with work permits and those born in the United States are paid significantly less.

So why do they come to the United States? An understanding of regional politics and economies is instructive. In recent years, the ability of families such as Yesenia and Josué's to work and provide for themselves on farms in their communities of origin has been hampered by international trade policies such as the Dominican Republic-Central American Free Trade Agreement (CAFTA-DR), which was signed into U.S. law in 2005 by George W. Bush and ratified by El Salvador in 2006, the first Central American nation to do so. Since that time, the Dominican Republic, Costa Rica, El Salvador, Guatemala, Nicaragua, and Honduras became other signatories. Undocumented migrants from Mexico—similarly impacted by the 1990s North American Free Trade Agreement (NAFTA) and its replacement, the United States-Mexico-Canada Agreement (USMCA) of 2020—and Central America have been displaced from agricultural work in their countries of origins and come to the United States as guest workers and undocumented migrant workers, as discussed in chapters 6, 8, and 9.

Since the passage of CAFTA-DR and NAFTA/USMCA, many critics note that the trade agreements have benefited U.S. agricultural corporations at the expense of small Central American and Mexican farmers. Small U.S. farmers have also been harmed by these agreements. In the 15 years since CAFTA-DR's passage, people in Central American countries such as El Salvador have experienced not just massive losses in farm income but also harmful laws and policies that risk health, the environment, the food system, and human rights. There has also been increased political instability and violence. Given the increased job opportunities in the United States, the country becomes a viable option for people such as Yesenia and Josué, even with the dangers involved with migrating and working with undocumented statuses.

CASE 4: I'M TIRED OF TRAVELING ACROSS TOWN TO GO GROCERY SHOPPING

Tonya is an African American woman who lives on the West Side of Chicago. Her community of Austin is the second largest in both geographic and population size in the city. Its population size makes it larger than many towns, at 95,260 residents as of 2017. Since whites fled for the suburbs in the 1960s and 1970s, the community has been an almost all African American one. That has recently started to change as Latinx people began to move into the Austin community, which is currently 81 percent African American, 13 percent Latinx, and 5 percent white. The median income there is $32,843, significantly lower than the city's overall median income of $52,497. On nights when Tonya comes home from work, she may stop by a local independent grocer to buy pasta and sauce for dinner and cereal and milk for her breakfast the next day. In the summer time, Tonya makes runs to a local corner store that is always well supplied with sodas and ice cream. When Tonya's nieces and nephew come for a weekend visit, it is never a problem to go on a quick walk to a nearby store to purchase cookies, chips, and popcorn for their ritual movie nights. However, when Tonya wants to go grocery shopping to fill her refrigerator and cabinets with foods to make nutritious meals, she travels to the more affluent suburb of Oak Park, Illinois, which shares a border with her community. In Oak Park, Tonya has her choice of three chain supermarkets, a Trader Joe's, numerous independent grocery stores, and a Target store with a better selection of fresh fruits and vegetables than many of the grocery stores where she lives. This is in addition to a food co-op that sources much of their produce and meats from local farms, as well as a number of specialty stores, including a high-end butcher and one that only sells gourmet olive oils and balsamic vinegars. This abundance of food shopping options amazes Tonya, since with a population of less than 52,000 people, the suburb is much smaller than her own community.

Tonya, who grew up in the neighborhood where she currently lives, remembers that it was not always like this. Every Thursday, she, her siblings, and their parents piled into the car to the chain supermarket two blocks away. That store closed down in the 1990s when she was in college, though the chain is still in business and has two locations in neighboring Oak Park that she regularly shops at. The building two blocks away from her childhood home was replaced by an independent grocer. Where there had been a light-filled and clean store with fresh produce and a full-time butcher, there is now a dingy, rather messy store with stacks of pack-aged boxes of fruit snacks and cans of processed beans where the apples, oranges, cherries, peppers, cucumbers, fresh beans, and greens had been. Ironically, though the store quality is much lower than the stores she fre-quents in the suburbs, its prices on staples such as bread, pasta, and milk are higher, giving her even less reason to want to shop locally. When Tonya hears people talk about the time, health, and other costs of food deserts, she wonders if they are basing their opinions on what they have read or heard or if their knowledge, much like hers, has been gained through first-hand experience. Tonya is tired of driving miles away from home when she needs to buy more than snacks or enough items to round out dinner, but what choice does she have?

Analysis

Tonya's experiences here are related to a number of the concepts and realities discussed in chapters 2, 3, 7, and 10. As seen here and in chapter 3, social statuses and geographic locations mean that some have abun-dance and others have scarcity in their options. Race—both in conjunc-tion with social class and other factors and independent of these—matters significantly for food access. On the whole, people with low incomes and low levels of education, people of color, women, and immigrants are all more likely to face a number of food inequalities. It is also clear that these factors compound each other and exacerbate inequality. People of color are more than twice as likely as whites to be food insecure. They are also less likely to live in places that sell high-quality foods and are less likely to live in places with adequate numbers of grocery stores and supermar-kets. They must travel longer distances to buy food and are less likely to have their own cars, further disadvantaging people of color in relation to whites when it comes to food access. Given their lower rates of home-ownership, education, employment, and wages, due to past and present forms of discrimination, people of color have lower economic security than whites do, which restricts their food—and other—purchasing power. People of color also have lower rates of health-care coverage and fewer health-care options while also being more likely to be obese, diabetic, and have diet-related diseases leading to increased health-care costs and debt and decreased life quality and expectancy. In Chicago, research finds that though African Americans account for one-third of Chicago's population, they make up 80 percent of those without consistent access to healthy food options.

As a middle-class homeowner living in a predominantly lower-income and African American neighborhood, Tonya experiences the realities of life in a food desert on an individual as well as a community and institutional level. For African Americans like Tonya, regardless of their social class, racist patterns of social exclusion that date back to redlining, sharecropping, and enslavement means that they live in neighborhoods that have the least supermarket access. This is the case in Chicago, Baltimore, Detroit, Los Angeles, Milwaukee, Minneapolis, Houston, and other cities across the United States. This is a consistent pattern, even when factors including income, college education, employment status, and population density are controlled for. Hence Tonya's frustrating experience, and the necessity to travel outside her community for healthy and abundant food options is certainly unjust but not uncommon.

CASE 5: WHY IS THAT IN YOUR CART?

As David and his two children, Elena and August, left the school, they were delighted. Both kids were on the honor roll and had been selected to represent the school at a district-wide art fair. Given their good mood, when Elena and August asked for cookies, chips, and soda when they stopped at the grocery store on the way home, it was easy for David to happily agree. After all, they were good kids. After everything they did to get good grades, work hard on their art, and only occasionally argue with each other, they deserved a treat or three. Elena and August were so surprised that their father granted their request. After all, they asked for snacks and other extra items from their father every time they went to the store. And almost every time they had gone to the store lately, the answer was no. In fact, David had grown so tired of saying no, creative ways of denying them had become something of a running joke. Ever since David and the children's mother divorced and David's hours were cut at work, money was a scarce resource. Six months ago, David swallowed his pride and applied for the Supplemental Nutritional Assistance Program (SNAP) and signed his kids up for reduced-fee lunches at their school to ensure they had enough to eat.

As the kids excitedly unloaded the cart, David engaged in small talk with the clerk ringing him up. When he took out his Electronic Benefits Card to complete the purchase, he heard a voice behind him. It took him a moment to realize that the person was talking about him as he heard someone say, "I am so tired of going to work every day and sacrificing just so some people can buy their kids a bunch of junk they don't need." David's lips tightened, and his face and neck grew hot. He tried to ignore the woman in line behind him, but she did not relent. She grew louder and louder, and other shoppers began to crane their necks to see exactly what was going on. David could see that his kids were getting upset, and that prompted him to respond. He turned around and told the woman, "Look, I'm just trying to pay for my groceries for me and my kids. Could you chill?" This set her off even more, and she yelled, "No, I'm paying for your groceries. Me and all these other people in line. I can't afford to buy all that junk, so why is that in your cart?" Elena ran out of the store so that no one would see her tears of shame, anger, and embarrassment. August mumbled to their father that he was sorry that he asked for the treats and that he no longer wanted to eat them as he had lost his appetite. David's good mood had certainly ended, and as he walked to the car, he wondered how he could make Elena and August get back the joy they lost.

Analysis

There is a long history of shaming the poor in the United States. The stigma of serving children cold cheese sandwiches or throwing away hot lunches for students with school lunch debt, discussed in chapter 13, is one example of this. The experience in the grocery store that ruined David, Elena, and August's evening is another one. This shaming and debate over what SNAP benefits should be used for—and what it should not—happens in grocery stores, talk radio shows, policy circles, and in congressional sessions as critics talk of "moochers" and "takers" and vow to reduce, if not end, such entitlement programs.

As shown in chapter 11, there are already numerous restrictions on what SNAP can be used to purchase. These include any foods not intended for home preparation or home consumption; foods cooked or heated by the retailer, whether before or after purchase, such as rotisserie chicken and other prepared meals; and baked goods. As discussed in chapter 11, this is rooted in a sense of paternalism and punitiveness that says that people who are poor are not capable of making their own decisions and are undeserving of anything other than the bare basics. Furthermore, multiple studies reveal that there are not any significant distinctions between how SNAP recipients and nonrecipients spend money on food.

This is not considered by those politicians, pundits, policy makers, and others who call for even further restrictions in the program if not its complete elimination. Current legislative proposals, even made in the midst of the COVID-19 crisis, seek to substantially decrease federal and other state allocations for food assistance. Recently, Republican politicians have been shown to be more likely to propose punitive and restrictive SNAP policies. In addition to the current presidential administration, New York State senator Patty Ritchie introduced legislation to bar SNAP recipients from buying lobster and energy drinks. In multiple unsuccessful tries, Maine governor Paul LePage has tried to restrict the purchase of sweetened beverages and candy with SNAP funds. Perhaps most famously is Ronald Reagan's fabricated campaign speeches about a Chicago woman who was amassing more than $150,000 a year through a complicated welfare—including what were then called "food stamps"—fraud scheme.

Rather than reflecting a personal failing or any moral judgment, assessing people such as David and the situations they are in should be understood as the result of low wages and weak economic policies to protect workers. Like David, more than half of SNAP recipients with children are the employed heads of their households. David's reliance on SNAP is an indictment of a lack of a national living wage more than anything else. University of Missouri communications professor Debbie Dougherty and her coauthors recommend destigmatizing and shifting the public's perception of who is in need. In summation, of this case and this book, it is important to point out that while food inequalities are certainly experienced at the individual level, they are not created there. Analyses of and remedies to these must move beyond attention to what people load into their carts at the grocery store, consumer attitudes, and behaviors toward food. Keeping an emphasis on the individual belies the impacts and roles of social statuses, such as race and class and their intersections, structures, institutions, and policies on food preferences and choices. Instead, a fuller understanding of the historical patterns, cultural understandings, contemporary practices, policies, and laws that create, reinforce, and maintain food inequalities is necessary.

Glossary

Cultural Capital: A collection of resources that allows its possessor to know and show the expected, yet unwritten, social rules in any given social setting.

Cultural Foodways: Foodways shine a light on both history and culture, as they are the behaviors, values, beliefs, stories, traditions, and rituals associated with food that are passed down across generations. Economic practices are also a part of cultural foodways, as are practices around how food is processed, prepared, and consumed.

Economic Capital: It is money, in the form of both liquid assets, such as the cash in one's wallet and the balance in one's savings account, and illiquid assets, such as any properties and stocks and bonds that can be converted (or liquidated) into liquid funds.

Environmental Racism: A term originated by Robert Bullard to describe the product of environmental injustice and both private and public policies and practices that benefit whites at the expense of people of color.

Food Apartheid: A term developed by Karen Washington to illuminate the conscious policy and other decisions that lead to the systematic inequality that make food in general and healthy food in particular scarce in communities inhabited by African Americans and other targets of social exclusion.

Food Desert: Places with persistent patterns of limited access to food.

Food Environment: This describes the kinds of foods that are readily available in one's local communities.

Food Insecurity: The limited or uncertain availability of nutritionally adequate and safe foods or limited or uncertain ability to acquire acceptable foods in socially acceptable ways.

Food Justice: Efforts designed to remedy food insecurity through grassroots efforts and responsive social policy to increase access to affordable, healthy, nutritious, and ethically sourced foods.

Food Mirage: A reference to when supermarkets and grocery stores open in areas considered food deserts while creating conditions that make food just as inaccessible as before they were opened.

Food Practices: These include etiquette, manners, and consumption patterns that are associated with one's social status, such as social class.

Food Security: The ready availability of nutritionally adequate and safe foods and the assured ability to acquire acceptable foods in socially acceptable ways.

Food Sovereignty: The right of people to healthy and culturally appropriate food produced through sustainable methods, and their right to define their own food and agriculture systems.

Food Space: The relationships between food practices, economic capital, and cultural capital.

Food System: The complex and interconnected arrangement of activities from the growing, processing, transporting, and warehousing to the distribution, sale, preparation, and consumption of food.

Human Capital: This is a collection of abilities, capacities, formal and informal education, skills, and talents.

Neurogastronomy: An emerging science that involves the nexus of neuroscience, food science, psychology, biochemistry, and culinary arts to understand the role of the senses in our perceptions of what we eat.

Social Capital: Social capital refers to how well social relationships can be leveraged to gain a host of personal benefits, especially the kinds that can lead to educational, employment, and financial success.

Social Exclusion: A term drawn from the work of Linda Burton and Whitney Welsh that describes when members of a marginalized social group lack full integration into society, have unequal access to necessary resources and opportunities for life choices, are oppressed by privileged members of society who retain control of necessary resources and opportunities, and experience clear boundaries between themselves and those who are the included in society.

Social Policy: These are actions, practices, regulations, and rules established by institutions, such as governments and legal systems, that are designed to address social issues and needs.

Structural Racism: Structural racism occurs when historical and contemporary social systems, made up of cultural understandings and representations, social norms, social policies, laws, institutional practices, and laws, work together to create, maintain, and deepen racial inequalities for members of racially marginalized groups.

Supermarket Greenlining: This occurs when grocery stores and supermarkets perceived as health-conscious and environmentally conscious open in low-income and gentrifying neighborhoods that attract more affluent customers and are seen as exclusionary of less privileged residents.

Supermarket Redlining: The practice of larger grocery retailers leaving low-income communities, creating economic and social exclusion.

Tastes: Tastes are reflections of the societal boundaries between social classes and other status groups. They create distinctions between groups that then reinforce and harden these boundaries, creating exclusion.

DIRECTORY OF RESOURCES

ACADEMIC JOURNALS

Food, Culture & Society: An International Journal of Multidisciplinary Research
https://www.tandfonline.com/loi/rffc20
Publishes critical reviews on food studies, including cross-cultural perspectives on eating behaviors and the social construction of culinary practices.

Food Policy https://www.journals.elsevier.com/food-policy
A bimonthly, peer-reviewed scientific journal covering food policy.

Gastronomica https://gastronomica.org
Represents the space where the breadth of academic scholarship on food cultures meets a public that is increasingly interested in questions of food, gastronomy, and the culinary arts. With a long history of accessible scholarship, exceptional production values, and varied, long-form writing, *Gastronomica* is uniquely positioned to enable food scholars to interact with the profession and the public.

Journal of Food Science https://onlinelibrary.wiley.com/journal/17503841
A peer-reviewed scientific journal that was established in 1936 and is published by John Wiley & Sons on behalf of the Institute of Food Technologists in Chicago, Illinois.

BOOKS

Bowen, Sarah, Joslyn Brenton, and Sinikka Elliott. *Pressure Cooker: Why Home Cooking Won't Solve Our Problems and What We Can Do about It*. New York: Oxford University Press, 2019.
Food is at the center of national debates about how Americans live and the future of the planet. Not everyone agrees about how to reform our relationship

to food, but one suggestion rises above the din: we need to get back in the kitchen. Amid concerns about rising rates of obesity and diabetes, unpronounceable ingredients, and the environmental footprint of industrial agriculture, food reformers implore parents to slow down, cook from scratch, and gather around the dinner table. Making food a priority, they argue, will lead to happier and healthier families. But is it really that simple?

Gottlieb, Robert, and Anupama Joshi. *Food Justice*. Cambridge, MA: MIT Press, 2010.

In today's food system, farmworkers face difficult and hazardous conditions, low-income neighborhoods lack supermarkets but abound in fast-food restaurants and liquor stores, food products emphasize convenience rather than wholesomeness, and the international reach of American fast-food franchises has been a major contributor to an epidemic of "globesity." To combat these inequities and excesses, a movement for food justice has emerged in recent years seeking to transform the food system from seed to table. In *Food Justice*, Robert Gottlieb and Anupama Joshi tell the story of this emerging movement.

Julier, Alice P. *Eating Together: Food, Friendship, and Inequality*. Champaign: University of Illinois Press, 2013.

Sharing and enjoying food together constitute a basic human expression of friendship, pleasure, and community, and in *Eating Together: Food, Friendship, and Inequality*, sociologist Alice P. Julier argues that the ways in which Americans eat together play a central role in social life in the United States. Focusing on the experiences of African American and nonethnic white hosts and guests, she explores the concrete pleasures of cooking as well as the discourses of food and sociability that shape the experience of shared meals.

Mihesuah, Devon A., and Elizabeth Hoover, eds. *Indigenous Food Sovereignty in the United States: Restoring Cultural Knowledge, Protecting Environments, and Regaining Health*. Norman: University of Oklahoma Press, 2020.

Centuries of colonization and other factors have disrupted Indigenous communities' ability to control their own food systems. This volume explores the meaning and importance of food sovereignty for Native peoples in the United States, and asks whether and how it might be achieved and sustained.

Orleck, Annelise. *"We Are All Fast-Food Workers Now": The Global Uprising against Poverty Wages*. Boston: Beacon Press, 2018.

Tracing a new labor movement sparked and sustained by low-wage workers from across the globe, Annelise Orleck's book is an urgent, illuminating look at globalization as seen through the eyes of worker-activists: small farmers, fast-food servers, retail workers, hotel housekeepers, home-health-care aides, airport workers, and adjunct professors who are fighting for respect, safety, and a living wage. With original photographs by Liz Cooke and drawing on interviews with activists in many U.S. cities and countries around the world, including Bangladesh, Cambodia, Mexico, South Africa, and the Philippines, it features stories of resistance and rebellion, as well as reflections on hope and on change as it rises from the bottom up.

Penniman, Leah. *Farming while Black: Soul Fire Farm's Practical Guide to Liberation on the Land.* White River Junction, VT: Chelsea Green Publishing Company, 2018.

With *Farming while Black*, Penniman extends her work by offering the first comprehensive manual for African-heritage people ready to reclaim their rightful place of dignified agency in the food system. This one-of-a-kind guide provides readers with a concise how-to for all aspects of small-scale farming.

Sbicca, Josh. *Food Justice Now! Deepening the Roots of Social Struggle.* Minneapolis: University of Minnesota Press, 2018.

The United States is a nation of foodies and food activists, many of them progressives, and yet their overwhelming concern for what they consume often hinders their engagement with social justice more broadly. *Food Justice Now!* charts a path from food activism to social justice activism that integrates the two. It calls on those who are food-focused to broaden and deepen their commitment to the struggle against structural inequalities both within *and* beyond the food system.

Warde, Alan. *The Practice of Eating.* Hoboken, NJ: John Wiley & Sons, 2016.

This book reconstructs and extends sociological approaches to the understanding of food consumption. It identifies new ways to approach the explanation of food choice, and it develops new concepts that will help reshape and reorient common understandings. Leading sociologist of food Alan Warde deals both with abstract issues about theories of practice and substantive analyses of aspects of eating, demonstrating how theories of practice can be elaborated and systematically applied to the activity of eating.

Williams-Forson, Psyche A. *Building Houses out of Chicken Legs: Black Women, Food, and Power.* Chapel Hill: University of North Carolina Press, 2006.

Chicken—both the bird and the food—has played multiple roles in the lives of African American women from the slavery era to the present. It has provided food and a source of income for their families, shaped a distinctive culture, and helped women define and exert themselves in racist and hostile environments. Psyche A. Williams-Forson examines the complexity of Black women's legacies using food as a form of cultural work. While acknowledging the negative interpretations of Black culture associated with chicken imagery, Williams-Forson focuses her analysis on the ways Black women have forged their own self-definitions and relationships to the "gospel bird."

Winne, Mark. *Closing the Food Gap: Resetting the Table in the Land of Plenty.* Boston: Beacon Press, 2008.

In *Closing the Food Gap,* food activist and journalist Mark Winne poses questions too often overlooked in our current conversations around food: What about those people who are not financially able to make conscientious choices about where and how to get food? And in a time of rising rates of both diabetes and obesity, what can we do to make healthier foods available for everyone?

WEBSITES

The Berkeley Food Institute https://food.berkeley.edu
> "The Berkeley Food Institute strives to transform food systems to expand access to healthy, affordable food and promote sustainable and equitable food production. We empower new leaders with capacities to cultivate diverse, just, resilient, and healthy food systems."

Civil Eats https://civileats.com
> "Civil Eats is a daily news source for critical thought about the American food system. We publish stories that shift the conversation around sustainable agriculture in an effort to build economically and socially just communities. Founded in January 2009, Civil Eats is a nonprofit news organization with more 150 contributors who report on the evolving food landscape from Capitol Hill to Main Street. Civil Eats was named the James Beard Foundation's Publication of the Year, and has been inducted into the Library of Congress."

The Counter https://www.thecounter.org
> "The Counter is a nonprofit, independent, nonpartisan newsroom investigating the forces shaping how and what America eats."

Feeding America https://www.feedingamerica.org
> "Feeding America is a United States–based nonprofit organization that is a nationwide network of more than 200 food banks that feed more than 46 million people through food pantries, soup kitchens, shelters, and other community-based agencies. *Forbes* ranks it as the second largest U.S. charity by revenue."

The Fight for $15 https://fightfor15.org
> "The Fight for $15 began in 2012 when two hundred fast-food workers walked off the job to demand $15 an hour and union rights in New York City. Today, we're a global movement in over 300 cities on six continents. We are fast-food workers, home health aides, child care teachers, airport workers, adjunct professors, retail employees—and underpaid workers everywhere."

The Food Insight Group https://www.foodinsightgroup.com
> "The Food Insight Group works to help communities build just, equitable, and resilient food systems."

The Good Food Purchasing Program https://goodfoodcities.org
> "Transforming the way public institutions purchase food by creating a transparent and equitable food system built on five core values: local economies, health, valued workforce, animal welfare, and environmental sustainability. The Good Food Purchasing Program is the first procurement model in the country to support these food system values in equal measure."

The Greenhouse Project https://nysunworks.org
> "NY Sun Works is a nonprofit organization that builds innovative science labs in urban schools. Through our Greenhouse Project Initiative we use hydroponic farming technology to educate students and teachers about the science of sustainability."

Heal Food Alliance https://healfoodalliance.org
> "HEAL's mission is to build our collective power to create food and farm systems that are healthy for our families, accessible and affordable for all communities,

and fair to the hardworking people who grow, distribute, prepare, and serve our food—while protecting the air, water, and land we all depend on."

National School Lunch Program https://www.fns.usda.gov/nslp

"Overseen by the U.S. Department of Agriculture's (USDA) Food and Nutrition Service, the National School Lunch Program (NSLP) provides free and reduced-cost lunches [for] thousands of children throughout the United States' public and nonprofit private schools."

The Okra Project https://www.theokraproject.com

"The Okra Project is a collective that seeks to address the global crisis faced by Black trans people by bringing home-cooked, healthy, and culturally specific meals and resources to Black trans people wherever they can be reached. During the Middle Passage, Africans snuck okra onto captive ships to sustain themselves and plant in the new world. Black diasporic cooking traditions often use the okra plant for its versatility, and it is often associated with health, prosperity, and community. In this spirit, the Okra Project hopes to extend free, delicious, and nutritious meals to Black trans people experiencing food insecurity."

Oldways https://oldwayspt.org

"Oldways is a nonprofit organization helping people rediscover and embrace the healthy, sustainable joys of the 'old ways' of shared cultural traditions."

Sankofa Farms https://www.sankofafarmsllc.com

"Sankofa Farms LLC is a multifaceted agricultural entity that seeks to assist [in] changing the food intake habits of those living in and affected by food deserts."

School Breakfast Program https://www.fns.usda.gov/sbp/school-breakfast-program

"Overseen by the U.S. Department of Agriculture's (USDA) Food and Nutrition Service, the School Breakfast Program (SBP) provides reimbursement to states for operating no- or low-cost breakfast programs in schools."

The Southern Foodways Alliance https://www.southernfoodways.org

"The Southern Foodways Alliance documents, studies, and explores the diverse food cultures of the changing American South. Our work sets a welcome table where all may consider our history and our future in a spirit of respect and reconciliation."

Spark-Y https://www.spark-y.org

"Spark-Y is a 501(c)(3) nonprofit based in Minnesota that empowers youth through hands-on education rooted in sustainability and entrepreneurship."

Supplemental Nutrition Assistance Program (SNAP) https://www.fns.usda.gov/snap/supplemental-nutrition-assistance-program

"Overseen by the United States Department of Agriculture (USDA), the Supplemental Nutrition Assistance Program (SNAP), commonly referred to as 'food stamps' is a federal program that provides food-purchasing assistance for individuals with little or no income."

Teens for Food Justice https://www.teensforfoodjustice.org

"Teens for Food Justice works to ensure universal equitable access to healthy, fresh, affordable food. We train youth in 21st century hydroponic, urban agricultural farming techniques, entrepreneurship, and health/nutrition education and advocacy, empowering them as change agents who can lead themselves and their own food insecure communities towards healthier futures."

The Union of Concerned Scientists https://www.ucsusa.org

"The Union of Concerned Scientists is a national nonprofit organization founded more than 50 years ago by scientists and students at the Massachusetts Institute of Technology."

United Farm Workers of America https://ufw.org

"Begun in 1962 by Cesar Chavez, Dolores Huerta, Gilbert Padilla and other early organizers, the United Farm Workers of America is the nation's first enduring and largest farm workers union. It continues its efforts in working for a safe and just food supply."

Urban Growers Collective https://urbangrowerscollective.org

"Urban Growers Collective is a nonprofit organization that builds urban farms, gardens, and provides fresh foods primarily in underprivileged areas in the West and South Side of Chicago. The organization was founded in Chicago, Illinois, in 2017 by Erika Allen and Laurell Sims."

BIBLIOGRAPHY

Adams, Kelly M., W. Scott Butsch, and Martin Kohlmeier. "The State of Nutrition Education at US Medical Schools." *Journal of Biomedical Education* 2015, no. 4 (2015): 1–7.

Agricultural Justice Project. "Food Justice Certification." https://www.agricultural justiceproject.org/en/.

Ahtone, Tristan. "Tribes Create Their Own Food Laws to Stop USDA from Killing Native Food Economies." *Yes!*, May 24, 2016. https://www.yesmagazine .org/democracy/2016/05/24/tribes-create-their-own-food-laws-to-stop-usda -from-killing-native-food-economies.

Allegretto, Sylvia A., and David Cooper. *Twenty-Three Years and Still Waiting for Change: Why It's Time to Give Tipped Workers the Regular Minimum Wage*. Washington, DC: Economic Policy Institute, 2014.

Allegretto, Sylvia A., Marc Doussard, Dave Graham-Squire, Ken Jacobs, Dan Thompson, and Jeremy Thompson. *Fast Food, Poverty Wages: The Public Cost of Low-Wage Jobs in the Fast-Food Industry*. Berkeley, CA, and Champaign, IL: University of California, Berkeley, Center for Labor Research and Education, and the University of Illinois at Urbana-Champaign Department of Urban & Regional Planning, 2013. https://laborcenter.berkeley.edu /pdf/2013/fast_food_poverty_wages.pdf.

Allen, Will. *The Good Food Revolution: Growing Healthy Food, People, and Communities*. New York: Penguin Random House, 2012.

Anderson, Jamie. "Whole Foods & Trader Joe's Provide a Healthy Boost to Nearby Homes." Zillow. https://www.zillow.com/research/whole-foods-trader-joes -home-value-11696.

Anderson, Sarah, and Sam Pizzigati. *Executive Excess 2019: Making Corporations Pay for Big Pay Gaps*. Washington, DC: Institute for Policy Studies, 2019.

Andrews, James. "Debate Grows over Poultry Worker Safety under Proposed HIMP Regulations." Food Safety News. https://www.foodsafetynews.com/2014/03 /debate-grows-over-poultry-worker-safety-under-proposed-regulations.

Anguelovski, Isabelle. "Healthy Food Stores, Greenlining and Food Gentrification: Contesting New forms of Privilege, Displacement and Locally Unwanted Land Uses in Racially Mixed Neighborhoods." *International Journal of Urban and Regional Research* 39, no. 6 (2015): 1209–1230.

Arnsdorf, Isaac. "How a Top Chicken Company Cut Off Black Farmers, One by One." ProPublica, June 26, 2019. https://www.propublica.org/article/how-a -top-chicken-company-cut-off-black-farmers-one-by-one.

Ashbrook, Alexandra, Heather Hartline-Grafton, Judy Dolins, Jean Davis, and Camille Watson. *Addressing Food Insecurity: A Toolkit for Pediatricians.* Washington, DC: American Academy of Pediatrics & Food Research and Action Council, 2017.

"Ask Code Switch: You Are What You Eat." NPR, March 27, 2019. https://www .npr.org/2019/03/27/704861884/ask-code-switch-you-are-what-you-eat.

Aubrey, Allison. "Tax Soda to Fight Obesity, WHO Urges Nations around the Globe." NPR, October 11, 2016. https://www.npr.org/sections/thesalt/2016/10/11 /497525337/tax-soda-to-fight-obesity-who-urges-nations-around-the-globe.

Babey, Susan H., Allison L. Diamant, Theresa A. Hastert, Stefan Harvey, Harold Goldstein, Rebecca Flournoy, Rajni Banthia, Victor Rubin, and Sarah Treuhaft. *Designed for Disease: The Link between Local Food Environments and Obesity and Diabetes.* Los Angeles: California Center for Public Health Advocacy, PolicyLink, and the UCLA Center for Health Policy Research, 2008.

Baltimore City Health Department. "Food Access." https://health.baltimorecity .gov/programs/food-access.

Baptist Edward. *The Half Has Never Been Told: Slavery and the Making of American Capitalism.* New York: Basic Books, 2014.

Baptiste, Nathalie. "Farmworkers Are Dying from Extreme Heat." *Mother Jones*, August 2018. https://www.motherjones.com/food/2018/08/farmworkers-are -dying-from-extreme-heat.

Baral, Susmita. "Neurogastronomy 101: The Science of Taste Perception How Chefs and Scientists Are Working Together to Change the Way We Taste." October 19, 2015. https://www.eater.com/2015/10/19/9553471/what-is -neurogastronomy.

Basu, Sanjay, Seth Berkowitz, and Hilary Seligman. "The Monthly Cycle of Hypoglycemia." *Medical Care* 55 (2017): 639–645.

Beals, Rachel Koning. "One Year In, Has Whole Foods Helped Fix One of Chicago's Toughest Neighborhoods?" *Marketwatch*, September 29, 2017. https:// www.marketwatch.com/story/one-year-in-has-whole-foods-helped-fix-one -of-chicagos-toughest-neighborhoods-2017-09-28.

Becker, Carolyn B., Keesha M. Middlemass, Brigette Taylor, Clara Johnson, and Francesca Gomez. "Food Insecurity and Eating Disorder Pathology." *International Journal of Eating Disorders* 50 (2017): 1031–1040.

Black, Rachel, and Aleta Sprague. "Republicans' Fixation on Work Require-
    ments Is Fueled by White Racial Resentment." *Slate*, June 22, 2018.
    https://slate.com/human-interest/2018/06/trump-administrations-fixation
    -on-work-requirements-for-snap-benefits-is-part-of-a-long-racist-policy
    -history.html.
Block, Daniel, John Bisegerwa, Kristin Bowen, Brent Lowe, John Owens, and
    Noah Sager. *Food Access in Suburban Cook County*. Oak Forest, IL: Cook
    County Department of Public Health, 2012.
Block, Daniel, and Joanne Kouba. "A Comparison of the Availability and Afford-
    ability of a Market Basket in Two Communities in the Chicago Area." *Public
    Health Nutrition* 9, no. 7 (2006): 837–845.
Bourdieu, Pierre. *Distinction: A Social Critique of the Judgement of Taste*. Trans-
    lated by Richard Nice. Cambridge, MA: Harvard University Press, 1979.
Bower, Kelly M., Roland J. Thorpe, Charles Rohde, and Darrell J. Gaskin. "The
    Intersection of Neighborhood Racial Segregation, Poverty, and Urbanicity
    and Its Impact on Food Store Availability in the United States." *Preventive
    Medicine* 58, no. 1 (2014): 33–39.
Bower, Kelly M., Roland J. Thorpe, Gayane Yenokyan, E. Emma E. McGinty,
    Lisa Dubay, and Darrell J. Gaskin. "Racial Residential Segregation and
    Disparities in Obesity among Women." *Journal of Urban Health* 92, no. 5
    (2015): 843–852.
Brones, Anna. "Karen Washington: It's Not a Food Desert, It's Food Apart-
    heid." *Guernica Magazine*, May 7, 2018. https://www.guernicamag.com
    /karen-washington-its-not-a-food-desert-its-food-apartheid.
Bullard, Robert D. "Dismantling Environmental Racism in the USA." *Local
    Environment* 4, no. 1 (1999): 5–19.
Burton, Linda, and Whitney Welsh. *Inequality and Opportunity: The Role of
    Exclusion, Social Capital, and Generic Social Processes in Upward Mobil-
    ity*. New York: William T. Grant Foundation, 2015.
Cairns, Kate. "Relational Foodwork: Young People and Food Insecurity." *Chil-
    dren & Society* 32, no. 3 (2018): 174–184.
Carlson, Steven, Dottie Rosenbaum, Brynne Keith-Jennings, and Catlin Nchako.
    SNAP Works for America's Children. Center for Budget Policies and Priori-
    ties, 2016.
Carr, Donald, and Chris Campbell. "USDA Bailout for Impact of Trump's Tariffs
    Goes to Biggest, Richest Farmers." AgMag. https://www.ewg.org/agmag
    /2019/07/usda-bailout-impact-trump-s-tariffs-goes-biggest-richest-farmers.
Carter, Prudence L. "'Black' Cultural Capital, Status Positioning, and Schooling
    Conflicts for Low-Income African American Youth." *Social Problems* 50, no.
    1 (2003): 136–155.
Center for Good Food Purchasing "The Program." https://goodfoodpurchasing.org.
Center on Budget and Policy Priorities. "House Farm Bill's SNAP Cuts, Work
    Requirements Would Hurt Children." https://www.cbpp.org/research/food-ass
    istance/house-farm-bills-snap-cuts-work-requirements-would-hurt-children.

Center on Budget and Policy Priorities. "A Quick Guide to SNAP Eligibility andBenefits." www.cbpp.org/research/food-assistance/a-quick-guide-to-snap -eligibility-and-benefits.

Centers for Disease Control and Prevention. "Adult Obesity." https://www.cdc .gov/vitalsigns/adultobesity/index.html.

Centers for Disease Control and Prevention. "Suicide Increasing among American Workers." https://www.cdc.gov/media/releases/2018/p1115-Suicide-american -workers.html.

Centers for Disease Control and Prevention. *Surveillance for Foodborne Disease Outbreaks, United States, 2015, Annual Report*. Atlanta, GA: U.S. Department of Health and Human Services, CDC, 2017.

Chicago Food Policy Council. "Our Mission." https://www.chicagofoodpolicy.com.

Chicago Metropolitan Agency for Planning. "Community Data Snapshot: Austin, June 2019." https://www.cmap.illinois.gov/documents/10180/126764/Austin .pdf.

Coalition of Immokalee Workers. "Fair Food Program." https://www.fairfood program.org.

Cohen, Nevin. *Feeding or Starving Gentrification: The Role of Food Policy*. New York: CUNY Urban Food Policy Institute.

Collier, Andrea King. "A Reparations Map for Farmers of Color May Help Right Historical Wrongs." Civil Eats, May 27, 2020. https://civileats.com/2018/06 /04/a-reparations-map-for-farmers-may-help-right-historical-wrongs.

Collins, Patricia Hill. *Black Feminist Thought: Knowledge, Consciousness, and the Politics of Empowerment*. New York: Routledge, 2000.

Conrad, Zach, Meredith T. Niles, Deborah A. Neher, Eric D. Roy, Nicole E. Tichenor, and Lisa Jahns. "Relationship between Food Waste, Diet Quality, and Environmental Sustainability." *PLoS One* 13, no. 4 (2018): e0195405.

Cooksey-Stowers, Kristen, Marlene B. Schwartz, and Kelly D. Brownell. "Food Swamps Predict Obesity Rates Better than Food Deserts in the United States." *International Journal of Environmental Research and Public Health*. 14, no. 11 (2017): 1366.

Cooper, David. *Raising the Federal Minimum Wage to $15 by 2024 Would Lift Pay for Nearly 40 Million Workers*. Washington, DC: Economic Policy Institute, 2019.

Daniel, Pete. *Dispossession: Discrimination against African American Farmers in the Age of Civil Rights*. Chapel Hill: University of North Carolina Press, 2013.

Danovich, Tove. "How A Seed Bank Helps Preserve Cherokee Culture through Traditional Foods." NPR, April 2, 2019. https://www.npr.org/sections /thesalt/2019/04/02/704795157/how-a-seed-bank-helps-preserve-cherokee -culture-through-traditional-foods.

Denham, Hannah. "The Mississippi Work Sites Targeted by ICE Raids." *Washington Post*, August 9, 2019. https://www.washingtonpost.com/business/2019/08/08 /what-we-know-about-five-companies-targeted-mississippi-ice-raids.

Detroit Food Policy Council. *Creating a Food Secure Detroit: Policy Review and Update*. Detroit, MI: Author, 2017. https://detroitfoodpolicycouncil .net/sites/default/files/images/DFPC%20Food%20Policy%20Document%20 021317%20%281%29.pdf.

Dixon, Vince. "How Wide Is the Wage Gap between Fast-Food CEOs and Their Workers?" https://www.eater.com/2017/6/5/15661110/fast-food-ceo-pay.

Donahue, Marie. "Dollar Store Fact Sheet." https://ilsr.org/wp-content/uploads /2018/12/Dollar_Store_Fact_Sheet.pdf.

Dougherty, Debbie S., Megan A. Schraedley, Angela N. Gist-Mackey, and Jonathan Wickert. "A Photovoice Study of Food (In)security, Unemployment, and the Discursive-Material Dialectic." *Communication Monographs* 85, no. 4 (2018): 443–466.

Drewnowski, Adam, and S. E. Specter. "Poverty and Obesity: The Role of Energy Density and Energy Costs." *American Journal of Clinical Nutrition* 79, no. 1 (2004): 6–16.

Drucker, Erin R., Angela D. Liese, Erica Sercy, Bethany A. Bell, Carrie Draper, Nancy L. Fleischer, Kate Flory, and Sonya J. Jones. "Food Insecurity, Childhood Hunger and Caregiver Life Experiences among Households with Children in South Carolina, USA." *Public Health Nutrition* 22, no. 14 (2019): 2581–2590.

Duggan, Tara. "Hidden Hunger." *San Francisco Chronicle*, November 18, 2018. https://www.sfchronicle.com/hidden-hunger.

Economic Policy Institute. "Worker Rights Preemption in the U.S." https://www .epi.org/preemption-map.

Elliott, Sinikka, and Sarah Bowen. "Defending Motherhood: Morality, Responsibility, and Double Binds in Feeding Children." *Journal of Marriage and Family* 80, no. 2 (2018): 499–520.

Elsheik, Elsadig. "Race and Corporate Power in the US Food System: Examining the Farm Bill." *Food First* 2, no. Summer (2016): 1–7.

Eslami, Esa. *Trends in Supplemental Nutrition Assistance Program Participation Rates: Fiscal Years 2010 to 2013*. Alexandria, VA: U.S. Department of Agriculture, 2015.

Fair Food Network. "Double Up Food Bucks: A Win for Families, Farmers & Communities." https://www.doubleupfoodbucks.org/about.

Falbe, Jennifer, Hannah R. Thompson, Anisha Patel, and Kristine A. Madsen. "Potentially Addictive Properties of Sugar-Sweetened Beverages among Adolescents." *Appetite* 133 (2019): 130–137.

Farmer, Ashley D. *Remaking Black Power: How Black Women Transformed an Era*. Chapel Hill: University of North Carolina Books, 2017.

Federal Trade Commission. *A Review of Food Marketing to Children and Adolescents: Follow-up Report*. Washington, DC: Federal Trade Commission, 2012.

Feeding America. "Facts about Poverty and Hunger in America." https://www .feedingamerica.org/hunger-in-america/facts.

Feeding America. *Hunger in America 2014*. Chicago: Feeding America, 2014.

Feeding America. *Mind the Meal Gap.* Chicago: Feeding America, 2018.

Feeding America. *The State of Senior Hunger in America*. Chicago: Feeding America, 2018.

Feeding America. "Understand Food Insecurity." https://hungerandhealth .feedingamerica.org/understand-food-insecurity/.

Fight for $15. "Why We Strike." https://fightfor15.org/why-we-strike.

First Nations Development Institute. "Stewarding Native Lands." https://www .firstnations.org/our-programs/stewarding-native-lands.

Fletcher Adam, Chris Bonell, and Annik Sorhaindo. "You Are What Your Friends Eat: Systematic Review of Social Network Analyses of Young People's Eating Behaviours and Bodyweight." *Journal of Epidemiology & Community Health* 65, no. 6 (2011): 548–555.

Food Chain Workers Alliance. "What Food Workers on the Front Lines Need Right Now." https://foodchainworkers.org/2020/03/what-food-workers -on-the-front-lines-need-right-now/.

Food Chain Workers Alliance and Solidarity Research Cooperative. *No Piece of the Pie: U.S. Food Workers in 2016*. Los Angeles, CA: Food Chain Workers Alliance, 2016.

Food Empowerment Project. "Fast Food." https://foodispower.org/access-health /fast-food.

Fram, Maryah Stella, Edward A. Frongillo, Sonya J. Jones, Roger C. Williams, Michael P. Burke, Kendra P. DeLoach, and Christine E. Blake. "Children Are Aware of Food Insecurity and Take Responsibility for Managing Food Resources" *Journal of Nutrition* 141, no. 6 (2011): 1114–1119.

Freudenberg, Nicholas. "How Better U.S. Food Policies Could Foster Improved Health, Safer Jobs, and A More Sustainable Environment." Scholars Strategy Network, October 2, 2014. https://scholars.org/contribution/how-better-us -food-policies-could-foster-improved-health-safer-jobs-and-more.

Freudenberg, Nicholas. *Lethal but Legal: Corporations, Consumption, and Protecting Public Health*. New York: Oxford University Press, 2014.

Freudenberg, Nicholas, Sara Goldrick-Rab, and Janet Poppendieck. "College Students and SNAP: The New Face of Food Insecurity in the United States." *American Journal of Public Health* 109, no.12 (2019): 1652–1658.

Fu, Jessica. "Countless American Families Are Saddled with Student Lunch Debt. Many Won't Be Able to Pay It Off." *The Counter*, April 22, 2019. https:// thecounter.org/school-lunch-debt-usda.

Funk, Cary, and Brian Kennedy. *The New Food Fights: U.S. Public Divides over Food Science*. Washington, DC: Pew Research Center, 2016.

Gaddis, Jennifer E. *The Labor of Lunch: Why We Need Real Food and Real Jobs in American Public Schools*. Berkeley: University of California Press, 2019.

Goldrick-Rab, Sara, Jed Richardson, and Anthony Hernandez. *Hungry and Homeless in College: Results from a National Study of Basic Needs Insecurity in Higher Education*. Madison: Wisconsin Hope Lab, 2017.

Gordon, Nora E., and Krista J. Ruffini. "School Nutrition and Student Discipline: Effects of Schoolwide Free Meals." NBER Working Paper, w24986. Cambridge, MA: National Bureau of Economic Research, 2018.

Grabell, Michael. "Tyson Foods' Secret Recipe for Carving Up Workers' Comp Over." ProPublica, December 11, 2015. https://www.propublica.org/article /tyson-foods-secret-recipe-for-carving-up-workers-comp.

Greenhouse, Steven, and Jana Kasperkevic. "Fight for $15 Swells into Largest Protest by Low-Wage Workers in US History." *The Guardian*, April 15, 2015. https://www.theguardian.com/us-news/2015/apr/15/fight-for-15-minimum -wage-protests-new-york-los-angeles-atlanta-boston.

Gundersen, Craig, and James P. Ziliak. "Food Insecurity and Health Outcomes." *Health Affairs* 34, no. 11 (2015): 1830–1839.

Guthman, Julie. "'If They Only Knew': Color Blindness and Universalism in California Alternative Food Institutions." *Professional Geographer* 60, no. 3 (2008): 387–397.

Guthrie, Joanne, and Constance Newman. "Eating Better at School: Can New Policies Improve Children's Food Choices?" https://www.ers.usda.gov /amber-waves/2013/september/eating-better-at-school-can-new-policies -improve-children-s-food-choices/#:~:text=ERS%20research%20found%20 that%20offering,foods%20by%20children%20and%20teens.

Harris, L. Kasimu. "Can Applesauce Help Close the Racial Health Gap? No, Wait, Hear This Chef Out." NPR, December 17, 2019. https://www.npr.org /sections/thesalt/161357412/food-for-thought.

HEAL Food Alliance. "Platform." https://healfoodalliance.org.

Hite, Emily Benton, Dorie Perez, Dalia D'Ingeo, Qasimah Boston, and Miaisha Mitchell. "Intersecting Race, Space, and Place Through Community Gardens." *Annals of Anthropological Practice* 41, no. 2 (2017): 55–66.

Horst, Megan, and Amy Marion. "Racial, Ethnic and Gender Inequities in Farmland Ownership and Farming in the U.S." *Agriculture and Human Values* 36 (2019): 1–16.

Hoynes, Hilary, and Diane Schanzenbach. "U.S. Food and Nutrition Programs." NBER Working Paper 21057. Cambridge, MA: National Bureau of Economic Research, 2015.

Hubbard, Kristina. "The Sobering Details behind the Latest Seed Monopoly Chart." https://civileats.com/2019/01/11/the-sobering-details-behind-the-latest -seed-monopoly-chart.

Institute of Medicine and National Research Council. *A Framework for Assessing Effects of the Food System*. Washington, DC: The National Academies Press, 2015.

"Inventory of US City and County Minimum Wage Ordinances." https://labor center.berkeley.edu/inventory-of-us-city-and-county-minimum-wage -ordinances.

Inverse. "Pixar's 'Bao' Dumpling Short Reveals a Clash in East-West Family Values." https://www.inverse.com/article/46388-pixar-bao-dumpling-short -audience-confusion-asian-families.

Ivanic, Aarti S. "To Choose (Not) to Eat Healthy: Social Norms, Self-Affirmation and Food Choice." *Psychology and Marketing* 33, no. 8 (2016): 595–607.

Jacobs, Ken, Ian Eve Perry, and Jenifer MacGillvary. *The High Public Cost of Low Wages*. Berkeley: University of California, Berkeley Labor Center, 2015. https://laborcenter.berkeley.edu/the-high-public-cost-of-low-wages.

Johns Hopkins University Center for a Livable Future. "Food System Primer: Industrialization of Agriculture." http://www.foodsystemprimer.org/food-production/industrialization-of-agriculture.

Johnson, Paul, David Betson, Lorraine Blatt, and Linda Giannarelli. *National- and State-Level Estimates of Special Supplemental Nutrition Program for Women, Infants, and Children (WIC) Eligibles and Program Reach in 2014, and Updated Estimates for 2005–2013*. Alexandria, VA: U.S. Department of Agriculture, 2017.

Johnston, Josée, and Shyon Baumann. *Foodies: Democracy and Distinction in the Gourmet Foodscape*. New York: Routledge, 2014.

Jurafsky Dan, Victor Chahuneau, Bryan R. Routledge, and Noah A. Smith. "Linguistic Markers of Status in Food Culture: Bourdieu's Distinction in a Menu Corpus." *Cultural Analytics*, October 18, 2016.

Jurafsky Dan, Victor Chahuneau, Bryan R. Routledge, and Noah A. Smith. "Narrative Framing of Consumer Sentiment in Online Restaurant Reviews." *First Monday*, April 2014.

Justice of the Pies. "Our Story." https://www.justiceofthepies.com/about.

Kanwal, Jessleen K. "Brain Tricks to Make Food Taste Sweeter: How to Transform Taste Perception and Why It Matters." http://sitn.hms.harvard.edu/flash/2016/brain-tricks-to-make-food-taste-sweeter-how-to-transform-taste-perception-and-why-it-matters.

Keith-Jennings, Brynne, and Vincent Palacios. *SNAP Helps Millions of Low-Wage Workers*. Washington, DC: Center on Budget and Policy Priorities, 2017.

Ken, Ivy. "Big Business in the School Cafeteria." *Contexts* 13, no. 3 (2014): 84–87.

Kershaw, Kiarri N., Whitney R. Robinson, Penny Gordon-Larsen, Margaret T. Hicken, David C. Goff Jr., Mercedes R. Carnethon, Catarina I. Kiefe, Stephen Sidney, and Ana V. Diez Roux. "Association of Changes in Neighborhood-Level Racial Residential Segregation with Changes in Blood Pressure among Black Adults: The CARDIA Study." *JAMA Internal Medicine* 177, no. 7 (2017): 996–1002.

King, Robert P., Molly Anderson, Gigi DiGiacomo, David Mulla, and David Wallinga. *State Level Food System Indicators*. St. Paul, MN: Healthy Foods, Healthy Lives Institute, University of Minnesota, 2016.

Kolak, Marynia, Daniel Block, and Myles Wolf. "Food Deserts Persist in Chicago Despite More Supermarkets." https://www.chicagoreporter.com/food-deserts-persist-in-chicago-despite-more-supermarkets.

Kolak, Marynia, Michelle Bradley, Daniel R. Block, Lindsay Pool, Gaurang Garg, Chrissy Kelly Toman, Kyle Boatright, et al. "Urban Foodscape Trends:

Disparities in Healthy Food Access in Chicago, 2007–2014." *Health and Place* 52 (2018): 231–239.

Kraak, V. I., and M. Story. "An Accountability Evaluation for the Industry's Responsible Use of Brand Mascots and Licensed Media Characters to Market a Healthy Diet to American Children." *Obesity Reviews* 16 (2015): 433–453.

Krantz, Matt. "Minimum Wage? 11 Top Fast-Food CEOs' Pay Averages $6,617 an Hour." *Investor's Business Daily*, June 5, 2019. https://www.investors.com/news/top-fast-food-ceos-pay-hourly-chipotle-starbucks-mcdonalds.

Krivkovich, Alexis, and Marie-Claude Nadeau. "Women in the Food Industry." https://www.mckinsey.com/~/media/McKinsey/Featured%20Insights/Gender%20Equality/Women%20in%20the%20food%20industry/Women%20in%20the%20food%20industry-web-final.ashx.

La Vía Campesina. "Food Sovereignty Now: A Future without Hunger." https://viacampesina.org/en/wp-content/uploads/sites/2/2018/02/Food-Sovereignty-A-guide-Low-Res-Vresion.pdf.

La Vía Campesina. "The International Peasant's Voice." https://viacampesina.org/en/international-peasants-voice.

"Labor and Workers in the Food System." https://foodprint.org/issues/labor-workers-in-the-food-system/#easy-footnote-bottom-17-1302.

Legrain, Milli. "Revealed: Restricting Breaks Keeps Poultry Industry Workers Living in Fear." *The Guardian*, November 26, 2018. https://www.theguardian.com/food/2018/nov/26/revealed-restricting-breaks-keeps-poultry-industry-workers-living-in-fear.

Liu, Jodi L., Han Bing, and Deborah A. Cohen. "Beyond Neighborhood Food Environments: Distance Traveled to Food Establishments in 5 US Cities, 2009–2011." *Preventing Chronic Disease* 12 (2015): 150065.

Liu, Yvonne Yen, and Dominique Apollon. *The Color of Food*. New York: Applied Research Center, 2011.

Ma, Jing, and Richard Ghiselli. "The Minimum Wage, A Competitive Wage, and the Price of a Burger: Can Competitive Wages Be Offered in Limited-Service Restaurants?" *Journal of Foodservice Business Research* 19 no. 2 (2016): 131–146.

Magnini, Vincent P., and Seontaik Kim. "The Influences of Restaurant Menu Font Style, Background Color, and Physical Weight on Consumers' Perceptions." *International Journal of Hospitality Management* 53 (2016): 42–48.

Mancino, Lisa, and Joanne Guthrie. *SNAP Households Acquire about as Many Calories as Non-SNAP Households, but Spend Less*. Alexandria, VA: U.S. Department of Agriculture, Economic Research Service, 2018.

Manring, Maurice M. *Slave in a Box: The Strange Career of Aunt Jemima*. Charlottesville: University of Virginia Press, 1998.

Martryis, Nina. "Tainted Treats: Racism and the Rise of Big Candy." NPR, October 30, 2015. https://www.npr.org/sections/thesalt/2015/10/30/453210765/tainted-treats-racism-and-the-rise-of-big-candy.

Marx, Karl, and Frederick Engels. *The German Ideology*. New York: International Publishers, 1970. First published 1848.

Meyersohn, Nathaniel. "Dollar Stores Are Everywhere. That's a Problem for Poor Americans." CNN, July 19, 2019. https://www.cnn.com/2019/07/19/business /dollar-general-opposition/index.html.

Meyersohn, Nathaniel. "How the Rise of Supermarkets Left Out Black America." *Philadelphia Tribune*, June 16, 2020. https://www.phillytrib.com/news /business/how-the-rise-of-supermarkets-left-out-black-america/article _00c1bb8b-4f07-50e0-90be-6eeb4c4922fc.html.

Mintz, Sidney W., and Christine M. Du Bois. "The Anthropology of Food and Eating." *Annual Review of Anthropology* 31, no.1 (2002): 99–119.

Mitchell, Stacy. "Walmart's Monopolization of Local Grocery Markets." https://ilsr.org/walmarts-monopolization-of-local-grocery-markets.

Moon, Emily. "Agriculture Census Data Shows the U.S. Has More Female Farmers Than Ever." *Pacific Standard*, April 12, 2019. https://psmag.com/news /ag-census-finds-more-female-farmers-than-ever.

Morehouse, Lisa. "Farming behind Barbed Wire: Japanese-Americans Remember WWII Incarceration." NPR, February 19, 2017. https://www.npr.org /sections/thesalt/2017/02/19/515822019/farming-behind-barbed-wire -japanese-americans-remember-wwii-incarceration.

Moss, Michael. "The Extraordinary Science of Addictive Junk Food." *New York Times*, February 20, 2013. https://www.nytimes.com/2013/02/24/magazine /the-extraordinary-science-of-junk-food.html.

Mozaffarian, Dariush. "Want to Fix America's Health Care? First, Focus on Food." The Conversation, September 12, 2017. https://theconversation.com /want-to-fix-americas-health-care-first-focus-on-food-81307.

Mozaffarian, Dariush, Sonia Y. Angell, Tim Lang, and Juan A. Rivera. "Role of Government Policy in Nutrition: Barriers to and Opportunities for Healthier Eating." *BMJ* 361 (2018): k2426.

Muth, Natalie D., William H. Dietz, Sheela N. Magge, Rachel K. Johnson, American Academy of Pediatrics, and American Heart Association. "Public Policies to Reduce Sugary Drink Consumption in Children and Adolescents." *Pediatrics* 143, no. 4 (2019): e20190282.

Naftulin, Julia. "Why We Get Hangry, according to Science." *Health,* June 13, 2018. https://www.health.com/nutrition/what-is-hangry.

Nargi, Lela. "Does Your Food Label Guarantee Fair Farmworkers' Rights? This One Does." https://civileats.com/2019/04/29/does-your-food-label-guarantee -fair-farmworkers-rights-this-one-does.

National Employment Law Project. "Report: 27 Workers a Day Suffer Amputation or Hospitalization, Acc. to OSHA Severe Injury Data from 29 States." http://www.nelp.org/news-releases/osha-severe-injury-data-report.

National Family Farm Coalition. "Home." https://nffc.net.

National Farm to School Network. "About National Farm to School Network." http://www.farmtoschool.org/about.

National Farm Worker Ministry. "Low Wages." http://nfwm.org/farm-workers/farm-worker-issues/low-wages.

National League of Cities. "Economic Costs of Obesity." http://www.healthy communitieshealthyfuture.org/learn-the-facts/economic-costs-of-obesity.

National Research Council. *Air Emissions from Animal Feeding Operations: Current Knowledge, Future Needs*. Washington, DC: National Academies Press, 2003.

National Research Council. *Food Insecurity and Hunger in the United States: An Assessment of the Measure*. Washington, DC: The National Academies Press, 2006.

Nestle, Marion. *Food Politics: How the Food Industry Influences Nutrition and Health*. Berkeley: University of California Press, 2013.

Neumann, Jeff, and Tracy Matsue Loeffelholz. "40 Acres and a Mule Would Be at Least $6.4 Trillion Today: What the U.S. Really Owes Black America." https://www.yesmagazine.org/issue/make-right/2015/05/14/infographic-40-acres-and-a-mule-would-be-at-least-64-trillion-today.

Nord, Mark, Margaret Andrews, and Steven Carlson. "Household Food Security in the United States, 2006." https://www.ers.usda.gov/webdocs/publications/45889/12211_err49_reportsummary_1_.pdf?v=965.1.

NYC Business. "Food Retail Expansion to Support Health (FRESH) Program. NYC Business Economic Development Corporation." https://www1.nyc.gov/nycbusiness/description/food-retail-expansion-to-support-health-fresh-program.

Oatman, Maddie. "California's Vineyard Workers Already Faced Long Hours, Low Pay, and Harsh Conditions. Then Came Trump's Immigration Crackdown." *Mother Jones*, July/August 2018. https://www.motherjones.com/food/2018/07/californias-vineyard-workers-wine-labor-shortage-guestworker-visas-immigration-crackdown.

Obama, Michelle. "Let's Move! Raising A Healthier Generation of Kids." *Childhood Obesity* 8, no. 1 (2012): 1.

O'Connell, Heather A., Lester King, and Jenifer L. Bratter. "Community Resources in a Diverse City: Supermarket Location and Emerging Racial Hierarchies." *Race and Social Problems* 8 (2016): 281–295.

Odoms-Young, Angela. "Examining the Impact of Structural Racism on Food Insecurity: Implications for Addressing Racial/Ethnic Disparities." *Family Community Health* 41 (2018): S3–S6.

The Okra Project. "We Are the Okra Project." https://www.theokraproject.com.

Oldways. "Traditional Diets." https://oldwayspt.org.

Ordway, Denise-Marie. "College Student Hunger: How Access to Food Can Impact Grades, Mental Health." https://journalistsresource.org/studies/society/education/college-student-hunger-food-pantry.

Paarlberg, Robert, Dariush Mozaffarian, Renata Micha, and Carolyn Chelius. "Keeping Soda in SNAP: Understanding the Other Iron Triangle." *Society* 55, no. 4 (2018): 308–317.

Partnership for a Healthier America. "What We Do." https://www
.ahealthieramerica.org.

Passel, Jeffrey S., and D'vera Cohn. "Size of U.S. Unauthorized Immigrant Workforce Stable after the Great Recession." Pew Research Center. https://www
.pewresearch.org/hispanic/2016/11/03/size-of-u-s-unauthorized-immigrant
-workforce-stable-after-the-great-recession.

Penniman, Leah. *Farming while Black: Soul Fire Farm's Practical Guide to Liberation on the Land*. White River Junction, VT: Chelsea Green Publishing,
2018.

Peterson, Cora, Aaron Sussell, Jia Li, Pamela K. Schumacher, Kristin Yeoman,
and Deborah M Stone. "Suicide Rates by Industry and Occupation—National
Violent Death Reporting System, 32 States." *MMWR Morbidity and Mortality Weekly Report* 69 (2016): 57–62.

Peterson, Hayley. "McDonald's Costs Taxpayers $1.2 Billion Annually." *Busi-
ness Insider*, October 2013. https://www.businessinsider.com/mcdonalds
-costs-taxpayers-12-billion-annually-2013-10.

Planting Justice. "The Modern/Colonial Food System in a Paradigm of War."
https://plantingjustice.org/resources/food-justice-research/the-moderncolonial
-food-system-in-a-paradigm-of-war.

Powell, Lisa M., Julien Leider, and Pierre Thomas Léger. "The Impact of a Sweetened Beverage Tax on Beverage Volume Sold in Cook County, Illinois, and
Its Border Area." *Annals of Internal Medicine* 172, no. 6 (2020): 390–397.

Powell, Lisa M., Sandy Slater, Donka Mirtcheva, Yanjun Bao, and Frank J. Cha-
loupka. "Food Store Availability and Neighborhood Characteristics in the
United States." *Preventive Medicine* 44, no. 3 (2007): 189–195.

Ramchandani, Ariel. "There's a Sexual-Harassment Epidemic on America's
Farms." *The Atlantic*, January 29, 2018. https://www.theatlantic.com/business
/archive/2018/01/agriculture-sexual-harassment/550109.

Rawls, Natalia. "Healthy Eating Plus Awareness Leads to Better Mindful-
ness." https://www.nami.org/Blogs/NAMI-Blog/July-2015/Healthy-Eating
-Plus-Awareness-Leads-to-Better-Mind.

Reese, Ashanté, and Randolph Carr. "Overthrowing the Food System's Planta-
tion Paradigm." Civil Eats, June 19, 2020. https://civileats.com/2020/06/19
/op-ed-overthrowing-the-food-systems-plantation-paradigm.

Reese, Ashanté M. *Black Food Geographies: Race, Self-Reliance, and Food
Access in Washington, DC*. Chapel Hill: University of North Carolina Books,
2019.

Restaurant Opportunities Centers United. *Ending Jim Crow in Restaurants*.
Berkeley: University of California, Berkeley, Labor Center, 2015.

Rhone, Alana, Michele Ver Ploeg, Chris Dicken, Ryan Williams, and Vince
Breneman. *Low-Income and Low-Supermarket-Access Census Tracts, 2010–
2015*. Alexandria, VA: U.S. Department of Agriculture, Economic Research
Service, 2017.

Roberto, Christina A., Jenny Baik, Jennifer L. Harris, and Kelly D. Brownell. "Influence of Licensed Characters on Children's Taste and Snack Preferences." *Pediatrics* 126, no. 1 (2010): 88–93.

Rosenberg, Nathan, and Bryce W. Stucki. "USDA Gave Almost 100 Percent of Trump's Trade War Bailout to White Farmers." http://www.farmbilllaw.org /2019/07/24/usda-gave-almost-100-percent-of-trumps-trade-war-bailout-to -white-farmers.

Rust Belt Riders. "What We Do." https://www.rustbeltriders.com/what-we-do.

Schechinger, Anne Weir. "In California, Latinos More Likely To Be Drinking Nitrate-Polluted Water." https://www.ewg.org/interactive-maps/2020 -california-latinos-more-likely-drinking-nitrate-polluted-water/.

Shannon, Jerry. "Beyond the Supermarket Solution: Linking Food Deserts, Neighborhood Context and Everyday Mobility." *Annals of the American Association of Geographers* 106, no. 1 (2016): 186–202.

"Sharpen Your Skills: A Toolkit to Lead." http://womenchefs.org/wp-content /uploads/2020/01/RestaurantHER_Guide_2_26_19.pdf.

Sheingate, Adam. "Still a Jungle." *Democracy: A Journal of Ideas* 25, no. 9 (2012): 48–59.

Sheingate, Adam. "Why America's Food Is Still Not Safe." Scholars Strategy Network, November 5, 2014. https://thesocietypages.org/ssn/2014/11/05 /food-not-safe.

Sherman, Arloc. "Census: Programs Eyed for Cuts Keep Millions from Poverty." *Off the Charts* (blog). https://www.cbpp.org/blog/census-programs-eyed-for -cuts-keep-millions-from-poverty.

Shierholz, Heidi. *Low Wages and Few Benefits Mean Many Restaurant Workers Can't Make Ends Meet.* Washington, DC: Economic Policy Institute, 2014.

Silver, Lynn D., Shu Wen Ng, Suzanne Ryan-Ibarra, Lindsey Smith Taillie, Marta Induni, Donna R. Miles, Jennifer M. Poti, and Barry M. Popkin. "Changes in Prices, Sales, Consumer Spending, and Beverage Consumption One Year after a Tax on Sugar-Sweetened Beverages in Berkeley, California, US: A Before-and-After Study." *PLoS Medicine* 14, no. 4 (2017): e1002283.

Simpson, April. "Neighbors Suing over Pig Fumes Spur 'Right-to-Farm' Push." Pew Stateline, May 22, 2019. https://www.pewtrusts.org/en/research-and -analysis/blogs/stateline/2019/05/22/neighbors-suing-over-pig-fumes-spur -right-to-farm-push.

Smolski, Andrew R. "Stemming the Exploitation of Immigrant Farm Labor." *Contexts* 18 no. 2 (2019): 70–71.

Social Security Administration. "The Decision to Exclude Agricultural and Domestic Workers from the 1935 Social Security Act." http://www.ssa.gov /policy/docs/ssb/v70n4/v70n4p49.html.

Solomon, Rivers. *An Unkindness of Ghosts.* New York: Akashic Books, 2017.

Stewart, Hayden. *Fruit and Vegetable Recommendations Can Be Met for $2.10 to $2.60 per Day.* Alexandria, VA: U.S. Department of Agriculture, 2016.

Sullivan, Daniel. "From Food Desert to Food Mirage: Race, Social Class, and Food Shopping in a Gentrifying Neighborhood." *Advances in Applied Sociology* 4 (2014): 30–35.

Szabo, Liz. "Big Soda and the Ballot: Soda Industry Takes Cues from Tobacco to Combat Taxes." NPR, November 5, 2018. https://www.npr.org/sections /thesalt/2018/11/05/664435761/big-soda-and-the-ballot-soda-industry-takes -cues-from-tobacco-to-combat-taxes.

Tahmincioglu, Eve. "The 8 Lowest-Paying Jobs in America." http://www.nbcnews .com/id/38168029/ns/business-careers/t/lowest-paying-jobs-america/# .X34g9GhKiM9.

Teens for Food Justice. "The TFFJ Mission." https://www.teensforfoodjustice .org/about-us/about-tffj.

Traditional Native American Farmers Association. "TNAFA." http://www.tnafa .org/history.html.

Tran, Diep. "Cheap Eats, Cheap Labor: The Hidden Human Costs of Those Lists." NPR, February 12, 2017. https://www.npr.org/sections/thesalt /2017/02/12/512905725/cheap-eats-cheap-labor-the-hidden-human-costs -of-those-lists.

Treuhaft, Sarah, and Allison Karpyn. *The Grocery Gap: Who Has Access to Healthy Food and Why It Matters*. Oakland, CA, and Philadelphia: PolicyLink /Food Trust, 2010.

"Understanding Food Gentrification's Impact on Hunger." The Takeaway, July 18, 2018. https://www.wnycstudios.org/story/understanding-food -gentrifications-impact-hunger.

Union of Concerned Scientists. "USDA Increases Line Speeds, Endangering Poultry Processing Plant Workers." https://www.ucsusa.org/resources/attacks-on -science/usda-increases-line-speeds-endangering-poultry-processing-plant.

University of California, Davis, Sustainable Agriculture Research and Education Program. "Sustainable Agriculture Research & Education Program." https:// sarep.ucdavis.edu/sustainable-ag.

U.S. Burden of Disease Collaborators. "The State of US Health, 1990–2010: Burden of Diseases, Injuries, and Risk Factors." *Journal of American Medical Association* 310 (2013): 591–606.

U.S. Bureau of Labor Statistics. *Characteristics of Minimum Wage Workers, 2018*. Washington, DC: Bureau of Labor Statistics, 2019.

U.S. Bureau of Labor Statistics. *Characteristics of Minimum Wage Workers, 2019*. Washington, DC: Bureau of Labor Statistics, 2020.

U.S. Bureau of Labor Statistics. "Consumer Expenditures—2018." https://www .bls.gov/news.release/cesan.nr0.htm.

U.S. Bureau of Labor Statistics. "National Census of Fatal Occupational Injuries in 2016." https://www.bls.gov/news.release/archives/cfoi_12192017.pdf.

U.S. Bureau of Labor Statistics. "Union Members Summary." https://www.bls .gov/news.release/union2.nr0.htm.

U.S. Census Bureau. "QuickFacts: Oak Park Village, Illinois." https://www.census.gov/quickfacts/oakparkvillageillinois.

U.S. Citizenship and Immigration Services. "H-2A Temporary Agricultural Workers." https://www.uscis.gov/working-united-states/temporary-workers/h-2a-temporary-agricultural-workers.

U.S. Department of Agriculture, Economic Research Service. "Ag and Food Sectors and the Economy." https://www.ers.usda.gov/data-products/ag-and-food-statistics-charting-the-essentials/ag-and-food-sectors-and-the-economy.

U.S. Department of Agriculture, Economic Research Service. "Beginning, Limited Resource, Socially Disadvantaged, and Female Farmers." https://www.ers.usda.gov/topics/farm-economy/beginning-limited-resource-socially-disadvantaged-and-female-farmers.

U.S. Department of Agriculture, Economic Research Service. "Economic Linkages Supplemental Nutrition Assistance Program (SNAP) Linkages with the General Economy." https://www.ers.usda.gov/topics/food-nutrition-assistance/supplemental-nutrition-assistance-program-snap/economic-linkages.

U.S. Department of Agriculture, Economic Research Service. "Environmental Quality: Overview." https://www.ers.usda.gov/topics/natural-resources-environment/environmental-quality.

U.S. Department of Agriculture, Economic Research Service. "Estimates of Distance to Supermarkets Using 2010 Data." https://www.ers.usda.gov/publications/pub-details/?pubid=45035.

U.S. Department of Agriculture, Economic Research Service. "Farm Labor." https://www.ers.usda.gov/topics/farm-economy/farm-labor.

U.S. Department of Agriculture, Economic Research Service. "Food Availability and Consumption." https://www.ers.usda.gov/data-products/ag-and-food-statistics-charting-the-essentials/food-availability-and-consumption.

U.S. Department of Agriculture, Economic Research Service. "Food Dollar Series: Quick Facts." https://www.ers.usda.gov/data-products/food-dollar-seriesquick-facts.

U.S. Department of Agriculture, Economic Research Service. "Food Prices and Spending." https://www.ers.usda.gov/data-products/ag-and-food-statistics-charting-the-essentials/food-prices-and-spending.aspx.

U.S. Department of Agriculture, Economic Research Service. "Food Security in the U.S.: Definitions." https://www.ers.usda.gov/topics/food-nutrition-assistance/food-security-in-the-us/definitions-of-food-security.aspx.

U.S. Department of Agriculture, Economic Research Service. "Food Security in the U.S.: Measurement." https://www.ers.usda.gov/topics/food-nutrition-assistance/food-security-in-the-us/measurement.

U.S. Department of Agriculture, Economic Research Service. "National School Lunch Program." https://www.ers.usda.gov/topics/food-nutrition-assistance/child-nutrition-programs/national-school-lunch-program.

U.S. Department of Agriculture, Economic Research Service. "School Break-fast Program." https://www.ers.usda.gov/topics/food-nutrition-assistance/child-nutrition-programs/school-breakfast-program.

U.S. Department of Agriculture, Food and Nutrition Service. "Child and Adult Care Food Program." https://www.fns.usda.gov/cacfp.

U.S. Department of Agriculture, Food and Nutrition Service. "The Community Eligibility Provision Fact Sheet." https://fns-prod.azureedge.net/sites/default/files/cn/CEPfactsheet.pdf.

U.S. Department of Agriculture, Food and Nutrition Service. "Farm to School Census." https://www.fns.usda.gov/cfs/farm-school-census.

U.S. Department of Agriculture, Food and Nutrition Service. "Farm to School Works!" https://farmtoschoolcensus.fns.usda.gov.

U.S. Department of Agriculture, Food and Nutrition Service. "Farming and Farm Income." https://www.ers.usda.gov/data-products/ag-and-food-statistics-charting-the-essentials/farming-and-farm-income.

U.S. Department of Agriculture, Food and Nutrition Service. "Foods Typi-cally Purchased by Supplemental Nutrition Assistance Program (SNAP) Households." https://www.fns.usda.gov/snap/foods-typically-purchased-supplemental-nutrition-assistance-program-snap-households.

U.S. Department of Agriculture, Food and Nutrition Service. "Healthy Hunger-Free Kids Act." https://www.fns.usda.gov/school-meals/healthy-hunger-free-kids-act.

U.S. Department of Agriculture, Food and Nutrition Service. "Is My Store Eli-gible?" https://www.fns.usda.gov/snap/my-store-eligible.

U.S. Department of Agriculture, Food and Nutrition Service. "The National School Lunch Program Fact Sheet." https://fns-prod.azureedge.net/sites/default/files/cn/NSLPFactSheet.pdf.

U.S. Department of Agriculture, Food and Nutrition Service. *Reaching Those in Need: State Supplemental Nutrition Assistance Program Participation Rates in 2015.* January 2018. https://fns-prod.azureedge.net/sites/default/files/ops/Reaching2015.pdf.

U.S. Department of Agriculture, Food and Nutrition Service. "A Short History of SNAP." https://www.fns.usda.gov/snap/short-history-snap#1964.

U.S. Department of Agriculture, Food and Nutrition Service. "Summer Food Ser-vice Program." https://www.fns.usda.gov/sfsp/summer-food-service-program.

U.S. Department of Agriculture, Food and Nutrition Service. "WIC Eligibil-ity and Coverage Rates." https://www.fns.usda.gov/wic/wic-eligibility-and-coverage-rates.

U.S. Department of Agriculture, National Agricultural Statistics Service. "Ameri-can Indian/Alaska Native Producers, October 2019." https://www.nass.usda.gov/Publications/Highlights/2019/2017Census_AmericanIndianAlaskaNative_Producers.pdf.

U.S. Department of Agriculture, National Agricultural Statistics Service. "Asian Producers, October 2019." https://www.nass.usda.gov/Publications/Highlights/2019/2017Census_Asian_Producers.pdf.

U.S. Department of Agriculture, National Agricultural Statistics Service. "Black Producers, October 2019." https://www.nass.usda.gov/Publications /Highlights/2019/2017Census_Black_Producers.pdf.

U.S. Department of Agriculture, National Agricultural Statistics Service. "Female Producers, October 2019." https://www.nass.usda.gov/Publications /Highlights/2019/2017Census_Female_Producers.pdf.

U.S. Department of Agriculture, National Agricultural Statistics Service. "Hispanic Producers, October 2019." https://www.nass.usda.gov/Publications /Highlights/2019/2017Census_Hispanic_Producers.pdf.

U.S. Department of Labor. *Findings from the National Agricultural Workers Survey (NAWS) 2015–2016: A Demographic and Employment Profile of United States Farmworkers*. January 2018. https://www.dol.gov/sites/dolgov/files /ETA/naws/pdfs/NAWS_Research_Report_13.pdf.

U.S. Department of Labor, Office of Foreign Labor Certification. "H-2A Temporary Agricultural Labor Certification Program: Selected Statistics, FY 2018." https://www.dol.gov/sites/dolgov/files/ETA/oflc/pdfs/H-2A_Selected _Statistics_FY2018_Q4.pdf.

U.S. Environmental Protection Agency. "Food Recovery Hierarchy." https://www .epa.gov/sustainable-management-food/food-recovery-hierarchy.

U.S. Environmental Protection Agency. "Sustainable Management of Food." https:// www.epa.gov/sustainable-management-food/sustainable-management -food-basics.

U.S. Equal Employment Opportunity Commission. "Marquez Brothers to Pay $2 Million to Settle EEOC Race Discrimination Suit." https://www .eeoc.gov/newsroom/marquez-brothers-pay-2-million-settle-eeoc-race -discrimination-suit.

U.S. Government Accountability Office. "Food Insecurity: Better Information Could Help Eligible College Students Access Federal Food Assistance Benefits." December 2018. https://www.gao.gov/assets/700/696254.pdf.

U.S. Government Accountability Office. *Workplace Safety and Health Better Outreach, Collaboration, and Information Needed to Help Protect Workers at Meat and Poultry Plants*. Washington, DC: Government Accountability Office, 2017.

Urban Growers Collective. "Home." https://urbangrowerscollective.org.

Van Sant, Shannon. "Philando Castile's Mother Wipes Out School Lunch Debt, Continuing Son's Legacy." NPR, May 7, 2019. https://www.npr.org/sections /thesalt/2019/05/07/721142955/philando-castiles-mother-wipes-out-school -lunch-debt-continuing-son-s-legacy.

Vasel, Kathryn. "Too Poor to Afford Food, Too Rich to Qualify for Help." CNN, May 30, 2018. https://money.cnn.com/2018/05/30/news/economy/food -insecurity-food-banks/index.html.

Wansink, Brian, James M. Painter, and Koert van Ittersum. "Descriptive Menu Labels Effect on Sales." *Cornell Hotel and Restaurant Administrative Quarterly* 42, no. 6 (2001): 68–72.

Wansink, Brian, and Jeffery Sobal. "Mindless Eating: The 200 Daily Food Decisions We Overlook." *Environment and Behavior* 39, no. 1 (2007): 106–123.

Watson, Molly. "Bourdieu's Food Space." *Gastronomica,* 2012. http://www.gastronomica.org/bourdieus-food-space.

Weber, Max. "Class Status and Party." In *From Max Weber: Essays in Sociology*, edited by H. H. Gerth and C. W. Mills, 180–195. Reprint, New York: Oxford University Press, [1922] 1946.

Wheaton, Laura. *Estimated Effect of Recent Proposed Changes to SNAP Regulations*. Washington, DC: Urban Institute, 2019.

White, Monica M. *Freedom Farmers: Agricultural Resistance and the Black Freedom Movement*. Chapel Hill: University of North Carolina Press, 2018.

Wilde, Parke. *Food Policy in the US*. New York: Routledge, 2018.

Yust, Alauna. "Change Is Afoot in the North Minneapolis Foodscape." https://www.tptoriginals.org/change-is-afoot-in-the-north-minneapolis-foodscape.

Zhong, Yichen, Amy H. Auchincloss, Brian K. Lee, and Genevieve P. Kanter. "The Short-Term Impacts of the Philadelphia Beverage Tax on Beverage Consumption." *American Journal of Preventive Medicine* 55, no. 1 (2018): 26–34.

Zhu, Luke Lei, Victoria L. Brescoll, George E. Newman, and Eric Luis Uhlmann. "Macho Nachos: The Implicit Effects of Gendered Food Packaging on Preferences for Healthy and Unhealthy Foods." *Social Psychology* 46, no. 4 (2015): 182–196.

Zukin, Sharon, Valerie Trujillo, Peter Frase, Danielle Jackson, Tim Recuber, and Abraham Walker. "New Retail Capital and Neighborhood Change: Boutiques and Gentrification in New York City." *City & Community* 8, no. 1 (2009): 47–64.

Index

ABOUT THE AUTHOR

Tennille Nicole Allen, PhD, is Professor and Chair of Sociology at Lewis University. She is also the director of both African American and Ethnic and Cultural Studies there. Her primary teaching and research interests are in the intersections of race, class, gender, identity, and place. She is the author of works on social networks, the sociological contributions of Zora Neale Hurston, as well as African American intimate relationships, and African American cultural and creative practices. Her studies focus on the ways that African American girls and women understand and navigate their identities while challenging the images and perceptions crafted by others. She also engages and teaches experiential learning courses in community-based participatory research in communities in Joliet and Chicago.